County Court
of
Williamson County
Tennessee

Lawsuits
- 1821-1872 -

Compiled by:
Louise G. Lynch

Southern Historical Press, Inc.
Greenville, South Carolina

This volume was reproduced
from a personal copy located in
the Publishers private library

Please direct all correspondence and book orders to:

www.southernhistoricalpress.com
or
SOUTHERN HISTORICAL PRESS, Inc.
1071 Park West Blvd.
Greenville, SC   29611

southernhistoricalpress@gmail.com

Originally printed: Franklin, TN   1975
ISBN #978-1-63914-702-1

Printed in the United States of America

Louise Lynch has done it again! She has lived up to her
reputation of being one of the most prolific publishers of
local historic material in the field of local history.

This, her latest publication, is an abstract of seven volumes
of early court records of Williamson County, Tennessee. These
unindexed volumes are locked in the basement archives of the
Williamson County Courthouse and are inaccessible to the
public. Everyone who is interested in local history is
indebted to Louise for making the contents of these volumes
available to the public.

The importance of court records cannot be over emphasized
in genealogical and historical research. Such records contain what is legally known as the lawyer's "best proof" and
are almost universally accepted as accurate.

The parties to a law suit would not be in court if there
were not some controversy. The reason for their being there
is to establish what is actual fact and thus settle the
controversy. The courts sometimes err, but this procedure
constitutes the American system for deciding both questions
of law and of fact.

The American court system followed the practice of its
English Common Law predecessor of classifying law suits
according to the type of suit that it was. The name of the
category of suit did not always fit the crime. Throughout
this volume the cases are classified with names like "debt"
or "scire facias." Debt might have been any suit to recover
money and not for simple debt as we know it today. "Scire
ficias" literally means to make known and may have been
used to add a party to the suit. On the other hand such
terms as "petition for distribution" and "petition for
partition" properly describes the case before the court.

The records of Williamson County, Tennessee, are especially
vital to historical and genealogical research. This county
lies in the heart of the Cumberland Country to which settlers
flocked from Virginia, North Carolina, and South Carolina
in the late 1700's and early 1800's. Many of those settlers
remained, but their descendants by the droves joined the
mighty westward movement that was the heart and soul of the
development of America. Williamson County became also a
literal cross-roads for those moving west. Many stayed long
enough to become a part of the county's official court records
before they moved on, thus adding to the significance of the
records of this county.

Again, we owe a tribute and debt to Louise Lynch for making
these records available to us.

Thomas Vance Little
Attorney at Law.

RECORD BOOK

LAWSUITS

No. 2

1821 - 1823

P. 1   NICHOLAS WILBURNE - pl. vs CHARLES MORAN - def.
            Oct. 1821   Debt

P. 4   JOHN W. POPE, Assignee - pl. vs ANDERSON
        BERRYMAN - def.   Oct. 1821   Debt

P. 6   STERLING WHEATON - pl. vs PORTER WILLIAMS - def.
            Debt

P. 10   HENRY R. W. HILL, JAMES C. HILL, & ELIZABETH
        McALISTER - pl. vs JOSHUA FARRINGTON - def.
            Oct. 1821   Debt
        Henry R. W. Hill, James C. Hill, & Elizabeth
        McAlister were merchants in trade under the
        name of H. R. W. Hill & Co.

P. 12   STATE OF TENNESSEE - pl. vs GEORGE GLASCOCK - def.
            Oct. 1821
        Indictment for an assault & battery on
        Oswald Edlin.
        (County Court Minutes - Oct. 1835 - Ordered that
        James H. B. & T. Edlin (son of Oswald Edlin who
        has abandoned his wife & children) at the age of
        fourteen years be bound apprentice to Fountain
        B. Carter to learn the mystery & occupation of
        shoe & boot making. Teach him to read & write
        & at the age of twenty-one, give him a suit of
        clother worth $25 & a set of tools. THE WEEKLY
        REVIEW - April 29, 1831 - NOTICE: I hereby fore-
        warn & caution all persons against trusting my
        wife Mary Edlin, as I am determined to pay no
        debts on her contracting. Oswald Edlin.)

P. 15   JOSEPH G. HALL - pl. vs THOMAS H. PERKINS - def.
            Jan. 1822   Case
        In 1819 did certain work & care in & about the
        healing & curing of the said defendant's family
        of divers diseases & malady - provided medicines
        & potions for them. Has not paid.

P. 16   JOSEPH G. HALL - pl. vs NICHOLAS PERKINS JR. - def.
            Jan. 1822   Case
        Debt for medicine & treating servants & family
        at sickness.

2

P. 18   ROBERT MURRAY - pl. vs BENJAMIN WHITE - def.
                Jan. 1822   Case
         Robert Murray was in business of merchandising.
         Debt.

P. 22   JOHN EDMONDSON - pl. vs NICHOLAS PERKINS SR. -
         def.   Debt

P. 23   SARAH HAYES - pl. vs JAMES SCOTT - def.
                     Jan. 1822   Debt

P. 25   Same as above.

P. 26   CHARLES CROOKS - pl. vs FOUNTAIN PARRISH - def.
                Debt

P. 28   WILLIAM & JONATHAN MONTGOMERY - pl. vs WILLIAM
         SHUTE - def.   Debt
         William & Jonathan Montgomery - merchants.

P. 30   JOSEPH BRADEN, Assignee & C - pl. vs. HENRY
         COOK - def.   Jan. 1822   Debt

P. 32   STEPHEN HODGE, Assignee & C - pl. vs STEPHEN
         SMITH - def.   Debt

P. 34   THOMAS H. PERKINS - pl. vs JAMES G. JONES - def.
                Jan. 1822   Debt

P. 36   MATCALF DeGRAFFENRIED, Assignee - pl. vs
         JOSHUA FARRINGTON - def.   Debt

P. 36   ANDREW PARKS, Assignee & C - pl. vs JAMES
         WILLIAMS - def.   Debt

P. 41   JAMES IRWIN - pl. vs GEORGE A. IRION
                     April 1822   Case
         Sold him brick.

P. 42   THOMAS L. ROBINSON - pl. vs THOMAS RIDLEY - def.
                Scire Facias
         Robinson obtained judgment against William Betts
         & William Royal - failed to take bail.

P. 45   BOYD McNAIRY & JOHN SHELBY - pl. vs NANCY
         DUPREE, Administratrix of James Dupree & C - def.
                April 1822   Case
         Boyd McNairy & John Shelby physicians. James
         Dupree died intestate. This was a debt for the
         treatment of a fractured thigh of John Dupree,
         his son. Also for treatment of other members of
         the family.

P. 48   THOMAS RIDLEY - pl. vs JOHN BLYTHE - def.
                April 1822   Case

P. 51   PETWAY BOND & CO. - pl. vs THOMAS RIDLEY - def.
                Scire Facias
         Hinchey Petway, Morris L. Bond & Stephen Cantrell
         were merchants. Judgment against Frederick
         Holland - no bail signed. Thomas Ridley, sheriff.

P. 53   ROBERT D. HAYDEN - pl. vs JAMES W. PERKINS - def.
                April 1822   Debt

P. 55   WILLIAM WILLIAMS - pl. vs FELIX STAGGS - def.
                Debt

P. 57   JAMES COCKRILL - pl. vs NICHOLAS T. PERKINS, JR. -
         def.

P. 58   MARTIN ADAMS, Assignee - pl. vs PATRICK
         CAMPBELL - def.   April 1822   Debt

P. 60   JOHN WILSON - pl. vs NICHOLAS T. PERKINS JR. -
         def.   Debt

P. 62   EDWARD G. CLOUSTON - pl. vs NICHOLAS P.
         PERKINS - def.   Debt

P. 63   HENRY R. W. HILL, Assignee & C - pl. vs WILLIAM
         P. DUKE - def.   April 1822   Debt

P. 65   THOMAS BRADLEY - pl. vs MATTHEW JOHNSTON - def.
                Case

P. 67   JOSEPH BRADEN - pl. vs SAMUEL POWERS - def.
                Debt

P. 69   JAMES W. PERKINS, Assignee & C - pl. vs
         NICHOLAS P. PERKINS - def.   April 1822 Debt

P. 70   JAMES W. PERKINS, Assignee - pl. vs NICHOLAS
         P. PERKINS - def.

P. 72   JOHN SMITH - pl. vs GEORGE & FINIS SHANNON,
         Executors of David Shannon, deceased & Alexander
         Craig - def.   Scire Facias

P. 76   JAMES CAROTHERS - pl. vs HENRY COOK & JAMES
         STANLEY - def.   Oct. 1821   Debt

P. 77   STATE OF TENNESSEE - pl. vs PHILIP T. McCABE
         & JOHN P. SMITH - def.
         Disturbing the peace by carrying pistols & dirks
         & threatening to commit murder.

4

P. 79   PHILS BEMON & MARTHA C. BEMON - pl. vs JANE B.
          CAMPBELL, Admrx. of Andrew Campbell- def.
                    Debt
          Martha C. Bemon, wife of Phils.

P. 83   BENJAMIN S. TAPPAN & JAMES W. BANKS - pl. vs
          SAMUEL D. WILSON - def.
                    July 1822   Debt

P. 85   PHILS BEEMON & MARTHA C. BEMON -pl. vs JANE
          B. CAMPBELL, Admrx. of Andrew Campbell, Deceased-
                    Debt

P. 88   LAWRENCE FLYE, use of Jeremiah Flye- pl. vs
          JOHN PORTER - def.   Debt

P. 89   HENRY R. W. HILL, JAMES C. HILL & ELIZABETH
          McALISTER -pl. vs JAMES H. WILSON - def.
                    July 1822   Debt
          Henry R. W. Hill, James C. Hill, & Elizabeth
          McAlister merchants.

P. 93   WILLIAM SCRUGGS -pl. vs JOHN SCRUGGS -def.
                    Debt

P. 95   WILLIAM COOPER, SR., Assignee & C. -pl. vs
          FELIX STAGGS -def.   July 1822 .. Debt

P. 97   JAMES SNEED -pl. vs. BENJAMIN S. TAPPAN -def.
                    Detinue
          That he render negro girl slave, Mira.

P. 99   JOHN BARBOUR - pl. vs LEONARD DUNAVANT -def.
                    Debt

P. 101   CALEB GARRETT -pl. vs PHILIP MAURY -def.
                    July 1822   Debt

P. 102   CALEB GARRETT -pl. vs PHILIP MAURY
                    Debt

P. 104   MOSES PRIEST -pl. vs ELISHA L. HALL -def.
                    Debt

P. 106   WILLIAM & JAMES M. BANKS -pl. vs SAMUEL D.
          WILSON -def.   Debt

P. 107   EDWARD G. CLOUSTON -pl. vs SAMUEL D. WILSON -
          def.   July 1822   Debt

P. 109   JOSEPH BRADEN, Assignee & C. -pl. vs WILLIAM
          SMITH -def.   Debt

P. 111   ROBERT SCALES -pl. vs JONATHAN HILL -def.
                    Debt

P. 113   JAMES SNEED - pl. vs BENJAMIN S. TAPPAN - def.
                  July 1822   Continue
         Render to him a negro girl slave by the name
         of Mira.

P. 115   JOHN SAPPINGTON - pl. vs JANE B. CAMPBELL,
         Admrx. of Andrew Campbell, deceased - def.
                  Debt

P. 116   BENJAMIN W. LANE - pl. vs JAMES G. JONES - def.
                  Debt

P. 118   PHILS BEMON & MARTHA C. BEMON - pl. vs JANE B.
         CAMPBELL, Admrx. of Andrew Campbell, deceased -
         def.   July 1822

P. 123   NOBLE LADD - pl. vs ANDREW S. MARTIN - def.
                  Oct. 1822   Debt

P. 125   WILLIAM P. DUKE - pl. vs JAMES TERRILL - def.
                  Case
         William P. Duke loaned a 4 wheel carriage to
         Terrill.

P. 127   WILLIAM & JAMES M. BANKS - pl. vs SAMUEL D.
         WILSON - def.
                  July 1822   Debt

P. 129   LAWRENCE FLYE, use of Jeremiah Flye - pl. vs
         JOHN PORTER   Debt   Same as page 88.

P. 131   HENRY R. W. HILL, JAMES C. HILL, & ELIZABETH
         McALISTER - pl. vs JAMES H. WILSON - def.
                  Debt
         Hill & McAlister are merchants.

P. 132   HENRY R. W. HILL, JAMES C. HILL, & ELIZABETH
         McALISTER - pl. vs JONATHAN HILL - def.
                  Oct. 1822   Debt
         Hill & McAlister are merchants.

P. 134   HENRY R. W. HILL, JAMES C. HILL, & ELIZABETH
         McALISTER - pl. vs JOHN WILSON - def.
                  Debt

P. 136   WILLIAM SCRUGGS - pl. vs JOHN SCRUGGS
                  Debt

P. 138   WILLIAM E. OWEN - pl. vs THOMAS S. ROBINSON -
         def.   Oct. 1822   Debt

P. 139   WILLIAM E. OWEN - pl. vs THOMAS S. ROBINSON
                  Debt

6

P. 141 WILLIAM & JAMES M. BANKS - pl. vs WILLIAM WILSON -
        def.   Case   (Debt)

P. 143 JASON C. WILSON - pl. vs JAMES W. CURRY - def.
              Debt

P. 145 RICHARD HUGHES - pl. vs JOHN WITHERSPOON - def.
              July 1822   Discontinuance of a Road
        Samuel Cummins, Samuel Kirkpatrick, Hugh Dobbins,
        William Porter, Richard Steele, William White,
        John K. Campbell, & John Atkinson are selected
        to mark & lay off a road beginning at the Natchez
        Road where it crosses Indian Creek near the
        mouth of said creek, then to Richard Hughes;
        then along present way passing Jones Meadows
        crossing South Harpeth ridge to Jonathan
        Stepletons then passing Lodowich Beachs, John
        Beaches, Samuel Powers to the Davidson County
        line - to discontinue road leading from Carters
        down Indian Creek on the North side of John
        Witherspoon's plantation on which road Isaac
        Short was appointed overseer. Hands of Richard
        Hughes, Isaac Short, Sterling Gunter, Charles
        Gunter, Frances Carter, Jonas Meadows, Ben-
        jamin Brown, Price Gray, Henry Betty,
        Edmund Wall, Elias Dodson, William Powers, Adam
        H. Berry, Andrew Boyd, Lodowick Beech, B. H.
        Anderson, Jonathan Stepleton, & John Berry work
        on road.

P. 147 BENJAMIN L. TAPPAN & JAMES M. BANKS - pl. vs
        JAMES WILSON - def.
              Oct. 1822   Debt

P. 149 HOLLAND S. WHITE, Assignee - pl. vs HENRY COOK,
        SR. - def.   Debt

P. 151 NETHERLAND TAIT - pl. vs THOMAS A. THOMPSON - def.
              Appeal   (Debt)

P. 152 THOMAS J. HARDEMAN, use of Thomas Hardeman - pl.
        vs ROBERT SCALES, Exr. Sc.   Debt
        Robert Scales, Exr. of Thomas H. Perkins, Jr.,
        deceased.
        Thomas J. Hardeman, guardian of D. Hardeman,
        Lavenia C. Hardeman & Sarah J. E. Hardeman,
        heirs of Nicholas P. Hardeman, deceased.

P. 154 CHAPMAN WHITE - pl. vs JOSEPH BURNETT - def.
              Jan. 1823   Covenant

P. 158 METCALF DeGRAFFENREID - pl. vs THOMAS RIDLEY -
        def.   Case

P. 164 PHILIP EVERLY - pl. vs JOSHUA FARRINGTON - def.
        Debt

P. 167 WILLIAM S. WEBB - pl. vs JOHN M. WATSON - def.
        Debt

P. 169 JESSE BENTON - pl. vs THOMAS STACY - def.
        Jan. 1823   Case
        Has cattle that strayed from his farm.

P. 171 TURNER SAUNDERS, LEVI GIST, BEVERLY REESE,
        LEWIS DILLIHUNTY, JOHN DONALDSON, BERN &
        McKERNAN & HINCHEY PETWAY, Commissioners of the
        Town of Dainbridge - pl. vs RICHARD ORTEN &
        STEPHEN SMITH   Debt

P. 172 HENRY R. W. HILL & CO. - pl. vs STERLING
        WHEATON - def.
        Jan. 1823   Debt

P. 174 HENRY R. W. HILL & CO. - pl. vs STERLING
        WHEATON   Case   (Debt)

P. 176 HENRY R. W. HILL & CO. - pl. vs STERLING
        WHEATON - def.   Debt

P. 178 HOLMES H. HOPKINS - pl. vs PATRICK H. DARBY -
        def.   Jan. 1823   Motion

P. 181 SAMUEL CROCKETT - pl. vs WILLIAM CRUTCHER &
        ALLEN BUGG - def.
        Jan. 1823   Debt

P. 182 JOHN CROUSE - pl. vs WILLIAM NALL - def.
        Debt

P. 187 W. S. J. MONTGOMERY, Assignee - pl. vs
        CHARLES PERKINS - def.   Debt

P. 189 JOHN McCLELLAN, use of Joseph B. Porter - pl.
        vs NICHOLAS T. PERKINS, SR. & NICHOLAS PERKINS,
        JR. - def.

P. 190 HENRY R. W. HILL & CO. - pl. vs JAMES & JAMES
        H. WILSON - def.
        April 1823   Debt

P. 192 STEPHEN PETTUS, use of Richard Herring &
        Richard Ellis - pl. vs JOHN TISDALE - def.
        Debt

P. 194 WILSON WOODRUFF - pl. vs RICHARD ORTON &
        WILLIAM GOFF - def.   Case
        Has Woodruff's mare in his possession.

P. 196   JAMES CAROTHERS - pl. vs JASON C. WILSON & JOHN
         WILSON - def.
                   April 1823   Debt

P. 199   JOHN LAWSON & ELEANOR HIS WIFE; WILLIAM HOWARD &
         ELIZA, his wife; JOHN BLYTHE; WILLIAM BLYTHE;
         WILLIAM CONNER; JOHN HUTSON & ELIZA, his wife;
         BLYTHE SPRATT; RACHEL SPRATT; JAMES SPRATT;
         ANDREW McCORKLE & MARTHA, his wife; JOSEPH BLYTHE;
         JOSEPH SPRATT; ARTHUR A. STEWART; RACHEL STEWART;
         BENJAMIN BLYTHE; ANDREW SPRATT & JANE, his wife;
         SAMUEL SPRATT; JOHN SPRATT; WILLIAM S. ALLIN &
         CATHERINE, his wife - pl. vs SAMUEL BLYTHE;
         JAMES ELLIOTT & ELIZABETH, his wife; & ELENOR
         RING - def.
         Joseph Blythe formerly of George Town, South
         Carolina died. He had a tract of land in
         Williamson & Davidson Counties (about 4800
         acres - Deed Book A - Page 455). He left a will
         & left the land to his brothers & sisters &
         their children equally, except to his nephew,
         Andrew Spratt & his sister Howard & her children,
         who shall have only 1/2 as much as the others.
         James Blythe, his brother - 22nd part. Joseph,
         William, Benjamin, & John, sons of James Blythe -
         22nd part. Martha McCorkle & Rachel Spratt,
         daughters of James Blythe. Andrew Spratt, Sr.
         & Jane, his wife, a sister - 22nd part.
         Samuel, John, Joseph; Blyth, Eliza Hutson, the
         wife of John Hutson, Catherine Allen, the wife
         of William J. Allin, Rachel Stewart - 22nd part
         each. William Conner, the son of Elenor Conner,
         deceased, sister of Joseph - 22nd part.
         Andrew Spratt, Jr., son of Andrew Spratt, Sr. &
         Eliza Howard, wife of William Howard & sister of
         Joseph; Sarah Bell, wife of Alexander N. Bell;
         Elenor Lawson, wife of John Lawson; Robert G.
         Howard; Jane Stevens, wife of Amos Stevens;
         Catherine Wolf, wife of Conrad Wolf; Samuel B.
         Howard; Eliza Fullward, wife of John M. Full-
         ward; Pensellea A. Howard; William McKee;
         Howard & Anne B. Howard, children of said William
         Howard & Eliza, his wife - 1/44 part.

P. 205   JOSEPH DWYER & JOHN DWYER - pl. vs THOMAS
         MONTGOMERY - def.
                   April 1823   Trespass & Force of Arms
         Erected a high fence on the land not his.

P. 207   AMOS MOORE, by his guardian Joseph Kimbroe Comp.
         vs JOSHUA CUTCHAN & SAMUEL MERRITT & WILLIAM
         ANTHONY, surviving Exrs. of Isaac Battle, deceased -
         def.
         Joshua Cutchan was appointed guardian to Amos
         Moore in January. Isaac Battle now deceased &
         Samuel Merritt became his securities. William
         (Continued on next page)

P. 207   Continued:
Anthony & Nathan Stancil, deceased, became Exrs.
of Isaac Battle, deceased, in 1822. Joshua
Cutchan became insolvent. Joseph Kinbro was
appointed guardian to Amos Moore. Joshua Cutchan
has money that belongs to Amos Moore that he
got in 1812.

P. 209 LUTHER BROWN - pl. vs THE CHILDREN OF CHARLES
BROWN - def.   April 1823
Charles Brown gave by deed of gift on Jan. 5, 1801
to Luther Brown & his brother, Joshua Brown, now
dead, a tract of land containing 640 acres in
Davidson County on the Little Harpeth & Beach
Creek. In 1806 or 1807, Joshua Brown, then a
minor about 7 yrs. old, died. He left brothers
& sisters: Luther Brown; William Brown; Elizabeth
Brown, now married to Jesse Cox; & Rebecca Brown.
In 1815 William Brown died. He was a minor
unmarried. He left brothers & sisters: Elizabeth;
Rebecka; Benjamin; Ephraim; Samuel; & Charles
Brown. About 10 days after the death of William,
Rebecca died. She was a minor & unmarried.
Luther wants 2/3 part of the land. He wants 1/2
by deed of gift & 1/6 part by the deaths of his
brothers, Joshua & William & his sister,
Rebecka. Elizabeth is entitled to 1/6 part.
Benjamin Brown, Ephraim, Samuel & Charles Brown
are entitled to 1/24 part. They are minors &
their mother, Michael Brown, is their guardian.
Charles Brown died in 1816.

P. 215 STATE OF TENNESSEE - pl. vs JAMES MURRELL - def.
          April 1823   Indictment for riot
Indictment against John A. Murrell, James Murrell,
& William Murrell.

P. 217 STATE OF TENNESSEE vs WILLIAM MURRELL
              Indictment for riot

P. 220 STATE OF TENNESSEE vs JOHN A. MURRELL
              Indictment for riot

P. 222 ALEXANDER M. HARWOOD - pl. vs STEPHEN SUTTON - def.
          April 1823   Covenant broken

P. 224 STATE OF TENNESSEE - pl. vs MATTHEW PINKERTON -
        def.   Indictment for assault & battery
Assault on the body of Margaret McMullen. Also
charged were William Stanfield, Henry Mullen, &
Matthew Pinkston.

P. 227 STATE OF TENNESSEE - pl. vs WILLIAM STANFIELD &
HENRY MULLEN (See above)
              Indictment for assault & battery

10

P. 230 HENRY L. GRAY - pl. vs FELIX STAGGS - def.
         Jan. 1823   Debt

P. 232 JOHN D. BOND, Assignee & guardian of the heirs
       of Richard L. Locke, deceased - pl. vs KNACY
       ANDREWS & SAMUEL SHELBURNE - def.   Debt

P. 234 JOHN P. ERWIN, BILLE WILLIAMS, JAMES McLAUGHLIN,
       use of Edmund Charlton & Joseph White - pl. vs
       JAMES RUTHERFORD & ROBERT MURRAY - def.
                        Debt
       Erwin, Williams & McLaughlin are merchants.
       James Rutherford & Robert Murry are Exrs. of
       Frances Murray, deceased.

P. 238 RICHARD SWANSON - pl. vs JOHN WITHERSPOON - def.
         July 1823   Debt

P. 239 JESSE STANCIL, Exr. of Nathan Stancil, deceased -
       pl. vs JOHN WAGGONER & JOEL STEVENS - def.
                  Debt

P. 241 JOHN HUGHS - pl. vs JOHN NICHOLS - def.
                  Debt

P. 242 SAMUEL CROCKETT, guardian for Stokley & Harvey
       Page - pl. vs JOHN WILSON, JASON C. WILSON,
       ELISHA DAVIS, Admrs. of Samuel Wilson, deceased -
       def.   July 1823   Debts

P. 244 JAMES H. WILSON - pl. vs WILLIAM SMITH - def.
                  Debt

P. 246 HENRY R. W. HILL, JAMES C. HILL, & ELIZABETH
       McALISTER - pl. vs NICHOLAS PERKINS, SR. - def.
                  Debt

P. 248 WILLIAM McMAHON - pl. vs THOMAS HILL - def.
                  Case   (Debt)

P. 252 JOHN STAGGS - pl. vs ROBERT BEARD - def.
       While intoxicated, he executed a note for a
       horse, saddle & bridle.

P. 256 NICHOLAS WILBURNE - pl. vs JOSHUA FARRINGTON -
       def.   Debt

P. 258 MATTHEW H. QUINN - pl. vs WILLIAM WILSON - def.
         Oct. 1823   Debt

P. 260 EDWARD G. CLOUSTON - pl. vs JASON H. WILSON - def.
                  Debt

P. 261 JONATHAN CURRIN & CO. - pl. vs WILLIAM RAY - def.
                  Debts
       Robert P. Currin & David Mason are merchants.

P. 263 VANLIER & ROBERT BAXTER - pl. vs BERNARD
        RICHARDSON - def.
                    Oct. 1823   Debt

P. 265 JASON THOMPSON - pl. vs DANIEL J. HUMPHREY,
        Admr. of Jane Orton - def.
                  Debt

P. 267 NICHOLAS PERKINS, JR. - pl. vs WILLIAM SHUTE - def.
                  Debt

P. 268 SAMUEL MOORE - pl. vs NICHOLAS PERKINS, SR. - def.
                    Oct. 1823   Debt

P. 270 BENJAMIN S. TAPPAN & WILLIAM BANK - pl. vs
        JASON H. WILSON - def.
                  Debt
        (Merchants trading under the name of Tappan &
        Banks).

P. 271 JOSHUA D. CLOUD - pl. vs WILLIAM SHUTE - def.
                  Debt

P. 273 JOHN SWINNEY - pl. vs JOHN PORTER - def.
                    Oct. 1823   Debt

P. 275 W. VANLIER & CO. - pl. vs BERNARD RICHARDSON -
        def.   Debt

P. 277 STATE OF TENNESSEE - pl. vs GEORGE REDMOND
                Oct. 1823   Indictment for assault & battery
        George & John Redmond, planters, did on the
        23rd day of this inst. violently assault & beat
        Daniel J. Humphrey at the house of M. Goddern
        in Nolensville; then followed him & struck him
        with a gun & snapped a loaded gun at him.

P. 279 HINCHEY PETWAY, MORRIS L. BOND & STEPHEN
        CANTRELL - pl. vs JOHN NICHOLS - def.
                  Debt
        (Merchants trading under the firm & style of
        Petway, Bond, & Co.)

P. 281 Same as above.

P. 283 HENRY COOK - pl. vs ROBERT W. RAGLAND - def.
                    Oct. 1823   Case   (Debt)

P. 287 RHODA DRAKE   Exparte   Petition for Dower
                    April 1824
        Zachariah Drake died intestate. He owned a
        large tract of land, about 407 acres on
        Murfree's Fork of Harpeth. James Neelly is the
        guardian of Lila Drake & C. W. McConnico is the
        guardian of John Drake.

12

P. 291 JOHN GIBSON; JAMES GIBSON; SALLY GIBSON; MOLLY
       GIBSON; BETSEY GIBSON; ELIJAH PARRISH & CATHERINE,
       his wife   Exparte   April 1824
               Petition for Partition
       They are the owners of a tract of land on the
       waters of the Harpeth containing 760 acres &
       another tract containing 936 acres.
             1/3 of the land to James Gibson.
             1/3 of the land to John Gibson.
             1/3 of the land to the rest of the petitioners.

P. 295 CHRISTOPHER W. McCONNICO & SUSAN, his wife;
       LILAH T. DRAKE by her guardian, James Neelly;
       JOHN N. DRAKE by his guardian, Christopher W.
       McConnico; & JAMES L. DRAKE by his guardian,
       Rhoda Drake   April 1824
            Petition for Partition of Zachariah Drake,
                    deceased, estate
       Zachariah Drake died in 1821 intestate. He owned
       tracts of land containing 407 acres & 100
       acres. Lot # 85, # 95, # 61, & # 71 in
       Franklin. He also owned many slaves.

P. 302 ALLEN BUGG - pl. vs WILLIS & WILLIAM CRUTCHER -
       def.   Jan. 1824   Debt

P. 304 JOHN PILLOW & OTHERS vs MATTHIAS ROSUMBUM
               Debt

P. 309 JAMES CHILDRESS vs NICHOLAS T. PERKINS, JR.
               Debt

P. 310 THOMAS STAGGS - pl. vs WILLIAM ANTHONY - def.
               Jan. 1824   Scire Facias
       William Anthony, sheriff, who by his debuty,
       Benjamin W. Lane, failed to take bail of
       Henry S. Gray.

P. 312 WILLIAM & JAMES M. BANKS - pl. vs JOHN WITHER-
       SPOON - def.   Case

P. 314 HENRY BETTY - pl. vs CHARLES ALLEN - def.
               Covenant broken

P. 316 MANOAH BOSTICK & RICHARD W. HYDE - pl. vs
       WILLIAM B. McCLELLAN - def.
               Jan. 1824   Debt

P. 319 THOMAS RIDLEY - pl. vs WILLIAM PEEBLES - def.
               Case

P. 322 JOHN NICHOLS - pl. vs BERNARD RICHARDSON - def.
               Debt

P. 324 JOHN NICHOLS - pl. vs NICHOLAS PERKINS, SR. - def.
             Jan. 1824   Debt

P. 326 AARON D. COHORN - pl. vs BENJAMIN W. LANE &
       THOMAS L. ROBINSON - def.   Scire Facias

P. 328 EDWARD STEPHENS - pl. vs ELISHA DAVIS & HUGH
       PINKSTON - def.   Debt

P. 330 BURWELL ROBINSON - pl. vs JOHN NICHOLS - def.
             Jan. 1824   Scire Facias

P. 333 OWEN T. WATKINS - pl. vs JOEL & AMOS ROUNSAVALL -
       def.   Debt

P. 334 DEMPSEY NASH -- pl. vs MAHLON STACY - def.
                  Debt

P. 335 HUGH BARR - pl. vs GEORGE GLASCOCK - def.
             Jan. 1824   Debt

P. 338 BENJAMIN S. TAPPAN & WILLIAM BANKS & JAMES M.
       BANKS - pl. vs WILLIAM M. WILSON - def.
                  Case

P. 341 EDWARD G. CLOUSTON, Assignee & Co. - pl. vs
       WILLIAM M. WILSON - def.   Debt

P. 343 ELEAZOR KIRKPATRICK - pl. vs NICHOLAS PERKINS,
       SR. - def.   April 1824   Debt

P. 345 THE MAYOR & ALDERMAN OF THE TOWN OF FRANKLIN -
       pl. vs JAMES BROWN - def.   Debt

P. 349 JOHN H. HOLT, Assignee & Co. - pl. vs JAMES
       & JAMES H. WILSON - def.   Debt

P. 351 NICHOLAS T. PERKINS, SR. - pl. vs JAMES
       STEWART - def.
                  April 1824   Case

P. 354 STATE OF TENNESSEE - pl. vs NELSON FIELDS - def.
             Indictment for extortion by collecting
             unlawful fees

P. 357 STATE OF TENNESSEE - pl. vs NELSON FIELDS - def.
             Dismission from office as a Constable

P. 358 STATE OF TENNESSEE - pl. vs RODDEN TUCKER - def.
             July 1824   (Same as next page)

P. 359 STATE OF TENNESSEE - pl. vs RODDEN TUCKER, DANIEL
       HUMPHRIES & DAVID RHEA - def.   Riot
       For assault, battery & riot committed on the body
       of Parsons Evans.

14

P. 360 STATE OF TENNESSEE - pl. vs JAMES DUPREE - def.
       Indictment for an assault & battery
       Assaulted Thomas Hallaway (bite, kick, bruise,
                                  beat, and stomp)

P. 363 STATE OF TENNESSEE - pl. vs WALLIS HARRIS - def.
       April 1824   Indictment for hog stealing

P. 367 MAYOR & ALDERMAN OF FRANKLIN - pl. vs JENKINS
       WHITESIDE'S HEIRS - def.   Debt

P. 369 WILLIAM BROWN - pl. vs JASON THOMPSON - def.
       Trespass with force & arms

P. 370 THOMAS G. MALLORY - pl. vs ATKINS NICHOLSON -
       def.   Jan. 1824   Garnishment

P. 374 THOMAS HARDEMAN - pl. vs DANIEL GERMAN - def.
                April 1824
       Thomas Hardeman petitions the court.
       The public road from Franklin to McConnico's
       meeting house passes through a valuable small
       tract of land which belongs to Thomas Hardeman,
       in the vicinity of Franklin, where he plans to
       build. Reports that land was damaged to the
       extent of $500. He thinks damages very low
       & wishes road to be changed.

P. 377 JOHN WITHERSPOON vs RICHARD HUGHES & Others
                July 1824
       An application to have an allowance ascertained
       by a jury for an injury which a road did to him.

P. 379 SINA GENTRY, LETSY GENTRY, BETSY GENTRY, MINOS
       GENTRY, JOHN GENTRY, NANCY GENTRY, & SAMUEL
       GENTRY, children & distributees of Samuel
       Gentry, deceased; who being infants petition
       by their guardian, Nicholas Gentry - pl. vs
       MINOS CANNON, JAMES BOYD & FANNY CHEATHAM, once
       Fanny Gentry, Admrx. & THOMAS CHEATHAM, Admr.,
       in right of his wife, Fanny, of all & singular
       the goods & chattels, rights & credits of
       Samuel Gentry, deceased - def.   July 1824
       Samuel Gentry died in 1816 intestate. He left
       petitioners & Fanny Cheatham, once Fanny
       Gentry. Letters of Administration were granted
       to Minos Cannon, James Boyd, & Fanny Gentry,
       who has since married Thomas Cheatham. He
       left slaves, who were hired out. The money
       has not been given to the children for the
       hiring of the slaves.

P. 387   SINA GENTRY, LETSEY GENTRY, BETSEY GENTRY, MINOS
         GENTRY, JOHN GENTRY, NANCY GENTRY, & SAMUEL
         GENTRY, children & distributee of Samuel Gentry,
         deceased, by their guardian, Nicholas Gentry - pl.
         vs MINOS CANNON, JAMES BOYD & FANNY CHEATHAM,
         once Fanny Gentry, Admrx. & THOMAS CHEATHAM,
         Admr. in right of his wife, Fanny - def.
                      July 1824
         Petition for distributive share of the estate of
         Samuel Gentry, deceased. Also, the sale of
         negroes.

P. 391   SAMUEL WINSTEAD; WILLIAM C. WINSTEAD; LEMUEL H.
         OLILVIE & MARTHA, his wife; WILLIAM EDMONDSON &
         ELIZABETH, his wife; POLLY D. WINSTEAD; & JOHN
         M. WINSTEAD, heirs & distributees of John
         Winstead, deceased
                      Exparte   Petition for Partition
                           Oct. 1824
         Lot # 1 - Martha Ogilvie - 60 acres.
         Lot # 2 - William Winstead - 55 1/4 acres.
         Lot # 3 - Polly D. Winstead - 55 acres.
         Lot # 4 - John M. Winstead - 86 3/4 acres.
         Lot # 5 - Elizabeth Edmondson - 72 acres.
         Lot # 6 - Samuel Winstead - 82 acres.

P. 393   GEORGE F. CRAFTON, DENNIS M. CRAFTON, RICHARD
         L. CRAFTON, & DANIEL CRAFTON, by their guardian,
         Daniel Wilkes; heirs & distributees of John
         Crafton, deceased
                      Exparte   April 1823
         John Crafton died in 1807 intestate. Petitioners
         ancestor owned 2 slaves & land on the waters of
         Hay's Creek (about 200 acres). In his lifetime
         he gifted & granted the said rented tract of
         land. George F. Crafton has reached the age
         of 21 years.

P. 396   JOHNSON JORDAN & ANN L. JORDAN, his wife; ROBERT
         E. BEASLEY, WILLIAM B. BEASLEY, & JOHN P. BEASLEY,
         by their guardian, John W. Phillips; widow &
         heirs of Philip Beasley, deceased
                      Exparte   Petition for Division
                           Oct. 1823
         In 1801, Ann L. Jordan was married to Philip
         Beasley. Philip Beasley died in 1819. He left a
         will. John W. Philips & James Hicks, Exr. Ann
         married March 1822 to Johnson Jordan. Philip
         Beasley left Ann property during her lifetime or
         widowhood. He had 3 sons, Robert E., William B.,
         and John P. Beasley.

P. 398 SAMUEL DUNLAP & NANCY, his wife; WILLIAM CRUTCHER
& ELIZABETH, his wife; DANIEL M. RIGGS, by his
attorney in fact, Aaron Boyd; JANE RIGGS; MIRIAM
RIGGS; JOEL RIGGS; & PATSY RIGGS, by their
guardian, Aaron Boyd - Heirs & distributees of
Zadoc Riggs, deceased
   Exparte Petition for Division
      Oct. 1823
Zadoc Riggs died intestate in 1816. He left about
65 acres on the waters of Spring Creek. He also
left 12 slaves.
   Lot # 1 - Miram Riggs
   Lot. # 2 - Jane Riggs
   Lot # 3 - Samuel Dunlap
   Lot # 4 - Patsey Riggs
   Lot # 5 - Daniel Riggs
   Lot # 6 - Joel Riggs
   Lot # 7 - William Crutcher

P. 401 HENRY LESTER - pl. vs JAMES TERRILL - def.
   July 1824 Trespass on the case
In December 1821, Henry Lester entered an
agreement with James Terrill. He leased for
8 years the land that had descended to the
heirs of Barnebus Balls (about 140 acres). He
got part alloted to Dempsey D. Balls, one of the
heirs. Lester was to pay $2.00 an acre for
the land that was cleared and he was to have
use of 30 acres of land without rent. Terrill
was to furnish the lease.

P. 404 HENRY R. W. HILL - pl. vs WILLIAM P. DUKE &
ARCHIBALD LYTLE - def.
   July 1823   Debt

P. 406 SAMUEL WINSTEAD, Assignee & C - pl. vs NICHOLAS
PERKINS, SR. - def. Debt

P. 408 ANTHONY W. VANLEER, BERNARD VANLEER, & ROBERT
BANTER - pl. vs BERNARD RICHARDSON - def.
   Debt

P. 410 EDWARD McLEMORE - pl. vs BERNARD RICHARDSON -
def. July 1824 Debt

P. 411 PATRICK H. DARBY, to use of James Grizzard &
JAMES HIGGINS, guardian of Polly Moore - pl. vs
SALA N. SHARP - def. Debt

P. 413 JAMES CAROTHERS - pl. vs NOBLE STOCKETT - def.
   Debt

P. 415 ROBERT HAYS - pl. vs HENRY RAGSDALE - def.
        July 1824   Debt

P. 417 ANTHONY W. & BERNARD VANLEER & ROBERT BANTER -
        pl. vs BERNARD RICHARDSON - def.
        Debt

P. 419 JOHN CODINGTON - pl. vs JOSHUA FARRINGTON &
        HENRY COOK, SR. - def.   Debt

P. 420 FOUNTAIN B. CARTER - pl. vs JAMES WILSON - def.
        July 1824   Debt

P. 422 JAMES CAROTHERS, Assignee & Co. - pl. vs
        WILLIAM SHUTE   Debt

P. 424 WILLIAM VAUGHN - pl. vs LEMUEL SMITH - def.
        Debt

P. 426 ELIZABETH MARSHALL, use of William Manning - pl.
        vs LEONARD DUNAVANT - def.
        July 1824   Debt

P. 427 MATTHEW WATSON - pl. vs JAMES H. WILSON - def.
        Debt

P. 429 FOUNTAIN B. CARTER - pl. vs JAMES H. WILSON &
        JOHN STEWART - def.   Debt

P. 431 SAMUEL WINSTEAD, Assignee & Co. - pl. vs
        NICHOLAS PERKINS, SR. - def.
        July 1824   Debt

P. 433 ETHELDRED EVANS - pl. vs JOHN STACY - def.
        Debt

P. 435 EDWARD G. CLOUSTON - pl. vs JAMES WILSON - def.
        Debt

P. 436 JOHN NICHOLS, Exr. & C. - pl. vs WILLIAM
        WILKINSON, guardian & C. - def.
        July 1824   Debt

P. 438 WILLIAM M. RICHARDSON - pl. vs WILKINS
        WHITFIELD - def.   Debt

P. 439 RICHARD DARY (?) - pl. vs WILLIAM SHUTE - def.
        Debt

P. 441 SAMUEL V. D. STOUT - pl. vs JOHN WITHERSPOON,
        THOMAS H. PERKINS, DANIEL PERKINS, & WILLIAM
        SHUTE - def.
        July 1824   Debt

P. 444 WILLIAM S. WEBB - pl. vs JOHN W. CRUNK & Others -
def.   Oct. 1824   Motion

P. 445 JAMES ROANE & ROSWELL P. HAYS, use of Roswell P.
Hays - pl. vs ALEXANDER SMITH - def.
          Case (Debt)
Roswell P. Hays & James Roane are partners in
medicine & surgery.

P. 447 WILLIAM BANKS & JAMES M. BANKS - pl. vs FRANCIS
M. DEAN - def.
          July 1824   Trespass on the case (Debt)

P. 449 HUGH McCABE - pl. vs THOMAS MONTGOMERY - def.
               Debt

P. 451 MATTHIAS B. MURFREE - pl. vs WILLIAM R. NUNN -
     def.   Debt

P. 453 JOHN N. CHARTER - pl. vs JAMES H. WILSON - def.
          Oct. 1824   Debt

P. 455 THOMAS L. ROBINSON - pl. vs NICHOLAS P. PERKINS -
def.   Case (Debt)

P. 458 JAMES PATTON - pl. vs SAMUEL O. WILSON, WILLIAM
WILSON, & JASON C. WILSON - def.   Debt

P. 460 WILLIAM H. DOUNING - pl. vs WILLIAM SMITH &
JAMES A. M. T. STEWART - def.
          July 1824   Debt

P. 462 RICHARD STEEL & B. SPENCE, Exr. & C. - pl. vs
JAMES BROWN - def.   Debt
Richard Steel & Brent Spence, Exr. of George
Culbert, deceased.

P. 464 PETER BASS - pl. vs JAMES BROWN - def.
               Debt

P. 466 GEORGE B. MEEK - pl. vs JOHN NICHOLS - def.
          July 1824   Debt - Appeal from a justice

P. 468 JOHN WHITE - pl. vs JAM & WRIGHT STANLEY - def.
               Debt

P. 470 THOMAS L. ROBINSON - pl. vs ANDREW L. MARTIN -
     def.   Case (Debt)

P. 473 HINCHEY PETWAY, MORRIS L. BOND, & STEPHEN
CANTRELL - pl. vs BERNARD RICHARDSON - def.
          July 1824   Debt
(Merchants)

P. 474 ROBERT J. MOORE - pl. vs NICHOLAS PERKINS, SR. -
def.   Oct. 1824   Debt

P. 476 JOSEPH ANDERSON & JAMES KNOX - pl. vs JOHN
WILSON - def.   Debt

P. 479 JAMES W. BUCKLEY - pl. vs JAMES VAUGHN - def.
          July 1824   Certiorari

P. 483 THOMAS A. JONES - pl. vs JOHN PORTER - def.
          Certiorari

P. 487 FRANCIS FLESHEART & HARDAWAY, his wife - pl.
vs LUCY G. LOCK, RICHARD S. LOCK, HENRY C. LOCK,
FRANCIS LOCK & ELIZABETH SECREST & JOHN SECREST -
The widow & heirs of Richard Lock, deceased - def.
          Oct. 1824   Petition for Partition
Richard S. (or L.) Lock died intestate. He left
negroes & a tract of land (150 acres).
          Lot # 1 - Francis Flesheart & Hardaway,
                    his wife - 10 acres
          Lot # 2 - Lucy Lock - 14 acres
          Lot # 3 - Henry C. Lock - 10 acres
          Lot # 4 - Richard S. Lock - 12 3/4 acres
          Lot # 5 - Francis Lock - 29 3/4 acres
          Lot # 6 - Knacy Lock - 20 acres
The dower is divided into 6 lots.

P. 491 ELIZABETH COLEMAN
          Jan. 1824   Exparte   Petition for Dower
Joshua Coleman, husband of Elizabeth Coleman,
died in 1821. He left a tract of land on the
waters of the West Harpeth. Wants 1/3 of
the land - with mansion house & outbuildings.

P. 494 RICHARD BURNETT & MARY, his wife; THOMAS COLEMAN;
FANNY COLEMAN & NANCY COLEMAN, by their guardian,
Joseph Burnett & Elizabeth Coleman
          Jan. 1824   Exparte
          Petition for Partition of Joshua Coleman,
               deceased   Estate
Joshua Coleman died in 1821 intestate. He left
negroes & a tract of land containing 134 acres
on the waters of the West Harpeth. Mary
Burnett, formerly Mary Coleman. Elizabeth
Coleman, widow of Joshua Coleman.

P. 494 LEWIS OGILVIE; POLLY OGILVIE, by her guardian,
Henry Bailey; ALEXANDER ROBERTSON & FRANCIS,
his wife; & HOUSTON McCLURE & ANNA, his wife
          Jan. 1824   Exparte   Petition for Partition o
                              John Ogilvie, deceased
John Ogilvie died in 1821. He left a will to
divide the slaves.

20

P. 499 JOHN W. POPE - pl. vs WILLIAM J. BOYD. - def.
          Oct. 1821   Debt

P. 501 GEORGE BURNETT - pl. vs ANDREW ROUNDTREE - def.
                         Debt

P. 503 THOMAS BRADLEY - pl. vs MATTHEW JOHNSTON - def.
          April 1822   Case
       Johnston has a water mill for grinding corn
       situated on a stream of the waters called,
       Little Harpeth - obstructing stream in free
       running of the water.

P. 507 RICHARD AMHURST - pl. vs NICHOLAS P. PERKINS -
       def.   Oct. 1821   Debt

P. 509 C. WALLACE - pl. vs ANDREW S. MARTIN - def.
                    Debt

P. 511 JOSEPH NOWELL - pl. vs JAMES WILSON - def.
                    Case (Debt)

P. 512 WILLIS MACLIN - pl. vs THOMAS GARRETT - def.
              Certiorari from a justices judgment

P. 523 ALEXANDER McCOWN - pl. vs AARON D. CAHORN - def.
          Oct. 1823   Trespass on the case
       William S. Murrell bought a 4 wheel carriage
       from McCown; Cahorn was a wittness to the
       transaction & was acquainted with Murrell &
       knew him to be insolvent. He signed a note
       on Murrell.

P. 515 JAMES McKNIGHT - pl. vs CHARLES GOODE &
       WILLIAM BLACK - def.
          Jan. 1821   Attachment

P. 520 JOSIAH WALTON - pl. vs EDWARD SWANSON, JR. -
       def.   Debt

P. 522 LEVI EDMONDSON - pl. vs MANOAH BOSTICK - def.
          July 1824   Debt

RECORD BOOK

LAWSUITS

No. 3

1823 - 1827

Justice of Peace Court

P. 1   JAMES C. A. RILEY - pl. vs RICHARD STEELE &
BRENT SPENCE - def.
            June 1823   Debt
Richard Steele & Brent Spence, Exr. of last will
of George Culbert, deceased. Execution of
George Culbert, June 23, 1823.

P. 4   JOHN STAGGS - pl. vs GARNER MAYS & SEARCY D. SHARP -
def.   Jan. 1825   Trespass

P. 7   LUKE WILLIAMS - pl. vs WILLIAM H. COUNCELLE -
def.   April 1825   Certiorari
Agreed to work on a house for John Tisdale.

P. 11   LEWIS TURNER, use of Henry Reams - pl. vs
WARE HURLEY & ALLEN BUGG - def.
            Sept. 28, 1924 Debt

P. 13   ROBERT NEAL - pl. vs JOHN PORTER - def.
            Debt

P. 15   WILLIAM & JAMES M. BANKS - pl. vs JAMES WILSON,
SR. - def.
            Aug. 16, 1824   Debt

P. 16   JOSHUA G. SIMMS - pl. vs JACOB H. RUDER - def.
            Sept. 18, 1824   Debt

P. 18   JOSHUA G. SIMMS - pl. vs JACOB H. RUDER - def.
            Sept. 18, 1824   Debt

P. 20   SALA N. SHARP - pl. vs JAMES S. CHUNN - def.
            June 26, 1824   Case
Renting of land.

P. 22   HUGH M. DUNLAP - pl. vs JOHN NICHOLS - def.
            June 29, 1824   Case
Horse.

22

P. 24   JOHN & THOMAS WOOD, Assignees of James Stewart -
        pl. vs JAMES H. WILSON - def.
                    Dec. 30, 1823   Case
        James Steward & ________Gill are merchants.

P. 26   ALICE EDMISTON - pl. vs PATRICK CAMPBELL &
        DAVID CAMPBELL - def.
                    Sept. 16, 1822   Covenant
        Alice Edmiston, survivor of John Edmiston.

P. 28   METCALF DeGRAFFENREID - pl. vs THOMAS RIDLEY
        & JOHN HOUSE - def.
                    Oct. 1823   Debt

______ JOSHUA G. SIMMS - pl. vs JACOB H. RUDER - def.
                    Oct. 1823   Debt

P. 31   THOMAS RIDLEY - pl. vs JOHN NICHOLS - def.
                    Oct. 1824   Trespass

P. 37   WILLIAM & JONATHAN MONTGOMERY - pl. vs WILLIAM
        & JAMES M. BANKS - def.
                    Case
        William & Jonathan Montgomery are merchants &
        partners in trade, trading under the name of
        W. & J. Montgomery.
        William & James Banks are merchants &
        partners under the name firm of W. & J. M.
        Banks.
        Nathaniel Moody (on July 28, 1819) - Giles Co.
        Moody S. Alexander of Giles Co.

______ STATE OF TENNESSEE - pl. against PLEASANT
        STAGGS - def.   Indictment for an assault &
                            battery & affray
        Assault on Henry Reams Aug. 23, 1824.
        $5.00 fine plus cost - 20 days jail fine.

P. 51   BERNARD RICHARDSON - pl. vs JOANNA MILLER,
        WILLIAM MILLER, S. THOMAS MILLER, JESSE S.
        FLIPPEN, WILLIAM & PAGE BOND, Admr. of Morris
        S. Bond, deceased - def.
                    Petition for counter security
        Joanna Miller, Extrx. of Thomas Miller,
        deceased. Exr. & Exrx. have become careless
        in management of the estate. William Miller
        is planning to leave the state.

P. 55   KNACY ANDREWS - pl. vs THOMAS RIDLEY - def.
                    Dec. 7, 1822   Debt

P. 57   LEVI GARDINER - pl. vs JASON THOMPSON - def.
                    Oct. 1824   Debt - appeal from a
                                    Justice

P. 59 BAILEY HARDEMAN - pl. vs HOLLON DAVIS - def.
           Dec. 1824   : Covenant

P. 60 HENRY R. W. HILL, JAMES C. HILL, CHARLES G.
       ALMSTEAD & ELIZABETH, his wife - pl. vs
       ARCHIBALD LYTLE - def.
           Dec. 1824   Debt
       Plaintiffs were partners & merchants trading under
       the name of R. W. Hill & Company.

_____ JOANNAH MILLER - pl. vs JOHN MAYFIELD - def.
           Sept. 1824   Debt
       J. H. Maury, attorney.

P. 63 MALACHI KERBY - pl. vs ADAM PEWITT, LEWIS PEWITT,
       HENRY PEWITT, JAMES PEWITT, JOHN PEWITT, &
       BARBARY PEWITT - def.
           July 1825   Petition for Partition
       Children of James Pewitt, deceased. James
       died _____. He left 120 acres. Malachi Kerby is
       entitled to part of the land.

P. 68 ADAM PEWITT, LEWIS PEWITT, HENRY PEWITT, JAMES
       PEWITT, JOHN PEWITT, & BARBARY PEWITT, heirs of
       James Pewitt, deceased
                     Petition for Partition
                     April 1825
       Lewis & Henry Pewitt are minors & sue by their
       next friend, William Bond. James Pewitt, John
       Pewitt, & Barbary Pewitt are minors & sue by
       their guardian, James Adams. James Pewitt,
       deceased, left 120 acres of land of the South
       Harpeth - (640 acres South Harpeth part of
       this tract).

P. 73 HENRY EELBECK - pl. vs ROBERT PARRISH - def.
           June 1824   Case   Trespass
       Joel Parrish & the daughter of Robert Parrish
       are of full age.

P. 76 JOANNA MILLER - pl. vs JOHN T. COOK & MARY
       BOYD - def.
           March 1825   Debt
       Joanna Miller is the Extrx. of Thomas Miller,
       deceased.

P. 81 THOMAS RIDLEY - pl. vs BERNARD RICHARDSON - def.
           March 1824   Case
       $1,000 debt.

P. 84 WILLIAM BANK - pl. vs ROBERT PARRISH - def.
           July 1825   Debt

24

P. 86   JESSE COX & ELIZABETH, his wife; BENJAMIN BROWN;
         EPHRAIM BROWN, JR.; SAMUEL BROWN; & CHARLES
         BROWN   1825   Petition for Partition
         Ephraim, Charles & Samuel Brown are minors & sue
         by their guardian, Michael Brown. Luther Brown,
         Elizabeth Cox, Benjamin Brown, Ephraim Brown, Jr.,
         Samuel Brown, & Charles Brown are legal heirs
         of Charles Brown, deceased. He left about
         640 acres of land formerly in Davidson Co. &
         now in Williamson County on the Little
         Harpeth River.

P. 89   JESSE COX & Others
                 Wed. 12th Jan. 1825   Petition for Partition
         The heirs of Charles Brown, deceased, are as
         follows: Luther Brown; Jesse Cox & his wife,
         Elizabeth; Benjamin, Ephraim, Samuel, &
         Charles Brown. Ephraim, Samuel, & Charles
         Brown are minors. Their guardian is Michael
         Brown. Charles Brown, deceased, left 418 1/2
         acres of land.

P. 94   JAMES SHELBURN
                 1825   Petition for Partition
         Jan. 1825 - Joseph H. Stockett, deceased. He
         made a last will. Bequeathed to Nicholas
         T. Perkins & William Edminston in trust
         for the use & benefit of ________________.
         The heirs of Joseph H. Stockett, deceased, are:
         Thomas Sappington, Susan Sappington, Rebecca
         Sappington, & Ann Sappington. 12 or 13
         slaves were left to them.

P. 95   WINSON EDNEY & NANCY, his wife - pl. vs
         THOMAS A. THOMPSON & SUSAN, his wife; MARIA
         POTTS; EDWIN POTTS; & JOSEPH POTTS - def.
                 April 1825   Petition for Partition
         The heirs of Peter Potts, deceased are: Nancy
         Edney, who married Winson Edney; Susan Potts,
         who married Thomas A. Thompson; Maria Potts;
         Edwin Potts; & Joseph Potts. Maria, Edwin, &
         Joseph Potts are minors & their guardian is
         Sion Hunt. Peter Potts, deceased, left slaves.

P. 97   JAMES SHELBURNE & SUSAN, his wife; REBECCA
         SAPPINGTON; ANN SAPPINGTON; & THOMAS SAPPINGTON
                 April 1825   Petition for Partition
         Rebecca, Ann, & Thomas Sappington are minors &
         sue by their guardian, John Thompson. Thomas
         W. Stockett, deceased, made a last will.
         He left negroes - slaves.

P. 99   PETITION FOR PARTITION   April 1825
William Thweatt, ancestor of Petitioners.
William, Peter, & Elizabeth, his heirs. He
left slaves. Elizabeth has married Samuel
Blake. Guardian is Erastus T. Collins.

P. 101 HEIRS OF WILLIAM MURRY, Deceased
            April 1825   Petition for Partition
William Murry died about 1802. He had land
granted by the state of North Carolina. His
heirs are: Ennis Murry, Alfred Murry, John M.
Murry, Elijah Peyton & Matilda, his wife, &
Ursula Murry. Henry Murry, the father of
William Murry, died in 1804. He left the
following heirs: Thomas Murrey, John Murrey,
Henry Murrey, Jane married to Kemp Holland, &
the heirs of William Murrey.

P. 104 HEIRS OF EDWARD RAGSDALE, deceased.
            April 1825   Petition of Partition
Edward Ragsdale, deceased. His heirs are:
Edward Ragsdale, James B. Ragsdale, Frances
Ragsdale (her guardian being John Allison &
Mark L. Andrews), & Elizabeth Crick. John
Ragsdale & Mark Andrews, Exr. to the will.

P. 107 HEIRS OF KEMP HOLLAND, deceased
            April 1825   Petition for Partition
Kemp Holland died on Aug. 4, 1824. He owned
224 acres of land. His heirs are: Jane
Holland, Margaret Holland, Newton Holland, &
Bird Holland (their guardian being Jan Holland),
Frederick Holland, Spearman Holland, James
Hughes & Rosanna, his wife, George Holland (his
guardian being James Hughes), Kemp J. Holland,
John M. Holland (their guardian being Kemp S.
Holland), Bird Dodson & Judith, his wife, &
Fielding Helm & Nancy, his wife.

P. 111 JANE HOLLAND, MARGARET HOLLAND, NEWTON HOLLAND,
BIRD HOLLAND (by their guardian Jane Holland),
JAMES HUGHES & ROSANNA, his wife, GEORGE HOLLAND
(by his guardian, James Hughes), KEMP J.
HOLLAND & JOHN M. HOLLAND (by their guardian, Kemp
J. Holland), BIRD DODSON & JUDITH, his wife,
FIELDING HELM & NANCY, his wife, FREDERICK
HOLLAND & SPEARMAN HOLLAND, heirs at law &
distributors of Kemp Holland, deceased - pl. vs
JOHN K. CAMPBELL & PAGE BOND, Admr. of Kemp
Holland, deceased - def.
            1825   Petition for Division of Slaves
Kemp Holland died Aug. 4, 1824 in Williamson
County.

P. 115 HEIRS OF JOHN ROWLETT, deceased
April 1825   Petition for Partition
John Rowlett, deceased, left slaves. His heirs
are: Benjamin Rowlett, deceased (Benjamin is the
son of John Rowlett & he has left children of his
own), Elizabeth Rowlett, Prudence, Philip,
Martin, Lucy, William, & John S. Rowlett. Their
guardian is William G. Boyd.

P. 118 HEIRS OF CHAPMAN WHITE
July 1825   Petition for Partition
Chapman White, deceased, left a will. Martha
White is his widow. His heirs are: William
C. White, Abram White, Lucinda M. White (her
guardian being Martha White), Moses White (His
guardian being Martha White), Moses C. Rags-
dale, Elizabeth M. Ragsdale, Martha W. Rags-
dale, Catharine M. Ragsdale, Henry Ragsdale,
Robert Ragsdale, William Ragsdale, & Edward
Ragsdale (they are the children of Edward
Ragsdale, who is deceased, and their guardian
is Spencer Buford).

P. 122 HEIRS OF ELISHA MORTON
Jan. 1825   Petition for Partition
Elisha Morton died in 1821. He left some
land. Tobitha, his widow, has since
married William L. Ross. Elisha Morton's
heirs are: Martha Allen & Solomon Morton (their
guardian being David R. Gooch).

P. 126 HEIRS OF ROBERT McLEMORE
Jan. 1825   Petition for Partition
Robert McLemore, deceased, owned 125 acres of
land. Peggy S., Sr., his widow, has since married
Thomas R. Mallory. Robert McLemore's heirs are:
Atkin J. McLemore, Sugars McLemore & Bethenia
A. G. McLemore, his wife, John D. McLemore,
Polly M. McLemore, Robert W. McLemore, & Peggy
S. McLemore. John D., Polly M., Robert W.,
& Peggy S. McLemore are minors. Their guardian
is Charles A. Dabney.

P. 131 HEIRS OF JANE WHEATON
July 1822   Petition for Partition
Jane Wheaton died in 1809. She left 9 negroes &
town lots. Her heirs are: Sterling Wheaton &
John S. Wheaton (their guardian being
William Wilkerson).

P. 134 HEIRS OF SAMUEL WILSON
Oct. 1825   Petition for Partition
Samuel Wilson died Oct. 1821. He left 9 heirs:
Jason C. Wilson, Robert Wilson, Almyra T. Wilson,
Margaret Ann Wilson, Malvyra Wilson, Catherine
Wilson (all infants of Samuel Wilson, their
guardian being Martha Wilson, his widow), CON'T.

P. 134 Heirs of Samuel Wilson CON'T.
Rebecca A. F. Hardeman, who is married to Bailey
Hardeman, & Emmeline Wilson, who is married to
James H. Wilson.

P. 146 EDWARD G. CLOUSTON - pl. vs IRA WALTON & JESSE
WALTON - def.
Feb. 1825   Debt

P. 152 JOHN A. MURRELL - pl. vs JAMES BROWN - def.
July 1825   Case

P. 155 ROBERT C. THOMPSON - pl. vs JAMES NEAL - def.
July 1825   Debt

P. 157 JOEL G. CHILDRESS - pl. vs RICHARD C. NAPIER -
def.   July 1825   Case

P. 159 THOMAS G. MALLORY - pl. vs ROBERT PARRISH - def.
July 1825   Debt

P. 161 NICHOLAS SCALES - pl. vs NICHOLAS PERKINS - def.
Term - July 1825   Debt

P. 163 JAMES S. WILLIAMS - pl. vs NOBLE STOCKETT - def.
Debt

P. 165 AARON BROWN & SUSAN, his wife; NICHOLAS T.
PERKINS; & WILLIAM EDMISTON, use of James
Shelburne - pl. vs JOHN PORTER - def.
Debt

P. 167 WILLIAM BANKS - pl. vs JOHN S. WHEATON &
EDWARD G. CLOUSTON - def.
July 1825   Debts

P. 170 WILLIAM BANKS - pl. vs WILLIAM SMITH & EDWARD
G. CLOUSTON - def.   Debt

P. 174 JOSIAH NICHOL & JAMES BELL - pl. vs JOHN S.
WHEATON - def.   Debt

P. 176 JOHN WHITE - pl. vs JAMES STANLEY & WRIGHT
STANLEY - def.
July 1825   Debt

P. 178 ANGUS McPHAIL - pl. vs THOMAS OLD - def.
Debt

P. 180 ROBERT B. EDMONDSTON - pl. vs WILLIAM WILSON -
def.   Debt

P. 181 RICHARD ARNOLD - pl. vs WILLIAM HARRISON - def.
July 1825   Debt

P. 183 ROBERT B. EDMONDSON - pl. vs WILLIAM WILSON - def.
     July 1825   Debt

P. 185 ARCHELUS P. HUGHES - pl. vs JOHN NICHOLS - def.
     Debt

P. 187 THOMAS OLD - pl. vs NICHOLAS PERKINS, SR. -
  def.   Debt

P. 189 JAMES STANLEY - pl. vs GEORGE E. COOK & MARY
  BOYD - def.
     Oct. 1825   Debt

P. 192 THOMAS SMITH - pl. vs JOHN M. WATSON & RICHARD
  H. RUDDER - def.   Debt

P. 194 LUKE TURMAN, CHARLES TURMAN, & SAMUEL WILLIAMSON -
  pl. vs ALFRED T. MOORE - def. Debt

P. 196 BENJAMIN W. WILLIAMS - pl. vs EDWARD G.
  CLOUSTON - def.
     July 1825 Debt

P. 198 RICHARD C. NAPIER - pl. vs PHILIP MAURY - def.
     Debt

P. 200 WILLIAM BANKS - pl. vs GEORGE E. COOK &
  EDWARD G. CLOUSTON - def. Debt

P. 203 JOHN DOE, lessee of William R. Nunn - pl. vs
  JAMES MAYFIELD - def.   Ejectment
  On tract of land granted to Thomas Polk by
  North Carolina, Grant # 6. Richard Roe with
  force & arms entered into the said tenements.

P. 205 STATE OF TENNESSEE - pl. against JOHN WITHER-
  SPOON, SR. - def.
    1826 Indictment for stopping a
      public highway

P. 211 JOHN WITHERSPOON - pl. vs RICHARD HUGHES &
  Others - def.
  On a petition for a road.

P. 212 RICHARD HUGHES - pl. vs JOHN WITHERSPOON - def.
    Petition for a road

P. 213 STATE OF TENNESSEE - pl. against GEORGE
  GLASCOCK - def.
    Presentment for an assault

P. 217 THOMAS SIMMONS - pl. vs JOHN T. COOK - def.
    Debt

P. 220 JOHN NEWMAN - pl. vs ALEXANDER SMITH - def.
         Debt

P. 222 PETITION FOR DISTRIBUTION
            Jan. 1824   Filed June 2, 1822
       David Robertson, deceased, died April 1821.
       Sarah Robertson is his widow. He left 2 infants,
       David R. Robertson & Nicholas T. Robertson. Their
       guardian is John Witherspoon. David Robertson
       was a farmer. He had slaves. His heirs are:
       John Robertson, Sally Robertson (she is the
       minor daughter of David Robertson's son,
       Joseph Robertson, who is deceased), Michael
       Robertson, & Polly, who is married to Andrew
       Roundtree.

P. 230 The schedule of Andrew Roundtree & Polly Roundtree,
       his wife, referred to in the foregoing answer -
       a list of property received of David Robinson,
       deceased, by way of gift by Andrew Roundtree &
       Polly Roundtree, his wife & the daughter of said,
       David Robinson, deceased. 1799.

P. 235 GEORGE HATHWAY - pl. vs RICHARD SUTTON - def.
            Jan. 1826   Case

P. 241 PETITION FOR PARTITION   Oct. 1825
       John Parks, Sr. died Dec. 20, 1822. He left a
       will. Cloe Weather, deceased, had property in
       North Carolina & he left a will. Cloe Weather's
       heirs are: Reuben Weathers, James Hutton &
       Winny, his wife, Sally Weathers, Patsy Weathers,
       Elizabeth Weathers, William J. Weathers, & John
       Weathers. Sally, Patsy, Elizabeth, William J.,
       & John Weathers are all under age & their
       guardian is Reuben Weathers. The heirs of John
       Parks, Sr. are: Rachel Parks, his wife, Sally
       Mayfield, Children of Reuben Parks, deceased,
       Nancy Smith & Children, John Parks, Benjamin Parks,
       & Andrew Parks. John, Benjamin, & Andrew Parks
       are the sons of John Parks, Sr., deceased.

P. 253 JOSEPH H. STOCKETT
            Jan. 1826   Petition for Partition
       Joseph H. Stockett, deceased, left a will. His
       heirs are: Rebecca B. Gentry, wife of Theophelus
       L. Gentry, Thomas Sappington (1/3 part - minor
       child of Thomas Sappington), Ann Sappington (1/3
       part - minor child of Thomas Sappington), & James
       Shelburne & Susan, his wife (one of the Children).

P. 255 PETITION FOR PARTITION   Jan. 1826
        Samuel Clark, deceased, left slaves. His heirs
        are: William & Samuel Clark.

P. 256 HEIRS OF MARTIN R. WORD
            April 1826   Petition for Partition
        Martin R. Word, deceased. His heirs are:
        Louisa A. Word, William B. Word, & Judith A.
        Word. Their guardian is James Swanson.

P. 260 WILLIAM HAMILTON - pl. vs LEAH STANFIELD,
        GOODLOE STANFIELD, & MARMADUKE STANFIELD - def.
            Oct. 1825
        Ephraim Stanfield, deceased, left a will. The
        executors are mismanaging the estate.

P. 260 EPHRAIM STANFIELD, deceased   Oct. 1825
        Exr. to the will of Ephraim Stanfield, deceased,
        are: Leah Stanfield, Marmaduke Stanfield, &
        Goodloe Stanfield. William Hamilton wants exr.
        removed. He believes they are mismanaging the
        estate.

P. 262 NELSON LAVENDER, use of Allen Bugg - pl. vs
        FELIX STAGGS - def.
                    Debt

P. 265 WILLIAM MASON - pl. vs HOLLAN DAVIS - def.
                    Covenant

P. 268 GARNER MAYS - pl. vs FELIX STAGGS - def.
                    Case

P. 271 THOMAS MONTGOMERY - pl. vs THOMAS CASH - def.
                    Appeal

P. 273 URIAH CUMMINS - pl. vs JOHN M. WATSON &
        WILLIAM WATSON - def.   Debt

P. 276 THOMAS SCURRY - pl. vs FELIX STAGGS - def.
                    Debt

P. 279 MICHAEL PAGE - pl. vs ENNIS DUFF - def.
            April 1826   Trespass

P. 282 SAMUEL A. WILSON - pl. vs CHARLES MORAN - def.
                    Case

P. 286 STATE OF TENNESSEE - pl. vs JOSEPH OWEN - def.
                    Peace Warrant

P. 288 STATE OF TENNESSEE - pl. vs JOSEPH STREET - def.
                    Peace Warrant

P. 290 STATE OF TENNESSEE - pl. against EDWARD PHILIPS &
JOHN WITHERSPOON, JR. - def.
Indictment for stopping public highway

P. 295 JOEL G. CHILDRESS - pl. vs RICHARD C. NAPIER -
def.   Case

P. 299 WILLIAM YOWELL - pl. vs CLARISA DUSHAN - def.

P. 301 STATE OF TENNESSEE - pl. vs WILLIAM WALTON -
def.
Feb. 10, 1826

P. 304 STATE OF TENNESSEE - pl. vs WILLIAM STEWART -
def.   Feb. 10, 1826   Larceny

P. 307 ABRAM M. DeGRAFFENREID, Admr. of Mary Ann
DeGraffenreid, deceased - pl. vs ROBERT WHITE -
def.   April 1826   Case

P. 310 KNACY ANDREWS - pl. vs EPHRAIM ANDREWS - def.
Jan. 1826

P. 313 SALA N. SHARP - pl. vs GEORGE HULME & BENJAMIN
WHITE - def.
July term 1826
Trespass - Force & Arms

P. 316 ANDREW ROUNDTREE & MARY, his wife; DAVID ROBERTSON;
& NICHOLAS T. ROBERTSON, by their guardian, John
Witherspoon - pl. vs JOHN ROBERTSON; MICHAEL
ROBERTSON; & SALLY ROBERTSON - def.
June 1824
David Robertson, Sr. died April 1821 intestate.
He owned land at Leepers Fork of West Harpeth
where he resided. It was purchased from
Mattocks & Moses Sprinkles. The land contained
about 400 acres. It was to be divided into 6
parts: Mary Roundtree in Hickman County; David
Robertson in Hickman County; Nicholas Robertson
in Hickman County; John Robertson in Hickman
County; Michael Robertson in Bedford County; &
Sally Robertson. Sally Robertson is the daughter
of David Robertson's son, Joseph, who is deceased.

P. 322 NATHANIEL DOOLM - pl. vs GEORGE GLASCOCK - def.

P. 324 BERRYMAN McDANIEL - pl. vs STEPHEN CHILDRESS - def.

P. 326 SAMUEL B. LEE - pl. vs JOHN BLYTHE - def.

P. 328 CHARLES MORAN - pl. vs SAMUEL (LEMUEL?) A. WILSON -
def.

P. 330 JESSE MEACHAM - pl. vs ROBERT PARRISH - def.
Debt

P. 334 SALA N. SHARP - pl. vs GEORGE HULME &
BENJAMIN WHITE - def.

P. 337 JOSEPH DWYER - pl. vs JOHN F. SMITH, EDWARD
BREATHITT, & ROBERT P. CURRIN - def.

P. 340 SUSANNA PARRISH, use of Stephen Cantrell - pl.
vs ROBERT PARRISH - def.

P. 343 ROBERT WEAKLEY; TURNER SAUNDERS; ROBERT P.
CURRIN; BEVERLY RESE; JOHN DONELSON, JR.; CHARLES
BOYLES; JURI I. GIST,   Trustee of the Muscle
Shoal Land Company, South of Tennessee River,
for the use of Turner Saunders - pl. vs AMOUS
ROUNSOVLLE - def.
Debt

P. 346 ROBERT WEAKLEY; TURNER SANDERS; ROBERT P. CURRIN;
BEVERLY RESE; JOHN DONALSON, JR.; CHARLES BOYLES;
LEVI J. GIST, Trustee of Muscle Shoal Land Com-
pany, South of Tennessee River, use of Turner
Saunders - pl. vs JACOB HALFACRE - def.
Debt

P. 350 JOHN WHITE - pl. vs JAMES STANDLEY & WRIGHT
STANLEY - def.
Debt

P. 353 ROBERT WEAKLEY, TURNER SAUNDERS, ROBERT P. CURRIN,
BEVERLY REESE, JOHN DONALSON, JR., CHARLES BOYLES,
& LEVI I. GIST, Trustee of Muscle Shoal Land
Company, South of the Tennessee River, use of
Turner Sanders - pl. vs THOMAS HAYNES - def.
Debt

P. 356 Same as above - pl. vs LEMUEL DONELSON - def.
Debt

P. 359 JOHN WHITFIELD - pl. vs LEWIS C. ALLEN - def.
Scirifacias against Bail

P. 361 JOHN WHITFIELD - pl. vs JOSHUA D. CLOUD &
LEWIS C. ALLEN - def.

P. 363 WILLIAM MOORE - pl. vs SAMUEL SHANNON & NANCY
PRIEST, Admr. of James Priest, deceased - def.

P. 367 DANIEL GRIFFITH - pl. vs ISHAM R. THWEATT - def.
Debt

P. 369 HENRY TOLAND & JOHN ROCKHILL - pl. vs ANDERSON
BERRYMAN - def.

P. 371 JOSEPH TANNER & ANN HARRISON - pl. vs NICHOLAS
SCALES - def.
Debt

P. 373 JOHN BRUNER (BROWN?) & SUSAN BRUNER (BROWN?)
July 1822   Partition for Dower
Susan Bruner (Brown?) was married to Peter Hardeman,
deceased, in 1810. Peter Hardeman died May 21,
1820. Peter Hardeman's heir is Franklin
Hardeman, whose guardian is John Hardeman.
Susan has since married John Bruner (Brown?).
Peter Hardeman left some land on Five Mile
Creek. Susan wants 1/3 of the land including the
house.

P. 378 WALTER C. HALEY - pl. vs THOMAS REYNOLDS, Admr.
of Susan Reynolds, deceased - def.
Dec. 16, 1823   Petition for Partition
Walter C. Haley married Bethenia Reynolds,
daughter of Susannah Reynolds. Susannah
Reynolds died in the summer of 1821. Thomas
Reynolds (her son).

P. 380 GERMAN G. STOKES - pl. vs JOHN B. HOUSTON - def.

P. 382 THOMAS WELLS - pl. vs WILLIAM WEBB - def.
Debt

P. 387 JOHN A. HOLLAND - pl. vs JASON C. WILSON - def.
Trespass

P. 389 JOHN WATSON - pl. vs JOHN P. IRION - def.

P. 392 BERNARD McKURNAN, use of John S. Russwurn? -
pl. vs NICHOLAS PERKINS, SR. - def.
Covenant

P. 395 JOHN WATSON - pl. vs JOHN TISDALE - def.
Debt

P. 398 JOHN WATSON - pl. vs JOHN TISDALE - def.
Covenant

P. 400 HUGH ELLIOTT - pl. vs JOHN NICHOL - def.
Debt

P. 403 JOHN WILSON, JASON C. WILSON, & ELISHA DAVIS,
Admr. of Samuel Wilson, deceased, use of
Elisha Davis - pl. vs JOHN WILSON & BAILEY
HARDMAN - def.
Debt

P. 406 ROBERT WEAKLEY, TURNER SAUNDERS, ROBERT P. CURRIN,
BEVERLY REESE, JOHN DONALSON, JR., CHARLES
BOYLES, & LEVI I. GIST, Trustee of Muscle Shoal
Land Co., South of the Tennessee River, use of
Turner Sanders - pl. vs HOLLON DAVIS - def.
Debt

P. 409 JOHN WATSON - pl. vs JOHN NICHOLS - def.
Debt

P. 413 TALBOT JONES - pl. vs NICHOLAS PERKINS, SR. - def.
Debt

P. 415 BENJAMIN S. TAPPAN - pl. vs SAMUEL D. WILSON -
def. Debt

P. 418 ROBERT WEAKLEY - pl. vs JOHN WILSON - def.
Debt

P. 421 WILLIAM M. WILSON - pl. vs JOHN NICHOLS - def.
Debt

P. 423 JOHN WATSON - pl. vs JOHN NICHOLS - def.
Debt

P. 426 CHARLES G. OBUSTEAD, guardian to the heirs of
Charles McAlister, deceased - pl. vs JOHN
NICHOLS - def. Debt

P. 428 BENJAMIN S. TAPPAN & CHARLES G. OLMSTEAD -
pl. vs JOHN NICHOLS - def.
Debt
Benjamin S. Tappan & Charles G. Olmstead are
merchants & partners trading under the firm
& style of Tappan & Olmstead.

P. 431 THOMAS K. PRICE - pl. vs THOMAS C. SMITH - def.
Debt

P. 433 THOMAS T. THORNHILL & CHARLES PHELPS - pl. vs
THOMAS WORTHAM & JOSHUA FARRINGTON - def.
Debt
Thomas T. Thornhill & Charles Phelps are
merchants & traders trading under the name of
Thornhill & Phelps.

P. 437 SIMPSON PERRY - pl. vs WILLIAM WEBB - def.

P. 440 JOANNAH MILLER - pl. vs MARY BOYD - def.
Debt

P. 443 JOANNAH MILLER - pl. vs MARY BOYD - def.
Debt

P. 445 BERNARD RICHARDSON - pl. vs HENRY L. GRAY, JOHN
F. SMITH, & CHARLES G. OLMSTEAD - def.
. Motion

P. 447 STATE OF TENNESSEE - pl. vs FRANCIS GIDDEONS - def.

P. 450 STATE OF TENNESSEE - pl. vs JESSE WATSON - def.
Indictment for Misdemeanor

P. 452 STATE OF TENNESSEE - pl. vs JESSE WATSON - def.
& BETSEY SMITH - def.
Indictment for Fornication

P. 454 STATE OF TENNESSEE - pl. vs JAMES THOMAS - def.

P. 457 SIMON BRADFORD & JOHN STACKER - pl. vs JOSHUA
FARRINGTON - def.
Case

P. 460 THOMAS J. CHILDRESS - pl. vs MAHALAN STACY - def.

P. 464 JACOB CARL - pl. vs JOANNAH MILLER, Exr. of
Thomas Miller, deceased - def.
Petition for Counter Security
Signed by: Joannah Miller, William Miller,
John Miller, Thomas Miller, & Joseph A. Miller.

P. 473 PETITION FOR PARTITION   Oct. 1824
Jane Goodrum was the mother of part of the
Petitioners. She was the widow of Thomas Goodrum
and she is now deceased. Slaves were left in
the estate which is to be divided into four
parts.
        Part # 1 - Stephen Frazier & Lucy (Jincy?),
                   his wife. She was formerly
                   Lucy Goodrum.
        Part # 2 - Archer Frazier & Polly, his wife.
                   She was formerly Polly Goodrum.
        Part # 3 - Heirs of Sterling Goodrum,
                   deceased. The heirs are: John,
                   Sterling, & Jane Goodrum. They
                   are minors and their guardian is
                   Arthur Frazier.
        Part # 4 - Heirs of Thomas Goodrum. They are
                   Anderson, Thomas, Jane, & James
                   Goodrum. They are infants, being
                   minors, their guardian is Stephen
                   Frazier.

P. 475 JOHN L. WHEATON - pl. vs MARY WHEATON - def.
        April 1825   Petition for Partition
Daniel Wheaton died intestate in 1804. He left the
surviving heirs: John L. Wheaton & Sterling Wheaton
Sterling Wheaton married Mary ___?_. He died shortly
afterwards. He left a will leaving the real
estate that came to him from Daniel Wheaton to
his wife, Mary. He named Samuel Crockett (CON'T.)

36

P. 475 John L. Wheaton vs. Mary Wheaton (CON'T.)
       as the guardian of Mary Wheaton. He owned 2
       lots in the town of Franklin. He also owned
       several tracts of land. Named in the division
       were: P. Crawford, heirs of James Tisdale,
       John Rutherford, W. T. Lewis, John Brown, Mary
       Wheaton, & John L. Wheaton.
            NOTE: See Will Book I, Page 322 for the
                   Will of Jane Wheaton (Mother).

P. 483 WILLIAM E. OWEN & ANDREW CAMPBELL - pl. vs
       JOHN BLYTHE - def.

P. 487 SUSANNAH INGRAM - pl. vs DANIEL CRENSHAW &
       WILLIAM H. SPENCER - def.
                 Debt

P. 489 MICHAEL KINNEL - pl. vs ROBERT MURRAY - def.
                 Debt

P. 490 WILLIAM McGELERARY - pl. vs NICHOLAS P. PERKINS -
       def.   Debt

P. 491 WILLIAM A. STEPHENSON - pl. vs NICHOLAS A.
       PERKINS - def.

P. 492 JONAS I. BELL, use of John Nichols - pl. vs
       NICHOLAS P. PERKINS - def.
                 Debt

P. 494 WILLIAM CARROLL - pl. vs PHILIP MAURY - def.
                 Debt

P. 495 JOHN SMITH - pl. vs THOMAS HILL - def.
                 Case

P. 497 ARCHIBALD LYTLE - pl. vs NICHOLAS P. PERKINS -
       def.   Debt

P. 498 JOHN M. PRICE, THOMAS YARDLEY, & WILLIAM
       YARDLEY, JR., Exr. of the last will & testament
       of Adam Ringmaker - pl. vs BERNARD RICHARDSON -
       def.
                 Debt

P. 500 JOHN BUCHANAN - pl. vs NICHOLAS SCALES - def.

P. 502 PETITION FOR PARTITION   Oct. 1826
       John Edmondson, Sr. died Sept. 1826. He left
       no wife. He had land on Mill Creek (220 acres).
       He had 2 tracts of land in Haywood Co. - Grants -
       (Tennessee grants). He had 1 tract of land in
       Lincoln Co. on the Elk River - North Carolina
       grant # 378. The North Carolina grant
       to Samuel Edmondson, the father of said John
       Edmondson, Sr., deceased.   (CON'T.)

P. 502 Petition for Partition (CON'T.)
The heirs of John Edmondson, Sr. are: David
Bell & Elizabeth, his wife; Mary W. Edmondson,
15 year old (her guardian is David Bell);
Robert McCutchen & Martha G., his wife; William
Edmondson; John Edmondson; & Charles Edmondson,
of Lincoln Co., Tennessee.

P. 509 JAMES H. HERON - pl. vs JOHN HERON; ANDREW HERON;
MARY HERON; THOMAS HERON; ELIZABETH C. HERON;
WILLIAM R. HERON; & GEORGE HERON - def.
April 1827   Petition for Partition
John, Andrew, Mary, & Thomas Heron are minor
children of Thomas Heron. Thomas Heron departed
this life in 1823. Mary Heron is his widow &
the Admrx. of Thomas Heron. James Henderson is
Co. Admr. of the estate.

P. 516 STATE OF TENNESSEE - pl. vs PLEASANT STAGGS - def.
Indictment for assault & battery

P. 518 SALLY WEATHERS, PATSY WEATHERS, ELIZABETH WEATHERS,
W. J. WEATHERS, & JOHN WEATHERS (by their
guardian, Ruben Weathers), RUBEN WEATHERS,
JAMES HUTTON & WINNIE, his wife - pl. vs
JOHN & ANDREW PARKS - def.
July 1825   Petition for Distribution
The name of the father of the petitioners is not
given. He left a will. Andrew Clark is
entitled to 1/3 of the crop on his father's
place.

P. 519 HEIRS OF JORDAN REESE
July 1824   Petition for Distribution
Jordan Reese, deceased. His widow has since
died. No name of his widow. His heirs are:
Beverly Reese, Patrick Reese, Thomas Old &
Elizabeth, his wife, John Watson & Jane, his
wife, & Matilda Puryear.

_______ PETITION FOR DISTRIBUTION   April 1827
Estate of William Bond, deceased. Want slaves
divided. The heirs of William Bond, deceased,
are: Eliza M. Bond, Thomas B. Bond, & Helen
D. Bond.

P. 522 PETITION FOR DISTRIBUTION   April 1827
Thomas A. King is the guardian for the heirs of
Elisha Kimbro, deceased. The heirs of Elisha
Kimbro are: widow & 2 children.

RECORD BOOK

LAWSUITS

No. 4

1827 - 1829

P. 1　　TURNER PINKSTON - pl. vs HOLLON DAVIS - def.
　　　　　　　Jan. 1827　　Case　(Trespass)

P. 4　　JAMES McFARLAND, JR., use of William Clark - pl.
　　　　vs ROBERT PARRISH - def.
　　　　　　　　　　Debt

P. 8　　WILLIAM EDWARDS - pl. vs WILLIS GORDON - def.
　　　　　　　　　Debt

P. 10　JAMES STEWART & JOHN N. CHARTER - pl. vs
　　　　PETER R. RISON - def.
　　　　　　　　　Debt

P. 13　WILLIAM DAVIS - pl. vs JAMES WILKINSON - def.
　　　　　　　　　Debt

P. 16　ANDREW GOFF, for the use of Wilson White -
　　　　pl. vs NICHOLAS PERKINS, SR. - def.
　　　　　　　Jan. 1827　　　Case　(Trespass)

P. 18　JOHN COCKRILL, for the use of Timothy D.
　　　　Lawrence - pl. vs NICHOLAS PERKINS - def.
　　　　　　　　　Debt

P. 21　MATTHEW D. COOPER & JAMES C. HILL - pl. vs
　　　　THOMAS CASH - def.
　　　　　　　　　　Case

P. 25　JAMES H. HOOPER - pl. vs JOHN NICHOLS - def.
　　　　　　　April 1827　　　　Debt

P. 28　MOSES LINDSEY - pl. vs STERLING BROWN - def.
　　　　　　　Case　(Trespass)

P. 32　CHESLEY DAVIS - pl. vs RICHARD BULLOCK - def.
　　　　　　　Case　(Trespass)

P. 35　BAILEY HARDEMAN - pl. vs JOHN WILSON - def.
　　　　　　　April 1827　　　Covenant Broken

P. 37　JOHN W. WHITFIELD - pl. vs BENJAMIN TARKINGTON -
　　　　def.　　　　　　　　Debt

P. 99   BENJAMIN S. TAPPAN & PETER PERKINS - pl. vs
         SALA N. SHARP - def.
                        Debt
         Benjamin S. Tappan & Peter Perkins are merchants
         & partners trading under the firm & style of
         Tappan & Perkins.

P. 101   JOANNA MILLER, use of Tappan & Perkins - pl. vs
         PETER R. RISON & JOHN L. WHEATON - def.
                 July 1827   Debt

P. 103   ELIJAH HUNTER, Assignee & C - pl. vs JOHN L.
         WHEATON - def.
                        Debt

P. 106   PHILIP SHUTE - pl. vs THOMAS RIDLEY - def.
                        Debt

P. 108   BENJAMIN S. TAPPAN & PETER PERKINS - pl. vs
         JOHN NICHOLS - def.
                 July 1827   Debt
         Benjamin S. Tappan & Peter Perkins are
         merchants & partners trading under the firm &
         style of Tappon & Perkins.

P. 111   SUMMER M. SHARP - pl. vs JOSHUA FARRINGTON -
         def.   Covenant

P. 113   DANIEL DWYER - pl. vs THOMAS MONTGOMERY -
         def.   Case (Trespass)

P. 115   JOHN SHUTE - pl. vs WYATT HALEY, SR. - def.
                 July 1827   Covenant

P. 117   BENJAMIN S. TAPPAN & PETER PERKINS - pl. vs
         ORANGE HAM - def.
                        Debt
         Benjamin S. Tappan & Peter Perkins are merchants
         trading under the firm & style of Tappan &
         Perkins.

P. 119   JAMES ARMSTRONG, Assignee & C - pl. vs
         WILLIAM CRAIG - def.
                        Debt

P. 122   THOMAS G. MALLORY & POLLY HUNT, Admr. of Sion
         Hunt, deceased - pl. vs WILLIAM MOOR &
         ZACHEUS GERMAN - def.
                 July 1827   Debt

P. 125   BEVERLY REESE, Assignee & C - pl. vs JOHN
         NICHOLS - def.
                 July 1827   Debt

P. 128 JOHN PORTER - pl. vs JOHN L. WHEATON -. def.
       July 1827
John Porter was employed by John Edney, an agent
of J. L. Wheaton in 1826. John Edney hired John
Porter to move the negroes of John L. Wheaton to
Haywood Co., Tennessee. John Porter only got
a part of his money for his services.

P. 133 SUMMER M. SHARP - pl. vs JOSHUA FARRINGTON - def.
       July 1827   Debt

P. 136 NICHOLAS WILBURNE - pl. vs WILLIAM A. A. KIRK -
       def.   Debt

P. 139 SAMUEL MORTON, JACOB MORTON, & SOLOMON G. MORTON,
       Exrs. of Samuel Morton, deceased - pl. vs
       WILLIAM S. KING - def.
                       Debt

P. 142 GEORGE W. MAYBERRY - pl. vs ROBERT PARRISH -
       def.
              July 1827   Debt

P. 147 SARAH B. SHELBURN, OPLEAS (?) SHELBURN, DENNIS M.
       CRAFTON & MARY A., his wife, JAMES SHELBURN &
       ELIZABETH by their guardian, Sarah B. Shelburne -
              April 1828   Exparte
              Petition for Partition & Division
James Shelburne died intestate. He left a
widow, Sarah B. Shelburn. The children & heirs
at law are: Opleas (?) Shelburne, Mary S.
Crafton (late Mary S. Shelburn), James Shelburn,
& Elizabeth Shelburne. James Shelburne left the
following negroes: Love, Mary, Ritta, Asa,
Edney, Henry, & William. Heirs want the slaves
sold & division made.

P. 149 MORDICA C. H. PURYEAR - pl. vs JOHN T. PURYEAR
       & JORDAN R. PURYEAR - def.
              April 1828   Petition for Distribution
Hezekiah Puryear died intestate in 1816. Mordica
C. H. Puryear is now of age. John T. Puryear &
Jordan R. Puryear are minors & John Watson is
their guardian. Hezekiah Puryear left many
negroes. They are: Old Hill, Old Jo, Little
Jo, Claburn, Old Frank, Maria, Peyton, Little
Lucy, Tabby, Phil, Tom, Brister, Jerry, Mose,
America, Mary, Nancy, Isaac, Sam, Old Charles,
Jenny, Patterson, Betsey, Charlotte, Minny,
Little Charles, Little Dinah, Old Dinah, Old Peter,
Jack, Kindor, Little Peter, Abram, Rachel, John,
Suly, Oliver, Agy, Becky, Lewis, Lucinda, Mariah,
Liby, Fanny, Mira, & Peggy. Wants division of
negroes & other personal property.

42

P. 151 PETER J. WALKER & ELIZABETH M., his wife, BENJAMIN
        F. CROCKETT & MATILDA CROCKETT - pl. vs ROBERT
        SAYERS, NANCY CROCKETT & ANDREW G. CROCKETT,
        JOHN H. CROCKETT, JANE J. CROCKETT, JAMES B.
        CROCKETT, SAMUEL T. CROCKETT, & FLANIUS J.
        CROCKETT, who defend by Nancy Crockett, their
        guardian - def.
                April 1828   Petition for Partition &
                                           Dower
        John H. Crockett died intestate Oct. 6, 1827.
        He left a widow, Nancy Crockett. John H.
        Crockett's children & heirs are: Elizabeth M.,
        who married Peter J. Walker, Matilda Crockett,
        Benjamin F. Crockett, Andrew G. Crockett,
        John H. Crockett, Jane J. Crockett, James B.
        Crockett, Samuel T. Crockett, & Flanius J.
        Crockett. Elizabeth M. Walker, Matilda, &
        Benjamin F. Crockett are of age. The others
        are minors & Nancy Crockett is their guardian.
        John H. Crockett left a tract of land (847
        acres) & another tract of land containing
        76 acres. The widow, Nancy Crockett, is
        entitled to her dower. Division of the land
        (847 acres) is to be made between Robert Sayers
        & the heirs of John H. Crockett, deceased.
        Robert Sayers gets 1/2 & the heirs get 1/2.
        John H. Crockett, deceased, also left
        negroes. They are: Isaac, Ephraim, Aaron,
        Charity, Sampson, Becky, Aggy, Mary Ann,
        Emeline, Patsey, Ruth, Rose, Holly, Felix,
        & Peyton.

P. 162 WILLIAM E. OWEN & ANDREW CAMPBELL - pl. vs
        JOHN BLYTHE - def.
                Jan. 1827   Debt
        Owen & Campbell representing Hudson Dawson.

P. 166 WILLIAM D. TAYLOR, use & C - pl. vs NICHOLAS
        P. PERKINS - def.
                Debt   Appeal from Justices Judgment

P. 167 WILLIAM R. GRIFFITTS, Assignee & C - pl. vs
        GEORGE E. COOK & MARY BOYD - def.
                July 1827   Debt

P. 169 ISAAC BATEMAN - pl. vs THOMAS REYNOLDS, ALLEN
        MEBANE, & SAMUEL SWISHER - def.
                Trespass, Force & Arms

P. 172 JOHN RAY - pl. vs WILLIAM STONE - def.
                Covenant Broken

P. 176 BENJAMIN S. TAPPAN & PETER PERKINS - pl. vs
JAMES WILSON - def.
Oct. 1827   Debt

P. 178 WILLIAM GATLIN, Assignee & C - pl. vs JOHN
ANDREWS - def.
Debt

P. 181 SAMUEL JAMISON & Others - pl. vs ROBERT RIDLEY,
BEVERLY RIDLEY & SAMUEL PATTON - def.
Debt
Marshall Jamison; Samuel Jamison; Bartly Bird,&
Jane, his wife; John Jamison; Thomas Jamison;
Drury Warren & Sally, his wife; Robert Newsom &
Hesey, his wife; Elizabeth Jamison of whom
Marshall Jamison is guardian; & James Jamison;
Wiley Jamison; & Samuel Jamison; Brown Jamison;
Peggy Jamison; Sally Jamison; & Jane Jamison of
who Ruffin Brown is guardian.

P. 184 JAMES CAROTHERS & JOHN F. McEWEN - pl. vs LEONARD
DUNNAVANT & THOMAS H. PERKINS - def.
Oct. 1827   Debt

P. 186 WILLIAM E. OWEN & ALEXANDER CAMPBELL - pl. vs
GEORGE WHITE -- def.
Debt

P. 188 DELIA S. HIGHTOWER - pl. vs HARRIS GOODWIN - def.
Debt

P. 191 PETER R. RISON, use of Thomas Campbell - pl. vs
CHARLES MORAN - def.
Oct. 1827   Debt

P. 193 WILLIAM E. OWEN & ANDREW CAMPBELL - pl. vs
THOMAS MONTGOMERY - def.
Debt

P. 195 DELIA S. HIGHTOWER - pl. vs THOMAS MONTGOMERY -
def.   Debt

P. 197 THOMAS HARDEMAN, use of Marshall Jamison &
others - pl. vs SAMUEL PATTON, WILLIAM PATTON,
& ROBERT RIDLEY - def.
(See list of names on original page 181)

P. 199 WILLIAM E. OWIN & ANDREW CAMPBELL, late merchants
trading under the firm & style of Owen & Campbell
pl. vs ROBERT PARRISH - def.
Debt

44

P. 201 WILLIAM ROBINSON - pl. vs BENJAMIN R. WHITE -
       def.   April 1827   Debt

P. 203 WILLIAM B. McCLELLAN, Agt. (Charles A. Scott &
       Robert W. Ashley) - pl. vs JOHN NICHOLS - def.
                         Debt

P. 204 DAVID MOORE & FRANCES, his wife; CAREY H. MOORE &
       MARY, his wife - pl. vs DICY ASHLIN, ROBERT W.
       ASHLIN, JOHN ASHLIN, WILLIAM ASHLIN, MARTHA
       ASHLIN, ANN ASHLIN, & VIRGINIA ASHLIN - def.
               July 1828   Petition for Partition
       William Ashlin died in 1821 intestate. He left
       a widow, Dicey Ashlin & eight children. The
       children are: Frances, Mary, Robert W., Martha,
       John, William, Ann, & Virginia Ashlin. He also
       left 2 tracts of land & 1 town lot. The land
       is on the waters of the West Harpeth. 1 tract
       of land contains 320 acres & the other tract
       contains 235 acres. Lot # 6 is located on
       Water Street. Personal property hasn't been
       divided nor has a dower been set aside.

P. 211 DAVID BELL & ELIZABETH, his wife; ROBERT
       McCUTCHEN & MARTHA, his wife; CHARLES H.
       EDMONDSON; WILLIAM EDMONDSON; JOHN EDMONDSON;
       JOHN McCUTCHEN & MARGARET W., his wife; & MARY
       EDMONDSON, by her guardian, David Bell
                  April 1828   Exparte
                  Petition for Partition
       John Edmondston died intestate in 1826. He left
       Petitioners his heirs. He left no real estate as
       it has already been divided. He left some
       negroes. They are: Bob, Hannah, Rose, Nero,
       Nicholas, Tom, Jefferson, Tenor, Nelly, Sterling,
       Rachel, & Isaac. Advancements made to some
       of the heirs.

P. 215 ANDREW ROUNDTREE - pl. vs BENJAMIN TROTTER -
       def.
               July 1828   Case (Covenant Broken)

P. 218 ISAAC WEST - pl. vs BENJAMIN TROTTER - def.
                         Debt

P. 221 HENRY ELMORE - pl. vs BERNARD RICHARDSON - def.
                         Debt

P. 224 WILLIAM GOOCH - pl. vs NICHOLAS PERKINS, SR. -
       def.   July 1828   Debt

P. 227 THOMAS W. PETTUS - pl. vs BENJAMIN TROTTER - def.
                         Debt

P. 232 JOSEPH WILSON - pl. vs WINSON EDNEY, HARRIS
       CABLAR, & GEORGE WHITE - def.   Debt

P. 235 WILLIAM S. WEBB, Endorsee of James P. Peters - pl.
vs. WARE HENLEY - def.
July 1828   Debt

P. 239 BENJAMIN S. TAPPAN & PETER PERKINS - pl. vs
JOHN G. WILLIAMS - def.
Debt
Benjamin S. Tappan & Peter Perkins are merchants
& partners in trade trading under the firm &
style of Tappan & Perkins.

P. 241 JOSEPH WILSON - pl. vs JAMES WILSON & JAMES
H. WILSON - def.
July 1828   Debt

P. 245 WILLIAM N. HOLT - pl. vs JAMES C. IRVIN - def.
Debt

P. 247 GIDEON RIGGS, use of William C. Bruce - pl. vs
REUBEN W. REYNOLDS - def.
Covenant Broken

P. 249 SIMEON WEST - pl. vs AMELIA LOYD & SAMUEL
EASTEP - def.
April 1828
Amelia Loyd & Samuel Eastep are the Exrs. of
the last will of Lewis Loyd, deceased. The
management of the Exrs. is in question &
Simeon West wants to be removed from the bond.

P. 253 WILLIAM H. SLAUGHTER & HANNAH G., his wife;
JOHN CRUMP; CHARLES C. CRUMP; SETTON M. CRUMP;
SARAH A. CRUMP, by their guardian Lemuel Pope;
& RICHARD CRUMP, by his guardian W. H.
Slaughter; MARTHA CRUMP
April 1828
Petition for Dower, Partition & Distribution
Fendal Crump died in 1823 intestate. He left a
widow, Martha Crump and children. His children
are: Hannah H., Charles C., John, Setton M.,
Sarah A., & Richard. He also left some
negroes. They are: Milly, Rose & her baby,
Anna & her child, Nelson, Nathan, & Betsey. He
also left a tract of land.

P. 258 RICHARD H. RUDDER; JAMES GARRETT; ABNER McCORD;
PARTHENIA SHORT; LISETTA SHORT; JOHN SHORT;
RICHARD SHORT; & POLLY SHORT, by their guardian,
Thomas Short
Jan. 1827   Petition for Distribution
Mary Rudder died intestate June 24, 1826. She
left children who are: Richard Rudder (son),
Nancy Rudder (daughter, who married James Garrett),
Polly Rudder (daughter, who married Abner McCord).
Mary Rudder left grandchildren: Parthenia Short,
Lisetta Short, John Short, Richard Short, &
Peggy Short. They are the children of (CON'T.)

P. 258 Mary Rudder, deceased (CON'T)
Sally Short, deceased. Sally Short was Mary Rudder's
daughter. Mary Rudder also left slaves. They are:
Silva, Cate, Jerry, Paulina, Minerva, & Jane.

P. 260 DEMSEY NASH; CORNELIUS NASH; SAMUEL WILES &
ELIZABETH, his wife; WILLIAM C. NICHOLSON &
MARY, his wife; EMMA NASH & CATHERINE NASH,
minors who sue by their guardian, John Nash
        Jan. 1827   Petition for Distribution
Demsey Nash is of Williamson County, Tennessee.
Cornelius Nash is of Norfolk County, Virginia.
Samuel Wiles & Elizabeth, his wife, are of
Norfolk Co., Virginia. William C. Nicholson &
Mary, his wife, are of Norfolk Co., Virginia.
Emma Nash & Catherine Nash, by their guardian,
are all of Norfolk Co., Virginia. These are
all heirs of Charles Nash, late of Virginia.
Charles Nash died June last having left a will.
His will named his wife, Rebecca Nash. She was
left with the negroes: Jim, Abraham, Quash,
William, Argal, Betsey, & Mary. Rebecca Nash
departed her life during the lifetime of said
Charles Nash. Charles Nash left no children
surviving him. Demsey & Cornelius Nash are
his brothers. Elizabeth, Mary, Emma, &
Catherine are the children of William Nash,
who was also a brother of Charles Nash.
William Nash is now dead. Wants a division to
be made.

P. 263 JAMES SWANSON, Guardian for the children of
Thomas H. Word
        Jan. 1827   Exparte
        Petition for Sale of Negro
James Swanson, Sr. is the guardian of the
children of Thomas H. Word, who conveyed to
his children by deed of gift or bill of sale
the right to all the property that he had.
This was in 1823. John Sweeny of Williamson
County, obtained a judgment in the Supreme
Court of Tennessee against Thomas H. Word.
The negro, Levi, was advertised & sold Jan. 1,
1825. Garner McConnico bought him. Bernard
Richardson was a creditor & had the right to
redeem Levi & Garner McConnico surrendered
him to Richardson. James Swanson, Sr.
bought the slave with his own funds so that
he could save a part of the value of the
slave for the children he was guardian to.
The estate is unable to pay him for the
slave & he wants to sell the slave to get
his money back.

P. 266   JOHN BOON & MATILDA, his wife; & MILLAGE S.
DURHAM, by his guardian, Spencer Reynolds
         Jan. 1829   Exparte
              Petition for Distribution
John Durham died intestate 15 years ago in the
state of Georgia, where he resided. He left a
wife, Matilda, who has since married John Boon.
He also left one child, Millage S. Durham, an
infant. The child's guardian is Spencer
Reynolds. Matilda was appointed Admrx. after
selling the said estate she had on her hands
a negro girl, Silva. Since Matilda has moved to
Williamson County, Tennessee, the said Silva has
had an increase of Martha, Haley, & Dinnaha. All
remain to be divided between John Boon in right
of his wife, Matilda, & Millage S. Durham. By

law of Georgia where John Durham resided at the
time of his death, the property is subject to
an equal division of 1/3 to the widow.

P. 269   ANDREW CROCKETT, by his next, John S. Crockett -
pl. vs ROBERT CROCKETT, LUCINDA CROCKETT, &
ESTHER CROCKETT - def.
         Jan. 1829   Petition for Partition
Samuel Crockett died Jan. 1827. He left a will.
Esther Crockett, Lucinda Crockett, & Robert
Crockett are the heirs of Samuel Crockett. He
bequeathed to them a tract of land containing
about 400 acres on the Little Harpeth River.
Wants a division made of the land.

P. 274   ALEXANDER C. CARTER & MILDRED, his wife; SAMUEL
J. CARTER & ELIZABETH, his wife; CATHERINE
PARRISH; & EBENEZER B. STAGGS, by his guardian,
Lemuel H. Ogilivie
         Jan. 1829 Exparte - Petition for Partition
                          & Distribution
Felix Staggs died in 1826. He left as his issue
& children: Mildred Carter (formerly Mildred
Staggs); Catherine Parrish (widow of Abraham
Parrish & formerly Catherine Staggs); Elizabeth
Carter (formerly Elizabeth Staggs); & Ebenezer
Bess Staggs (an infant by his guardian, Lemuel
H. Ogilvie). Felix Staggs left a will & was
probated in 1826. He owned several tracts of land.
One tract of land was conveyed by Spencer & Edward
Buford, Exrs. of James Buford, containing 100
acres. One tract of land was conveyed by
Thomas Ridley. It contained 280 acres. One tract
of land was conveyed by Beverly Reese. It is
near the town of Franklin and contains 10 acres.
One tract of land was conveyed by John Bell
in the town of Franklin, known as the new part
of the town.   (CONT)

48

P. 274 Felix Staggs, deceased (CONT'D)
        Felix Staggs also left negroes: Philip, Gabriel,
        Ned, Randle, Jim, Ben, Isaac, Lewis, Washington,
        Isaac, Rose, Minnah, Rachel, Sear, Sissy, Nelly,
        Sindy, Rachel, Jenny, Milley, Charlotte,
        Huldah, Fanny, Cosly, Ellison, Hays, Miles,
        Elbert, Caroline, Anderson, Mary, Rofe, Henry,
        Elviza, & Mannerva. Copied from will: Son -
        Ebenezer Bess Staggs - tract of land I now
        live on. Daughter - Catherine Parrish.
        Heirs of the body of Eliza Carter. Heirs of the
        body of my daughter, Mildred Staggs. Brother,
        John Staggs - his support from the land he now
        lives on & a negro, Washington. The will was
        dated 3 Oct. 1826.

P. 283 JOHN GORDON & KALISTA, his wife; PATRICK GIBSON;
        JAMES GIBSON; JOSEPH GIBSON; WILSON GIBSON;
        MARY JANE GIBSON, by their guardian, Elijah
        R. Parrish
               Jan. 1829   Exparte
               Petition for Partition &
                    Distribution
        John B. Gibson died several years ago intestate.
        He left the Petitioners his heirs. Kalister has
        married John Gordon. John B. Gibson left a
        tract of land on the Duck River Ridge con-
        taining 348 acres. Elijah R. Parrish is
        named Admr. of the estate. John B. Gibson
        left the following negroes: Chainey, Nancy,
        & Nancy's children, Spencer & Fanny; Ned,
        Henderson, Rachael, Sarah, Andrew, & Stephen.
        The estate is to be divided into 6 parts.

P. 288 HENRY G. WILLIAMSON & MINERVA WILLIAMSON, by
        her guardian & next friend, Henry Elbeck
               Oct. 1828   Petition for Partition
        Thomas Williamson died Jan. 1817. He left a
        will & it was probated July 1817. Named in
        the will were: Henry G. Williamson (son) -
        the tract of land where I now live & a part of
        my 50 acres of land joining the tract I have
        given my son, Benjamin Williamson. The land
        is to be Henry G. Williamson's when he
        reaches the age of 21 years old except for
        the part loaned to his mother & that is to
        be his at her death or marriage. Also named
        in the will is: Minerva Williamson (daughter) -
        She is to get the rest of the tract of land
        I live on. (Martha Williamson, mother of
        Henry G. Williamson, died in June 1828)
        Henry G. Williamson is now 21 years old &
        he wants a division made.

P. 292 SAMUEL PRATT & POLLY, his wife; ABNER BOYD;
JAMES G. SWISHER & ELIZABETH, his wife; GEORGE
G. BOYD; HENRY H. SWISHER & SINAI, his wife;
JOHN G. BOYD; JONATHAN AMIS & NANCY, his wife;
JAMES W. BOYD & MIRA L. BOYD, by their guardian,
George G. Boyd; & NICHOLAS H. BOYD, by his
guardian, Abner Boyd
   Oct. 1828 Petition for Partition &
         Distribution
James Boyd died May 24, 1821. He left a will.
He left a widow, Nancy Boyd. The Petitioners are
the children of James Boyd. The Petitioners
have received the following:
Samuel Pratt & Polly, his wife - They have
 received 110 acres of land & a negro girl,
 Nancy, etc.
Abner Boyd - He has received a negro boy, Peter, &
 a negro girl, Sarah, etc.
James G. Swisher & Elizabeth, his wife - They
 have received the negro girls, Lotty &
 Harriett, etc.
George G. Boyd - He has received the west end of
 a tract of land which contains 91 acres, etc.
Henry H. Swisher & Sinia, his wife - They have
 received the negro girls, Mille & Mary, etc.
Jonathan Amis & Nancy, his wife - They have
 received 110 acres of land off of the east
 end of a tract of land, etc.
John G. Boyd - He has received a tract of land
 on the Southeast corner of the original tract,
 (101 acres), etc.
John G. Boyd has an extra bequest of $500 for his
 education.
James Boyd left a tract of land where he lived
containing 400 acres. He also left 13 slaves.
They are: David - 35 yrs.; Cynthia - 45 yrs.;
Fanny - 30 yrs.; Matilda - 27 yrs.; Tom - 13 yrs.;
Grace - 15 yrs.; Sine - 9 yrs.; Alfred - 9 yrs.;
Hannah - 7 yrs.; Mahala - 7 yrs.; Jemima - 5 yrs.;
Lewis - 3 yrs.; Lethe - 3 yrs. James Boyd also
left furniture, tools, livestock, etc. His
Exrs. are Abner Boyd & John G. Boyd. Nancy Boyd,
the widow of James Boyd, died May 24, 1828. The
Petitioners wish a division to be made.

P. 299 MARY MORRIS; ROBERT T. MORRIS; WILLIAM MORRIS;
JAMES T. MORRIS; JACOB T. MORRIS, by their
guardian, Mary Morris; NATHAN E. MORRIS & GEORGE
W. MORRIS, by their guardian, Simpson Perry
   Oct. 1820 Petition for Distribution
        of Negroes
William Morris died intestate. Mary Morris is his
widow. He left the following children: James
T. Morris, Jacob T. Morris, Robert T. Morris,
William Morris, Nathan E. Morris, & George W.
Morris. William Morris left slaves. Simpson
Perry, a guardian, is of Maury Co., Tennessee. He
states that Robert T. & William Morris have received
their part of the personal estate upon reaching
the age of 21. They have not received (CONT'D)

50

P. 299 William Morris, deceased (CONT'D)
        their part of the slaves. The slaves are:
        Cherry - 30 yrs.; Harry - 27 yrs.; Booker - 17
        yrs.; Dick - 15 yrs.; David - 12 yrs; Crissy -
        10 yrs.; Mina - 9 yrs.; Harriet - 7 yrs.; Gileo -
        5 yrs. - Tom - 3 yrs. - Rosanna - 4 months.
        The widow & children of William Morris, deceased,
        are entitled to 1/7 part.

P. 302 GIDEON RIGGS, who sues as well in his own right
        as Admr. of his wife, Polly Riggs & JOHN M. DAWSON
        & PHEBE, his wife
             Oct. 1828   Petition for Distribution
        Richard C. Reynolds died 182_ & left a will. Reuben
        Reynolds & Prepare Reynolds are the Exrs. The will
        was probated at the April session 1826. Petitioners
        have applied to Reuben Reynolds for their share
        of the estate. Richard C. Reynolds left his
        estate to his wife, Prepare & his daughters. His
        daughters are: Polly Riggs, Pheobe Dawson, &
        Reuben W. Reynolds. Polly Riggs has since died.
        The Petitioners want the court to force Reuben
        Reynolds to pay them their share of the estate.

P. 304 RICHARD C. HANCOCK, THOMAS W. HANCOCK, & WILLIAM
        GUY, guardians of John W. Guy, James J. Guy, &
        William W. Guy
               Jan. 1829   Petition for Distribution
        The Petitioners want a division of the slaves of
        John Guy, deceased, divided into 5 parts. The
        slaves are: Johnson, Fan, Tom, Sarah & her 3
        children, Ned, Peg, Handy, Linds, Jude, Peter,
        Little Peter, Flora & her 5 children, Lind,
        Scilla, Big Cilia & her child, & Little Celia &
        her child.

P. 306 THOMAS G. MALLORY & POLLY HUNT; THOMAS H. PERKINS
        & ELIZABETH G. B., his wife; & ANDREW W. HUNT.
             Jan. 1829   Petition for Partition &
                                        Dower
        Thomas H. Perkins & Elizabeth, his wife, & Andrew
        Hunt are minors under the age of 21 years & they
        sue by their guardian, Nicholas Perkins, Jr.
        Sion Hunt died Sept. 1826 intestate. Thomas G.
        Mallory & Polly Hunt are the Admrs. of the estate.
        Sion Hunt left a widow, Polly Hunt. His children
        are: Elizabeth G. S., wife of Thomas H. Perkins,
        & Andrew W. Hunt. Sion Hunt left the following
        negroes: Elly - 60 yrs.; Anthony - 23 yrs.;
        Dick - 21 yrs.; Lunne ? - 20 yrs.; Tennessee -
        22 yrs.; Horace - 28 yrs.; Sucky - 25 yrs.;
        Peggy - 23 yrs.; Hester - 20 yrs.; Elvira - 17
        yrs.; Minerva - 17 yrs.; Sarah - 16 yrs.; Mira -
        9 yrs.; Harriett - 8 yrs.; Bethenia - 7 yrs.;
        Bob - 5 yrs.; William - 1 yrs.; John - 1 yr.;
        Daniel - 1 yr.; Jane - 10 mos.; Mahala - 2 wks.;
        Margery - 2 wks. (22 negroes in all)   (CONT'D)

P. 306 Sion Hunt, deceased (CONT'D)
Sion Hunt had the following tracts of land:
Tract # 1 - formerly owned by Evans.
Tract # 2 - formerly owned by Thomas S. Spencer.
Tract # 3 - parts of tracts
The parts of Tract # 3 consist of:
Part # 1 - 1 part of a tract of land formerly owned by Isaac Mairs, Joshua Farrington, & William Spencer.
Part # 2 - 94 acres on the North of the Big Harpeth River.
Part # 3 - 1/10 part of an undivided tract on the Big Harpeth River, conveyed by William Shute to Alson Edney. This consists of 142 acres. (That 1/10 part being the part of John D. Edney of his father, Alson Edney, deceased)
Part # 4 - 400 acres on the Big Harpeth River.
Part # 5 - 601 acres conveyed by Randal McGavock & part of it sold to John Cartwright.
Part # 6 - 70 acres conveyed by Isaac Johnson, Jr.
Part # 7 - 119 acres on the north side of the Big Harpeth conveyed by George Stranler.
Part # 8 - 100 acres on the Big Harpeth. This is a part of a tract of land given to Daniel Perkins to his son, Harden.
Part # 9 - 105 acres on the north side of the Big Harpeth River conveyed by James W. Perkins.
Polly Hunt is entitled to 1/3 part and the children of Sion Hunt, deceased, are entitled to 1/2 part.

P. 316 JEREMIAH MORGAN; AARON A. WILSON; LITTLEBERRY TONEY & MARY, his wife; ROBERT MONTGOMERY & ELIZABETH, his wife; SAMUEL WILSON, THOMAS WILSON, & MATILDA WILSON, by their guardian, Richard C. Hancock
April 1828   Petition for Partition
Thomas Wilson died intestate. He left a widow, Magart Wilson & children: Aaron A. Wilson, Joseph Wilson, Samuel Wilson, Thomas Wilson, Elvy Toney, the wife of John Toney, formerly Elvy Wilson, Polly Toney, formerly Polly Wilson, Jane Wilson, who is since dead, Elizabeth Wilson, & Matilda Wilson. Aaron A. Wilson is the Admr. of the estate.
Thomas Wilson left the following negroes: Nat, Ben, Rose. He also left the following tracts of land:
Tract # 1 - 117 acres on the waters of the Harpeth.
Tract # 2 - Part of a 2000 acre tract originally granted to David & William Wilson, dated 17 Dec. 1794.

(CONT'D)

P. 316 Thomas Wilson, deceased (CONT'D)
    Tract # 3 - 100 acres granted to Thomas
        Wilson from David Russel on the
        waters of the Harpeth River.
    Tract # 4 - Part of the 2000 acre tract granted
        to David & William Wilson.
    Tract # 5 - 500 acres held by a quit claim
        deed from Spencer Griffin in
        Bedford County on the Caney
        Spring Creek, waters of the
        Duck River.
    Tract # 6 - Part of 1000 acre tract granted
        to Robert Hays by North Carolina,
        Grant # 82.
Petitioner Jeremiah Morgan states that the part
of the estate which descended to John Toney &
his wife, Elvy, may be allotted.

P. 323 JAMES H. HERRON; JOHN HERRON; MARY HERRON;
ANDREW HERRON, MARY HERRON, THOMAS HERRON,
CAROLINE HERRON, WILLIAM R. HERRON, & GEORGE
HERRON, by their guardian, Mary Herron
    April Session 1829
    Petition for Distribution
Thomas Herron died in 1824 intestate. Mary Herron
is his widow. His children are: James H., John,
Andrew, Mary, Thomas, Caroline, William R.; &
George. Thomas Herron left several negroes.
They are: Harriet - 32 yrs.; Jeremiah - 17
yrs.; Milly - 15 yrs.; Chaney - 13 yrs.;
Young Harriet - 12 yrs.; Coswell - 11 yrs.;
Alexander - 9 yrs.; Henderson - 5 yrs.; Mary -
2 yrs.; Rachel - 2 yrs. The Admrs. of Thomas
Herron are James Henderson & petitioner, Mary
Herron.

P. 326 WILLIAM E. OWEN - pl. vs SUSANNAH PARRISH,
RANDAL McGAVOCK, & JOHN D. BENNETT - def.
    April 1829   Petition for Partition
Joel Parrish, Sr. died in 1811. He had a tract
of land adjoining Franklin containing 63 acres.
He left a widow, Susannah Parrish & 6 children.
The children are: Caroline, wife of Hinchey
Petway, Matthew F. M. Parrish, Joel Parrish,
Robert Parrish, Abram M. Parrish, & David W.
Parrish. They are all living & are of legal
age. Joel Parrish, Sr. left a will. Hinchey
Petway & his wife have conveyed their interest
in the land to Randal McGavock. Matthew F.
M. Parrish & Joel Parrish have conveyed their
share of the land to John D. Bennett.

P. 329 JOSEPH L. THOMPSON; JAMES E. THOMPSON; NEIL
        CAMPBELL & ELIZABETH C., his wife; NANCY L.
        WILKINS; SARAH B. WILKINS; & JOHN A. WILKINS
              April 1829   Petition for Division &
                                Distribution
        Nancy L. Wilkins, Sarah B. Wilkins, & John A.
        Wilkins are minors & sue by their next friend &
        father, John Wilkins.
        Joseph Sea of Chatham County, North Carolina, died
        about 1804. He left a will. He willed to his
        daughter, Rachel Thompson, 2 negroes. The 2
        negroes are Fender & Hannah. At Rachel Thompson's
        death, the 2 negroes, Fender & Hannah go to
        her children. Joseph L. & James E. Thompson
        are her children by her first husband, William
        Thompson. At his death, Rachel married John
        Wilkins. She had children by him. They are
        Elizabeth C., Nancy L., Sally B., & John A.
        Wilkins. Rachel died in 1828 leaving 6 children.
        She left the following negroes: Fender - 35
        yrs.; Ben - 18 yrs.; Jim - 14 yrs.; Sam - 12 yrs.;
        Phillis - 7 yrs.; Madison - 5 yrs.; Hannah -
        27 yrs.; Mille - 9 yrs.; Dan - 7 yrs.; Nan - 5
        yrs.; Parlee - 3 yrs; & Lucy - 1 yr. James E.
        Thompson was of Dixon County, Tennessee.

P. 331 MARY WILLIAMS - pl. vs ELISHA C. WILLIAMS,
        WILLIAM C. WILLIAMS, MARY C. WILLIAMS, JOSEPHUS
        WILLIAMS, & SUSAN L. WILLIAMS - def.
              July 1829
        William Williams died in the fall of 1824 intestate.
        He left a widow, Mary Williams. He left the
        following minor children: Elisha C., William C.,
        Mary C., Josephus, & Susan L. Williams. Their
        guardian is James S. Williams. John Hardin is
        the Admr. & he has since moved to Alabama.
        William Williams left 9 negroes. They are:
        Richard, Tom, Hester, Sally, Harriet, Caroline,
        Minerva, Mary, & Young Tom. William Williams
        has also left a tract of land (about 200 acres),
        where he lived at the time of his death. He
        also had one tract of land containing 103 1/2
        acres on the waters of the Big Harpeth River
        conveyed by James Williams, Sr. & another tract
        of land containing 100 acres conveyed by
        Elijah Williams. This tract of 100 acres adjoins
        the other tract containing 103 1/2 acres.

P. 335 JAMES BERRY, an infant by his guardian, Alexander
        Ralston - pl. against WILLIAM WILSON & ROBERT
        SAWYERS - def.
              Oct. 1827
        William Wilson, as guardian of James Berry, received
        money for the rent of slaves & land. Division
        was made among the heirs of James Berry, deceased,
        & petitioner James Berry was one of the (CONT'D)

54

P. 335 James Berry (CONT'D)
       heirs. James Berry needs his money for tuition,
       board, clothing, etc.

P. 340 JAMES N. CHARTER - pl. vs THOMAS CASH - def.
            April 1827   Case (Trespass)

P. 342 STATE OF TENNESSEE - pl. vs JAMES G. JONES - def.
            Indictment, assault & battery

P. 344 STATE OF TENNESSEE - pl. vs JAMES G. JONES - def.
            Indictment, Assault & Battery
       Assault on Francis Graham by Jones, Yeoman, late
       of this county.

P. 345 NICHOLAS T. PERKINS & WILLIAM EDMISTON, use of
       Thomas Hardeman - pl. vs NICHOLAS PERKINS, SR. -
       def.
            Jan. 1828   Debt

P. 347 ANDREW CRAIG, Exr. of David Craig, deceased - pl.
       vs WILLIAM MONTGOMERY & DANIEL WILKES - def.
                     Debt

P. 349 ANDREW CRAIG, Exr. of David Craig - pl. vs
       ALEXANDER MONTGOMERY & JAMES CRAIG - def.
                     Debt

P. 351 ALEXANDER MORPHIS & SAMUEL A. ALSOBROOK,
       endorsers & c, use of James P. Peters - pl.
       vs TURNER PINKSTON - def.
                     Debt   Jan. 1828

P. 353 WILLAIM G. DICKINSON - pl. vs BERNARD
       RICHARDSON - def.
                     Debt

P. 355 DANIEL W. MAURY; ABRAM P. MAURY; JAMES P. MAURY;
       CAREY A. HARRIS & MARTHA, his wife; WILLIAM C.
       MAURY, by his next friend, James P. Maury - pl.
       vs ZEBULON M. P. MAURY, by his guardian
       pendente lite, John Marshall - def.
            April 1829   Petition for Partition
       Abram Maury died intestate in 1825. His heirs at
       law are Elizabeth B. Reid & Zebulon M. P. Maury, a
       minor with no guardian, & the petitioners. Abram
       Maury had real estate. He had 3 lots in the town
       of Franklin. They are:
                 Lot # 1 - Lot # 134
                 Lot # 2 - Lot # 144
                 Lot # 3 - The lot on which the old
                           Methodist Meeting House was
                           situated fronting Water Street.
       Elizabeth Reid executed a deed of release of her
       interest to the said Maury, deceased. 1/6 share to ea

P. 358 THOMAS J. PARHAM & WINIFRED L., his wife; MARY
C. POPE; WILLIAM R. POPE; JANE O. POPE; CANDIS
J. POPE; WILLAIM BAUGH & AMARILLA, his wife;
ANN L. POPE, & GUSTAVUS A. POPE, by their
guardian, Thomas J. Pope
        July 1829   Petition for Distribution
William Lucas died & left a will. Ann Pope is the
mother of the petitioners. William Lucas had
the following negroes: Easter & George & their
increase of Hannah, Aphia, Harriet, Sibba,
Jerry, Annica, Chesley, Penelope, Jesse, Washington,
Jordan, Martha, & Wisey. William Lucas executed
a deed of trust to George Lucas, Winship
Stedman, & William Scurlock for the use & benefit
of Ann Pope during her life & then to her
children the following negroes: Sarah & Ross
& their increase of Mark, Mary, Green, Jack,
Cinderilla, & Guilford. Since the death of John
Pope, the husband of Ann Pope, she has released
& conveyed by deed all of the negroes. The
petitioners want a division made.

P. 359 CAREY A. HARRIS & MARTHA, his wife - pl. vs
DANIEL W. MAURY, Admr. of Abram Maury, deceased -
def.
        July 1829
Abram Maury died Jan. 1825 intestate. He left a
widow, Martha Maury. He left the following
children: Elizabeth B. Reid, Daniel W. Maury,
Abram P. Maury, James P. Maury, Martha F. Maury,
William H. Maury, & Zebulon M. Maury. Daniel
W. Maury was appointed Admr. April 1825. An
inventory & account of sales was made. There
was no settlement made. Martha F. Maury has
lately married Carey A. Harris & she wants a
settlement made.

P. 361 JOSHUA SPEER, WILLIAM H. LOGAN, & JAMES H. LOGAN
        July 1829   Exparte - Petition for Partition
William Logan died. He left a will. He owned
some land. One large tract of land lying in
Wilson's Valley between the heads of Caney Spring
Creek & the Big Harpeth River. This land was
granted by the state of North Carolina to Robert
Archibald. One tract of land was purchased from
James Sheppard joining 2000 acres of land
granted to Joseph Karr by North Carolina.
William Logan willed to his wife, Catherine,
200 acres of land. 817 acres of land was to be
divided between his 6 "male" children as they
become of age. The sons who are of age are:
James H., William, & John Logan. John Logan has
conveyed by deed his undivided interest to Joshua
K. Speer. The minor children are: Newton W.,
Robert F., & Cotesworth P. Logan. Their guardian
is Richard C. Hancock.

56

P. 366 POLLY HUNT; DANIEL P. PERKINS; SOLOMON ODEN;
CHARLOTTE EDNEY; EMILY EDNEY & MILTON EDNEY, by
their guardian, Thomas Montgomery
        Oct. 1829   Exparte   Petition for Partition
Alson Edney died intestate. He owned a tract of
land on the Big Harpeth River. This tract of land
contains 142 1/5 acres. Alson Edney left the
following children: Sally, who married Harris
Cobler; Nancy, who married Orion S. Perry; John
D. Edney; Alfred A. Edney; Polly, who married
Joel Childress; Levin Edney; Henry Edney;
Charlotte Edney; Emily Edney; & Milton Edney.
Polly Edney, the mother of the petitioners,
purchased the share left to Alford A. Edney. She
has died intestate & her share is to go to her
children. Polly Hunt has purchased the share
of Harris Cobler & Sally, his wife; Joel
Childress & Polly, his wife; John D. Edney;
& Levin Edney. Daniel P. Perkins has purchased
the share of Orion S. Perry & Nancy, his wife.
Solomon Oden has purchased the share of Henry
Edney. Alford A. Edney gave his part to
Charlotte, Emily, & Milton Edney.

P. 370 SHEARWOOD BETTY & JOHN BETTY, by his guardian,
Thomas B. Porter
        Oct. 1829   Petition for Distribution
John Betty is an infant & he sues by his
guardian, Thomas B. Porter. Shearwood Betty &
John Betty are the heirs of Roland Betty,
deceased. They are entitled to a negro woman,
Eliza & her child, Stafford. Sherwood Betty
has arrived of age & wants a division.

P. 372 JOHN RIVERS & SALLY, his wife; DANIEL GLENN
& LUCY, his wife; WILLIAM ROWLETT; & JAMES
ROWLETT
        Oct. 1829   Petition for Distribution
William Rowlett & James Rowlett are minors
& they sue by their guardian, William G. Boyd.
Sally Rivers is the widow of Benjamin Rowlett.
Lucy, William, & James are the children of
Benjamin Rowlett. They are entitled to 2
negroes and they want a division made. The
2 negroes are Anthony & Douglas.

P. 374 WILLIAM ROWLETT & JAMES ROWLETT, by their
guardian, William G. Boyd; & DANIEL GLENN
& LUCY, his wife
        Oct. 1829   Petition for Distribution
Lucy, William, & James are the children of
Benjamin Rowlett, deceased. They are entitled
to the slaves which came to them by their
grandfather, John Rowlett, deceased. The slaves
are Abram, Celia, Alice, & Billy. They want a
division made.

P. 376 ELIZABETH CURTIS - pl. vs BENJAMIN CURTIS, JR. - def.
      Oct. 1829   Petition for Dower
Benjamin Curtis died intestate in 1826. He left
a widow, Elizabeth. Joshua Curtis is appointed
Admr. Shortly after the death of Benjamin,
Elizabeth had a child named Benjamin, Jr., which
is the only child. Benjamin Curtis owned a tract
of land bound by Benjamin Curtis, Sr. & Moses
Curtis (about 93 acres). Benjamin Curtis, Jr.
has appointed Ranson Dudley as his special
guardian.

P. 380 SARAH S. BROWNLEE
            July 1829   Petition for Dower
James Brownlee died intestate in 1827. John
C. Simmons is appointed Admr. James Brownlee
left a widow, Sarah S. Brownlee. He also left
2 children: Arabilla Crawford & Lanes Jones.
They are infant daughters & Thomas Simmons is
appointed their guardian. James Brownlee had
a tract of land containing 172 acres. The land
joins the land of Andrew Crisswell, David
Chrisman, & Harris Goodwin.

P. 384 JOSHUA CURTIS, Admr. of Benjamin Curtis
      July 1829   Petition for Sale of Negro
The sale of a negro girl, Sylva, is necessary
so the debts can be paid & the estate of
Benjamin Curtis, deceased, settled.

P. 385 JAMES McCUTCHEN, Admr. of John Porter
          Jan. 1829   Petition for the Sale of Negroes
James McCutchen must sell the slaves of John
Porter, deceased, to be able to pay the debts of
the estate. The slaves are: Cain, Jacob,
Hannah & his child, & Old Jim.

P. 387 DRURY SCRUGGS, Admr. of Keziah Scruggs
          April 1829   Petition for Sale of Negroes
Mrs. Keziah Scruggs died last Sept. intestate.
Drury Scruggs is appointed Admr. in the last term
of court. Mrs. Keziah Scruggs owned 6 slaves;
London, Creed, Will, Dinah, Jude, & Lucy. London
& Creed are very valuable, but the other 4
are very old & of very little value. Keziah
had 8 children living & 1 dead. The one child,
who is dead, left children & they are entitled
to the share due their father. Is to be
divided into 9 parts. (Does not give name
of heirs).

58

P. 389 WILLIAM H. HILL, Admr. of Nancy Creacy
        July 1829   Petition for Sale of Negroes
    William H. Hill, Admr. of the estate of Nancy
    Creacy, deceased, states that the debts are more
    than can be paid unless the slaves are sold.
    Slaves are Zilpah, a crippled negro woman, 25
    years old, who has 3 children; Margaret - 5 yrs.,
    Aaron - 3 yrs., & Charity - 1 yr. old. Zilpah
    is so crippled that she is worthless to the
    estate to hire out. Nancy Creacy was the sister
    of William H. Hill. She left as her next of
    kin, her 2 sons. They are Calvin Creecy - 15
    yrs. old & Luther Creecy - 11 yrs. old. Sell
    slaves to pay debts.

P. 390 JAMES ARMSTRONG, Admr. of Thomas Lapsley
        July 1829   Petition for Sale of Negroes
    Thomas Lapsley, an uncle of the Petitioner & a
    citizen of Georgia, died intestate. He had 2
    slaves. They are: Jerry - about 21 or 22
    yrs. & Sally - about 19 or 20 yrs. They are
    both the issue of a female slave of said Thomas
    Lapsley. No regular administration was ever
    had upon the estate in the State of Georgia.
    The business was settled by James Lapsley,
    another uncle of James Armstrong. James Lapsley
    is the brother of Thomas Lapsley, deceased.
    William L. Armstrong also aided in settling
    the business of Thomas Lapsley. Thomas Lapsley
    left no will nor legitimate children. His
    distributees were his brother, James Lapsley
    & Elizabeth Lapsley, Thomas Armstrong, James
    Armstrong, William L. Armstrong, & Mary Tinnen.
    Elizabeth Lapsley since died intestate &
    without issue. Thomas Armstrong, James Armstrong,
    & William L. Armstrong, are the nephews of
    Thomas Lapsley. Mary Tinnen is his niece. She
    is also a widow. All of the above mentioned
    are above the age of 21 yrs. James Lapsley
    afterwards died & he left a will appointing
    Thomas Armstrong, Exr. James Armstrong,
    Thomas Armstrong, William L. Armstrong, &
    Mary Tinnen are the next of kin of James Lapsley,
    not bequeathed by his will. They (the Arm-
    strongs) are interested in liberating the
    slaves, Jerry & Sally, & locating them in Ohio.
    The slaves, Jerry & Sally, were sent from
    North Carolina in 1827 (where they had been
    taken from Georgia) to Williamson County.
    Petitioner, Thomas Armstrong, has asked his
    sister, Mary, to consent to this emancipation.
    Petitioner has no notice of debts due from the
    estate. He just wants to sell the slaves.

P. 392 ISAAC BIZZELL - pl. vs BENJAMIN TROTTER &
ISAAC TIGNOR - def.
Jan. 1828   Debt

P. 395 JOHN L. McEWEN - pl. vs BENJAMIN TROTTER - def.
Debt

P. 397 EDWARD G. CLOUSTON - pl. vs GEORGE WHITE &
ROBERT H. CAMPBELL - def.
Debt

P. 399 THOMAS HUGHES - pl. vs BERNARD RICHARDSON - def.
Jan. 1828   Case (Trespass)

P. 401 GEORGE McLEAN - pl. vs JESSE EVANS, WOODSON
HUBBARD, & ISAAC SMITH - def.
April 1828   Debt

P. 401 JOSEPH CROCKETT - pl. vs LEMUEL SMITH - def.
April 1828   Debt

P. 406 JOSEPH CROCKETT - pl. vs LEMUEL SMITH - def.
April 1828   Debt

P. 408 DAVID S. GARLAND, Assignee & C - pl. vs JOHN
NICHOLS - def.   Debt
David S. Garland, Assignee of James W. Smith,
Assignee of Allen Bugg.

P. 410 ROBERT PEEBLES - pl. vs JOHN NICHOLS - def.
Debt

P. 412 JOSHUA W. McCOWN, Assignee & C - pl. vs ALLEN
MEBANE - def.
April 1828   Debt

P. 414 JOHN H. CRISP & WILLIAM WILLIS - pl. vs FINIS
W. SHANNON - def.
Debt

P. 416 JOSEPH HASSELL - pl, vs NICHOLAS PERKINS, SR. -
def.   Debt

P. 418 JOHN NICHOLS, Assignee - pl. vs ALLEN MEBANE -
def.   April 1828   Debt

P. 420 JOSEPH HASSELL - pl. vs NICHOLAS PERKINS, JR. -
def.   Debt

P. 422 STATE OF TENNESSEE - pl. vs LEWIS JOHNSON - def.
George W. Maberry & Lewis Johnson for an
assault on the body of William Lea.

P. 424 STATE OF TENNESSEE - pl. vs GEORGE W. MABURY
        & LEWIS JOHNSON - def.
                   April 1828
        George W. Mabury & Lewis Johnson for an assault
        on the body of William Lea.

P. 425 STATE OF TENNESSEE - pl. vs THOMAS STAGGS - def.
        Indictment for gaming.

P. 427 & P. 428
        STATE OF TENNESSEE - pl. vs THOMAS STAGGS - def.
                April 1828
        Indictment for gaming.

P. 429 REUBEN REYNOLDS - pl. vs REUBEN W. REYNOLDS -
        def.
                Oct. 1829   Debt

P. 431 JACOB HALFACRE - pl. vs JOHN C. SIMMONS &
        THOMAS SIMMONS - def.
                            Debt

P. 433 WILLIAM WALLACE & MASON PILCHER - pl. vs
        BENJAMIN TROTTER - def.
                    Oct. 1829   Debt
        Wallace & Pilcher are merchants.

P. 436 BENJAMIN S. TAPPAN & CHARLES G. OLMSTED - pl.
        vs GEORGE E. COOK & MARY BOYD - def.
                        Debt
        Tappan & Olmstead are merchants.

P. 439 ROBERT P. CURRIN & CHARLES G. OLMSTED - pl. vs
        JOHN S. WHEATON - def.
                    Oct. 1829   Debt
        Currin & Olmstead are merchants.

P. 441 ROBERT P. CURRIN & CHARLES G. OLMSTED - pl.
        vs JOHN S. WHEATON - def.
                        Debt
        Currin & Olmstead are merchants.

P. 444 GEORGE CATHEY, Assignee & C - pl. vs WARE
        HENLEY - def.
                    July 1829   Debt

P. 447 BENJAMIN S. TAPPAN & PETER PERKINS - pl. vs
        JAMES R. TISDALE - def.
                        Debt
        Tappan & Perkins are merchants.

P. 449 BENJAMIN S. TAPPAN & PETER PERKINS - pl. vs
        SALA N. SHARP - def.
                        Debt
        Tappan & Perkins are merchants.

P. 451 ROBERT H. JACKSON - pl. vs PHILIP MAURY - def.
        July 1829   Debt

P. 454 JOHN WATSON, Assignee & C - pl. vs JAMES W.
       CURRY & ELI McGAN - def.
              Debt

P. 457 SAMUEL S. WILLIAMS, Assignee & C - pl. vs
       THOMAS W. CASH - def.
              Debt

P. 459 BENJAMIN F. CROCKETT - pl. vs ELISHA DAVIS -
       def.
              Oct. 1829   Debt

P. 462 ISHAM R. THWEATT - pl. vs CAREY A. HARRIS -
       def.   Debt

P. 465 ROBERT JOHNSTON - pl. vs ANDREW D. BATEMAN
       & THOMAS HOLT - def.
              Debt

P. 468 SUMNER M. SHARP - pl. vs JOSHUA W. McCOWN -
       def.   Covenant Broken
                         Oct. 1829

P. 470 LEMUEL B. McCONNICO, County Trustee of Williamson
       County - pl. vs JOSHUA FARRINGTON, ELI McGAN,
       WILLIAM CRAIG, TAYLOR H. BLAIR, & ROBERT
       PEEBLES - def.
                    Motion
       Joshua Farrington is the late county trustee of
       Williamson County & Eli McGan, William Craig,
       Taylor H. Blair, & Robert Peebles, were his
       securities. To make a settlement.

P. 472 J. G. BRODY - pl. vs ANDREW CROCKETT, Exr. of
       Samuel Crockett, deceased - def.
              July 1829   Trespass   (Debt)

P. 476 JAMES CRAIG - pl. vs NATHANIEL H. THOMAS - def.
              Debt

P. 478 ELI McGAN - pl. vs JAMES COPERTON - def.
              Trespass

P. 484 THOMAS GRAY - pl. vs JAMES COPERTON - def.
              Oct. 1829   Trespass

P. 487 STEPHEN NOLEN - pl. vs WILLIAM P. HAYS - def.
              Debt
       William P. Hays is of Davidson County.

P. 494 DENNY P. HADLEY - pl. vs THOMAS WELLS - def.
              Case   (Trespass)

62

P, 496 THOMAS H. BELL, Assignee & C - pl. vs JAMES
        MARSHALL & GILBERT MARSHALL - def.
                July 1829   Debt

P. 499 ISAAC SHORT - pl. vs DANIEL VAUGHAN & ELIAS
        DODSON - def.
                        Debt

P. 501 MARY MORRIS - pl. vs PETER R. RISON, JOHN L.
        WHEATON, & ISHAM R. THWEATT - def.
                        Debt
        Mary Morris is Assignee of Thomas H. Perkins.

P. 506 JOSEPH W. CAMP - pl. vs JOHN G. WILLIAMSON -
        def.
                April 1829   Debt

P. 508 THOMAS G. MALLORY - pl. vs JAMES GAREY &
        LEVIN H. WOOLDRIDGE - def.
                        Debt

P. 510 THOMAS G. MALLORY - pl. vs HENRY CHRISTMAS
        & RICHARD CHRISTMAS - def.
                        Debt

P. 513 WILLIAM T. BRYANT - pl. vs JAMES GAREY - def.
                April 1829   Debt

P. 516 STERLING GUNER, use of Abner White - pl. vs
        NATHANIEL HARRISON, COLEMAN HALEY, & RICHARD
        REYNOLDS - def.
                    Covenant Broken

P. 520 ROBERT H. JACKSON - pl. vs MARY BOYD &
        DANIEL P. PERKINS - def.
                        Debt

RECORD BOOK

LAWSUITS

No. 5

1830 - 1831

P. 1   JAMES SHELBURN & SUSAN, his wife & THEOPILUS L.
GENTRY & WIFE - pl. vs AARON BROWN & WIFE; N.
T. PERKINS; WILLIAM EDMISTON; & ANN & THOMAS
SAPPINGTON - def.
        Jan. 1831   Petition for Partition
Joseph H. Stockett died in 1821. He left a will.
He left all of his estate to: Mrs. Susan
Stockett (now Mrs. Susan Brown), Nicholas T.
Perkins, & William Edmiston, the Exrs. All of
his debts were to be paid first. The balance of
the estate is to go to the children of his deceased
sister, Elizabeth. She is the late wife of
Doctor Thomas Sappington. His sister's children
are: Susan, Rebecca, Ann, & Thomas. Susan married
James Shelburn. Rebecca married Theophilus L.
Gentry. Ann & Thomas Sappington are minors &
their guardian is John Thompson. Joseph H. Stockett
left the following tracts of land:
        1.   One tract of land containing 320 acres
             in Williamson & Davidson Counties. It
             crosses the Little Harpeth River. It is
             part of a 640 acre tract granted to
             Samuel McCutchin by North Carolina.
        2.   One tract of land containing 2 1/4 acres
             on the Little Harpeth.
        3.   One tract of land containing 320 acres
             joining Samuel McCutchin's land.
(Copy of will included) Mrs. Susan Stockett is
his step-mother - to William Edmiston, son of
Samuel Edmiston - to heirs of my Uncle Noble
Stockett, deceased - date 27 July 1819 - probated
April Term 1821.

P. 7   JAMES ARMSTRONG & JAMES SWANSON - pl. vs WILLIAM
WILLET & MARY, his wife; SARAH, JAMES, WILLIAM,
& JOHN WILLET, infants by their guardian, William
B. McClellan & Mary Tyrrill; JOHN D. BENNETT &
BETSEY, his wife; and JOSEPH & WILLIAM TYRRILL;
and HEZEKIAH, TIMOTHY, MARY, NANCY, MARTHA, &
JAMES TYRRILL, last 6 infants by their guardian,
John D. Bennett - def.
        Jan. 1831   Petition for Partition
Alesalom Tatum died in 1802 in Orange County,
North Carolina. He left a will. He left to
Mary Willitt, wife of William Willet, and to
the child she has & should thereafter have, (CONT'D)

P. 7   Absalom Tatum, deceased (CONT'D)
500 acres of land. This 500 acres is a part of
a 5000 acre tract of land on the West Harpeth
River. The children of the said Mary Willet are:
Hannah, Absalom T., Lewis A., Joseph W., Sarah,
James, William, & John. Hannah is now the wife
of Reuben Littleton. Sarah, James, William, &
John are infants & without guardian. James Armstrong
has purchased the part of Absalom T. Willett &
Lewis A. Willett. This consist of 2/9 part of
the undivided tract. James Swanson has
purchased from Joseph W. Willett 1/9 part of
said tract (this being Joseph W. Willett's share).
Some years ago, James Tyrrill purchased from
Reuben Littleton & his wife & William Willett &
his wife some interest in the said tract of land.
The said James Tyrrill afterwards died intestate
leaving a wife, Mary, & children. His children
are: Betsey (wife of John D. Bennett), Joseph
& William (both now of full age), & Hezekiah,
Timothy, Mary, Nancy, Martha, & James. Hezekiah,
Timothy, Mary, Nancy, Martha, & James are
minors without guardian.

P. 13   JOHN JOHNSTON, SALLY JOHNSON, JOSHUA JOHNSON,
POLLY JOHNSON, KEZIAH JOHNSON, & CAROLINE
JOHNSON
        Jan. 1831   Petition for Partition
Sally, Joshua, Polly, Keziah, & Caroline
Johnson are minors and they petition by their
guardian, John Jordan. Stephen Johnson died
intestate. He owned a tract of land (about
100 acres). His widow has had her dower
allotted. The petitioners want the land
divided into 6 parts.

_____   JOSIAH WOOD & MARTHA, his wife; JOHN JOHNSON;
SALLY JOHNSON; JOSHUA JOHNSON; POLLY JOHNSON;
KEZIAH JOHNSON; & CAROLINE JOHNSON.
        Jan. 1831   Petition for Partition
Sally, Joshua, Polly, Keziah, & Caroline
Johnson are minors. Their guardian is John
Jordan. Stephen Johnson died intestate. He
left a widow, Martha. He left the following
children: John, Sally, Joshua, Polly, Keziah,
& Caroline. He left Archer Jordan his Admr.
He left slaves. The petitioners want to sell
the slaves.

_____   JANE HOLLAND, JAMES HUGHES & ROSANNA, his
wife, JOHN M. HOLLAND, MARGARET HOLLAND, NEWTON
HOLLAND, BIRD HOLLAND, & GEORGE HOLLAND - pl.
vs JOHN K. CAMPBELL, PAGE BOND & JANE, his wife,
FIELDING HELM & NANEY, his wife, BIRD DOTSON &
JUDITH, his wife, SPIERMAN HOLLAND, KEMP L.
HOLLAND, & FREDERICK HOLLAND - def.   (CONT'D)

_____ Kemp Holland, deceased (CONT'D)
    Jan. 1831   Petition for Distribution
Kemp Holland died in 1824 intestate. Page Bond
& John H. Campbell are the Admrs. John H.
Campbell is now of Henry County. Kemp Holland
left a widow, Jane. He left the following
children: John M., Rosanna, George, Margaret,
Newton, Bird, Frederick (now of Perry County),
Speerman (now of Henry Co.), Kemp S. (now of
Henry Co.), Nancy (wife of Fielding Helm),
Jane (wife of Page Bond), & Judith (wife of Bird
Dotson). The estate is to be divided into 13
parts. Kemp Holland, deceased, left slaves.
Each of the heirs has been asked to give an
account of the items that they have received
from Kemp Holland during his lifetime.

P. 32   JAMES McCUTCHEN, Admr. of John Porter, deceased
    Jan. 1831   Petition for Sale of Negro
James McCutchen, Admr., has sold the rest of
John Porter's estate & now he must sell the
slave to pay the debts.

P. 34   ANN POPE
    Jan. 1831   Petition for Dower
John Pope died Jan. 1829. He left a widow,
Ann. He had a tract of land (about 800 acres)
on the West Harpeth & Murfree's Fork. He had
another tract of land (about 250 acres) in
Williamson & Maury Counties on the waters of
Carters Creek. Ann Pope wants her dower.

P. 37   JOSEPH CARSON - pl. vs ALEXANDER WOOD - def.
    April 1829

P. 39   JAMES TURNER, Assignee & C - pl. vs WILLIAM
    B. JONES - def.
    Debt

P. 42   REUBEN REYNOLDS - pl. vs GEORGE WHITE - def.
    Debt

P. 44   WILLIAM K. McALISTER, SAMUEL D. McALISTER, &
    JAMES C. HILL - pl. vs BENJAMIN TROTTER - def.
    April 1829   Debt
William K. McAlister, Samuel D. McAlister, &
James C. Hill are merchants trading under the
firm & style of McAlister Hill & Company.

P. 47   DANIEL W. MAURY, Admr. of Abram Maury, deceased -
    pl. vs PHILIP MAURY - def.
    Debt

P. 49   ANDREW W. NORRIS - pl. vs GEORGE G. BOYD - def.
    Debt

P. 52   SAMUEL B. BRIDGES - pl. vs SAMUEL H. DUVAL - def.
                April 1829   Case

P. 55   HENRY R. W. HILL, Endorsee & C - pl. vs HENDLEY
            STONE & STERLING IRVI - def.
                        Debt

P. 58   ABRAM M. WHITE - pl. vs ALLEN MEBANE - def.
                        Debt

P. 62   BURWELL EVERETT - pl. vs LAWRENCE O. BRYAN - def.
                Jan. 1829   Debt

P. 64   HENRY R. W. HILL - pl. vs HENDLEY STONE &
            STERLING IVIE - def.

P. 68   JAMES PARK - pl. vs THOMAS CASH - def.
                (Debt for 3 fine hats at $10 each)

P. 70   WILLIAM MOORE - pl. vs CHRISTOPHER E. McEWEN
            & JOHN L. McEWEN - def.
                Jan. 1829   Debt

P. 73   DANIEL MASON - pl. vs THOMAS RIDLEY & JOHN P.
            IRION - def.
                        Debt

P. 76   TILMAN PERRY - pl. vs LOVING H. WOOLDRIDGE -
            def.   Debt

P. 78   HENRY HALFACRE - pl. vs NICHOLAS P. PERKINS -
            def.
                Oct. 1829   Debt

P. 81   NICHOLAS PERKINS, JR. - pl. vs LEONARD
            DUNNAVANT & MICHAEL L. McCRORY - def.
                        Debt

P. 84   RODHAM TOLLOSSE - pl. vs LEVI CROSBY - def.
            Crosby shot the slave of Tolloss & he died
            from the wound. Tolloss wants $700 for
            damages.

P. 86   MATTHEW WATSON & JOHN R. BURKE - pl. vs SAMUEL
            H. DUVAL - def.
                Oct. 1828   Debt
            Matthew Watson & John R. Burke are merchants
            trading under the firm & style of Watson &
            Burke.

P. 90   ANDREW CAMPBELL & WILLIAM P. CAMPBELL - pl. vs
            JAMES WILSON & JAMES H. WILSON - def.
                        Debt

P. 94   ROBERT P. CURRIN for Daniel Mason - pl. vs THOMAS
         RIDBY & RICHARD C. HANCOCK - def.
                        Debt

P. 97   BARTON RICHMOND - pl. vs BENJAMIN TROTTER - def.
                Oct. 1828   Case

P. 100   PATRICK REESE - pl. vs BENJAMIN TROTTER - def.
                        Case

P. 103   PATRICK REESE - pl. vs BENJAMIN TROTTER - def.
                        Debt

P. 106   EDWARD H. CHAFFIN - pl. vs WILLAIM B. JONES - def.
                Oct. 1828   Certiorari
         Edward H. Chaffin of Maury County owed a debt.
         He gave a tract of land in Maury Co. in
         exchange for the debt. Reuben Reynolds failed
         to give him a receipt for the same.

P. 111   ULYSES FITTS - pl. vs GEORGE GLASCOCK - def.
                        Case
         George Glascock followed the occupation of hauling
         goods & merchandise by a certain wagon. He
         carried about 1475 lbs. of tobacco to Nashville
         and he did not take the proper care of it.

P. 116   JOHN NICHOLS - pl. vs WILLIAM E. ANDERSON &
         NICHOLAS P. PERKINS - def.
                Oct. 1828   Debt

P. 119   JOSEPH WILSON - pl. vs JAMES WILSON - def.
                        Debt

P. 123   STATE OF TENNESSEE - pl. vs WILLIAM SMITH - def.
                        Gaming

P. 126   STATE OF TENNESSEE - pl. vs ABNER PISTOLE - def.
                July 1828   Assault & battery
         Assault & battery on the body of William Watton.

P. 129   STATE OF TENNESSEE - pl. vs JOHN STOKES - def.
                        Assault & Affray
         Assault on the body of William Mathews & James
         Matthews.

P. 132   WILLIAM LIGGITT - pl. vs REUBENE HAMILTON - def.
                July 1828
         John Beck bought some slaves from Liggitt.
         Beck was insolvent. Reubene Hamilton was
         acquainted with Beck & recommended him to
         Liggitt.

P. 137   ROBERT BAXTER & EDWARD D. HICKS - pl. vs JOHN
         CHADWELL - def.
                        Debt

68

P. 141 ANDREW & WILLIAM P. CAMPBELL - pl. vs HENRY
SWEENEY - def.
Debt

P. 142 JAMES HUGHES, Assignee & C - pl. vs NICHOLAS
PERKINS, SR. - def.
July 1828   Debt

P. 145 CHRISTOPHER E. McEWEN & JOHN L. McEWEN, Assignee
& C - pl. vs NICHOLAS PERKINS, SR. - def.
Debt

P. 148 NETHERLAND TAIT for the use of Bacon Tait - pl.
vs EZEKIEL CHANEY - def.
Debt

P. 150 JOHN N. CHARTER & MICHAEL DOYLE - pl. vs JOHN
L. WHEATON - def.
July 1828   Debt
John N. Charter & Michael Doyle are merchants
& partners trading under the firm & style of
Charter & Doyle.

P. 152 JOEL SMITH, Assignee & C - pl. vs JOSHUA
FARRINGTON & WILLIAM NICHOL - def.
Debt

P. 156 GEORGE WHITE - pl. vs STEPHEN S. BRADLEY - def.
Debt

P. 158 WILLIAM G. DICKINSON - pl. vs JOHN M. WOTSON -
def.   July 1828   Debt

P. 161 JOHN C. McLEMORE, Assignee & C - pl. vs PETER
R. RISON & JOHN L. WHEATON - def.
Trespass

P. 163 BENJAMIN S. TAPPAN & PETER PERKINS - pl. vs
JAMES R. TISDALE - def.
Debt
Tappan & Perkins are merchants.

P. 166 ELIZABETH MARSHALL - pl. vs JOSHUA FARRINGTON
& ROBERT PEEBLES - def.
July 1828   Trespass

P. 168 BENJAMIN S. TAPPAN & PETER PERKINS, Assignee
& C - pl. vs JESSE COX & EPHRAIM BROWN - def.
Debt
Tappan & Perkins are merchants & partners
under the firm of Tappan & Perkins.

P. 172 WILLIAM SHUTE, use of John N. Charter & MICHAEL
DOYLE - pl. vs PHILIP MAURY - def.
July 1828   Debt
William Shute & Michael Doyle are merchants &
partners in trade trading under the firm & style
of Charter & Doyle.

P. 174 WILLIAM SHUTE, Assignee & C to the use of Tappan
& Perkins - pl. vs JOHN WITHERSPOON - def.
Debt

P. 176 WILLIAM B. McCLELLAN - pl. vs NATHANIEL H. THOMAS
& PHINEAS THOMAS - def.
July 1828   Debt

P. 179 WILLIAM B. McCLELLAN - pl. vs PHINEAS THOMAS &
NATHANIEL H. THOMAS - def.
Debt

P. 181 BENNETT SMITH - pl. vs CHARLES WHITLOCK & JOSHUA
FARRINGTON - def.
Debt

P. 185 ABRAM M. WHITE - pl. vs JOSHUA FARRINGTON - def.
July 1828   Debt
Abram M. White is endorsee of Elizabeth White.

P. 187 ANDREW ROUNTREE - pl. vs SAMUEL DODD & JOSHUA
MITCHELL - def.
Debt

P. 190 JEREMIAH BYRN - pl. vs JOHN H. SCRUGGS - def.
Trespass

P. 193 ROBERT JOHNSTON - pl. vs NANCY BALLOW & THOMAS
W. BALLOW - def.
Oct. 1829   Debt

P. 195 WILLIAM B. WORD - pl. vs LOUISA A. WORD; AMERICA
WORD; & JAMES SWANSON, their guardian - def.
April 1830   Petition for Distribution
James Swanson, Sr. was appointed guardian to
William B., Louisa A. & America Word in 1825.
William B., Louisa A., & America Word own slaves
jointly. William B. Word has reached the age of
21 & he wishes to have his part.

P. 197 THOMAS BRADLEY, in his own right & as Admr. of
William Norton, deceased; & THOMAS TALBOT & ELIZABETH,
his wife
1830   Exparte - Petition for Sale &
                         Distribution
Stephen Norton of North Carolina died & left a
will. He left the slaves to his wife, Jane, during
her life & then to his children. His children
are: Richmond (who died under age), William (who
died in Williamson County with Thomas Bradley,
Admr.), Margaret (who married Thomas Bradley & she
is dead), Ann (who is dead & left 1 child, Jane, who
married Bartholomew White & whose interest Thomas
Bradley has purchased), Elizabeth (who married
                                        (Cont"d)

P. 197 Stephen Norton, deceased (CONT'D)
Thomas Talbot). The children are to get 1/4
share each. Jane, Stephen Norton's widow,
died Oct. 1829. The slaves Stephen Norton
left are: Hannah - 60 yrs., Aggy - 35 yrs.,
Ann - 23 yrs., Lette - 23 yrs., Jinny - 19 yrs.
& her 3 children (Hannah - 6 yrs., Elmore - 3
yrs., & Anne - 6 mos.), Hannah - 18 yrs,
Ruben - 19 yrs., Albert - 17 yrs., & Andrew -
16 yrs. Will - Orange County, North Carolina.
Wife - Jane Norton. Sons - John Norton,
William Norton, & Richard Norton. Daughters -
Anne Norton, Margaret Norton, & Elizabeth
Norton. Elizabeth Norton's son, John, is to
get the land on the branches of the Rattle-
snake (200 acres). The Exrs. are: Jane
Norton, Stephen Norton's wife; Mans Armstead;
& John Armstrong. The will is dated 7 July
1773. Probated August 1774.

P. 201 THOMAS COOPER, use of Fountain B. Carter - pl.
vs WILLIAM MOORE - def.
Jan. 1830   Debt

P. 203 ARTHUR A. STEWART - pl. vs ISAAC SMITH - def.
Debt

P. 205 MAYOR & ALDERMAN OF FRANKLIN - pl. vs ALLEN
T. NOLEN - def.

P. 208 WILLIAM W. GOODWIN, Assignee & C - pl. vs
SALA N. SHARP - def.
Jan. 1830   Debt

P. 210 ROBERT C. FOSTER - pl. vs SOLOMON P. CATT - def.
Trespass

P. 213 ROBERT H. JACKSON - pl. vs PHILIP MAURY &
DANIEL P. PERKINS - def.
Debt

P. 216 JOHN N. CHARTER & MICHAEL DOYLE - pl. vs
ALEXANDER C. CARTER - def.
Jan. 1830   Debt

P. 218 ROBERT BAXTER & EDWARD D. HICKS, merchant &
C - pl. vs JOHN NICHOLS - def.
Debt

P. 221 EDWARD G. CLOUSTON - pl. vs JOHN L. WHEATON -
def.   Debt

P. 224 KEMP S. HOLLAND - pl. vs NATHANIEL HARRISON &
COLEMAN HALEY - def.
Debt

P. 228 The PRESIDENT DIRECTOR & COMPANY of the BANK of
the STATE OF TENNESSEE, for the use of their
Branch Bank at Franklin - pl. vs JOHN WILSON &
THOMAS WILSON - def.
        Debt

P. 231 GEORGE HAYNES - pl. vs BENJAMIN J. BASS - def.
        Debt

P. 234 DAVID THOMPSON, JOHN DRENNEN, WILLIAM B. McCLELLEN,
use of Richard H. Rudder - pl. vs WILLIAM B.
JONES & ALEXANDER Y. SIMMONS - def.
        Jan. 1830   Debt

P. 237 JAMES CAROTHERS - pl. vs ALEXANDER McCOWN - def.
        Debt

P. 240 NICHOLAS P. PERKINS - pl. vs JOHN GRAHAM - def.
        Debt

P. 242 THE STATE OF TENNESSEE - pl. vs THOMAS B.
GARRETT - def.
        April 1830
Thomas B. Garrett, as constable, failed to execute
a warrant.

P. 245 STATE OF TENNESSEE - pl. vs JAMES G. JONES - def.
        Assault, battery, & affray on Hollan Davis

P. 249 STATE OF TENNESSEE - pl. vs JAMES G. JONES - def.
        July Session, 1830
        Assault, battery, & affray on John Turner

P. 251 MARSHALL JAMISON; SAMUEL JAMISON; BARTLEY BYRD &
JANE, his wife; JOHN JAMISON; THOMAS JAMISON;
DRURY WARREN & SALLY, his wife; ROBERT NEWSOM &
HESSEY, his wife; ELIZABETH JAMISON, by her
guardian, Marshall & James Jamison; WILEY
JAMISON; BROWN JAMISON; PEGGY JAMISON; SALLY
JAMISON; & JANE JAMISON, orphans of William Jamison,
deceased, by their guardian, Ruffin Brown.
        Exparte - Petition for Partition
John Jammerson died in 1824 intestate. He left a
widow, Ellen Jimmerson, who has since died
intestate. Marshall Jamison was appointed the
Admr. They left the following children (heirs):
Marshall Jamison, John Jamison, Thomas Jamison,
Samuel Jamison, Elizabeth Jamison, Bartley Byrd
& Jane, his wife, Drury Warren & Sally, his wife,
Robert Newsom & Hessey, his wife, & the following
orphans of William Jamison, deceased: Wiley,
Brown, Peggy, Sally, & Jane Jamison. William
Jamison died intestate. John Jamison left the
following negroes: Jacob, Dice & her infant
child, Betsy & her children Jane & Charles,
Rachel, & Suckey.

P. 256   ALEXANDER B. MORTON, Admr. of Abner W. Morton,
deceased
              July 1830   Exparte - Petition for
                          Sale of Negroes
Alexander B. Morton was appointed Admr. of the
estate of Abner W. Morton at the Oct. Session,
1827. Alexander B. Morton has sold the
personal property of the estate except the slaves.
The slaves must be sold to have enough money
to pay the debts. Abner W. Morton died intestate.
John Marshall for the petitioners. Abner W.
Morton left a slave, Nathan. Nathan was sold
at the store of William Allison. He was sold to
Jesse Evans for $320.00.

P. 258   JOHN L. McEWEN, Admr. of Nancy Barfield,
deceased
              April 1830   Exparte - Petition for Sale
                          of Negro Slaves
Nancy Barfield died Nov. 1829 intestate. She
left 2 slaves. They are: Peter - 36 yrs. old
& Clara - 30 yrs. old. Nancy Barfield left her
7 children as next of kin. Her children are:
          1.   Lewis Barfield
          2.   John Barfield
          3.   Blake Barfield
          4.   Willie B. Barfield (Willie is a minor
               & his guardian is John L. McEwen.)
          5.   Penelope Carothers (She is the wife of
               James Carothers.)
          6.   Mary (She is the wife of John Brown.)
          7.   Tabitha (She is the wife of John L.
               McEwen.)
The children want to sell the slaves for a
division.

P. 259   GABRIEL BUFORD & AMANDA, his wife; SPENCER
BUFORD & JAMES PUGH, Exrs. of the last will of
Edward Buford, deceased; & ELIZABETH BUFORD,
MARY FRANCIS BUFORD, WILLIAM W. BUFORD, EMILY
BUFORD, & LOUISA BUFORD, who are minors & sue
by their guardians Spencer Buford & James Pugh
              April 1830   Exparte
          Petition for Division of the Personal Estate
          of Edward Buford, deceased, & Distribution
          of Share of Gabriel Buford & Amanda, his wife
Edward Buford died in 1828. He left Amanda,
his widow. His children & heirs are: Elizabeth,
Mary Francis, William W., Emily, & Louisa, &
Jane. Jane is now deceased & she was the child
of petitioner, Amanda. Edward Buford left a
will. It was probated in 1828. Amanda, Elizabeth,
Mary Francis, William W., Emily, Louisa, &
Jane were entitled to 1/7 part of the slaves
according to the will. Now that Jane is dead,
the survivors are entitled to 1/6 part each.
Amanda has since married Gabriel.   (CONT'D)

P. 259 Edward Buford, deceased   (CONT'D)
Edward Buford, deceased, left the following slaves:
Dick, Bower, Jim, Frank, Stephen, Dave, Poseley,
Edmund, Alce, Lucinda, Tabb, Jinny, Maria,
Caroline, Martha, Mille, Ellinder, Siley, Olly,
Ellick, & Mira. (Complete will given.) The
will is dated 5 March 1828. Wit: G. Buford &
William B. Hardy. Wife, Amanda, to get a child's
part. 6 children - not named. Bro. Spencer
Buford & James Pugh, Exrs.

P. 262 MIRIAM PORTER; JAMES H. PORTER; THOMAS B. PORTER;
JOSEPH M. PORTER; MARY PORTER; JOSEPH S. BARTLETT
& AMANDA F., his wife; GEORGE W. HULME & SYRENA
G., his wife; REBECCA B. PORTER & JOHN B. PORTER,
last 2 are minors & sue by their guardian George
W. Hulme & James McCutchen.
        April 1830   Exparte - Petition for
                        Distribution
John Porter died intestate in 1827. James McCutchen
was named Admr. Jan. 1828. The Admr. has used
all the funds except the money from the slaves.
The slaves are: Matilda - 28 yrs.; Frank - 4 yrs.;
Elenor - 2 yrs.; Hannah - 6 mos.; Charlotte - 21
yrs. & her children, Nancy - 3 yrs., Elenor - 6
mos.; Lucy - 24 yrs. & her children, Cinda - 7
yrs.; Zilpha & Sylva - 5 yrs., Mary - 3 mos.;
Franky - 18 yrs.; Daniel - 11 yrs.; Zilpha - 60
yrs.; Samuel - 16 yrs. Miriam is the widow of
John Porter. His children & next of kin are:
James H., Thomas B., Joseph M., Mary, Amanda F.,
Syrena G., Rebecca B., & John B. Miriam, the
widow & the 8 children are entitled to 1/9 part
each.

P. 264 NICHOLAS P. SMITH & ELIZABETH J. WEST, by her
guardian, Stephen J. West
        April 1830   Exparte - Petition for Partition
Henry Childress died intestate. He left the
following children: Eliza Childress, Margery
Childress, Sarah C. Childress, & Thomas M. Childress.
He owned a tract of land (about 200 acres) on the
waters of the West Harpeth River bounded as
follows: Beginning at William Montgomery's
southwest corner (now Nicholas P. Smith's)------
a tract of land granted to Samuel Moore now
belonging to Nicholas P. Smith------to Price
Gray's southeast corner------Henry Betty's
northeast corner------to a tract of land sold by
John Childress, Sr. to Matthew Barrow------to
Murfree's south line------middle of West Harpeth
River-----south line of Thomas H. Perkins----to
tract of land sold to said Henry Childress by
Francis May. Elizabeth Childress, the widow of
Henry Childress, has since married Stephen West
& she wants her dower. Sarah C. Childress has
died intestate & without issue.   (CONT'D)

P. 264 Henry Childress, deceased (CONT'D)
Thomas M. Childress has died & he left a will &
left his share of the land to Elizabeth J. West.
After the death of Sarah C. Childress, Nicholas
P. Smith purchased the share of Eliza Childress,
(she was then Eliza Bosley) & of Margery Childress.
Nicholas P. Smith is entitled to 2/3 part of the
tract of land.

P. 268 STEPHEN WEST, Exr. of Thomas M. Childress
           April 1830   Exparte - Petition for Sale
                                    of Negroes
Thomas M. Childress died. He left a will. He
named Stephen West, Exr. He left the negro,
George, who is 60 yrs. old. George must be
sold to pay his debts.

P. 270 THOMAS H. PERKINS & SAMUEL SMITH - pl. vs AMELIA
       LOYD & SAMUEL EASTEP - def.
             April 1830
Thomas H. Perkins & Samuel Smith are bound as
securities for Amelia Loyd & Samuel Estep as
Exrs. for the Will of Lewis Loyd. They asked
to be released from the bond.

P. 271 JOHN GORDON & CALISTA, his wife; PATRICK GIBSON,
JAMES GIBSON, JOSEPH GIBSON, & NANCY GIBSON,
minor heirs of John B. Gibson, deceased, by
their guardian, Elijah R. Parrish
          Oct. 1830   Exparte - Petition for Sale
                                    of Negro
The petition of Elijah R. Parrish, guardian of
Patrick Gibson, James Gibson, Joseph Gibson, &
Mary J. Gibson: Calista Gibson is now married
to John Gordon. All of the estate of John B.
Gibson, deceased, has been divided except for
the negro boy, Spencer. Calista is the
orphan of John B. Gibson, deceased. John
Gordon in right of his wife for 1/6 part.

P. 273 HOLLAND L. WHITE; MILES WHITE; CAREY WHITE;
WILLIAM D. TAYLOR & ELIZABETH, his wife
          Jan. 1830   Exparte
Benjamin White died Sept. 1827. He left a will.
He left to his wife, Abiah White, the mansion
house, inclusive of 3 lots & the meadow tract
of land, furniture, livestock, slaves, & etc.
The estate is to be sold if the wife should
marry or die & then be divided between 4 heirs.
They are: Holland L. White, Miles White,
Elizabeth Taylor, & Cary White. Benjamin White
left negroes. They are: Ellick, Moses, Fereby,
Virgin, Judy, & Joseph. Abiah White gave a bill
of sale & deed of release 10 Oct. 1829 for all
of her interest in the negroes.   (CONT'D)

P. 273   Benjamin White, deceased (CONT'D)
         Holland L. White, Miles White, Elizabeth Taylor,
         & Carey White want to sell the negroes for
         division.

P. 277   JAMES MARSHALL, Exr. of Patrick McCutchen
              Oct. 1830   Exparte - Petition for
                               Emancipation of Negro Slaves
         Patrick McCutchen died in 1812. He left a will
         naming his wife, Hannah McCutchen, & Samuel
         McCutchen, Exrs. Hannah McCutchen & Samuel
         McCutchen have since died intestate. Patrick
         McCutchen stated in his Will that he wanted his
         slaves to be set free after the death of his
         wife, Hannah & his brother, Samuel McCutchen.
         The slaves are: Jack - 24 yrs., Ben - 19 yrs.,
         Rose - 26 yrs. & her children, Eliza - 11 yrs.,
         Scinthia - 7 yrs., Thomas - 4 yrs., Harriet - 2
         yrs., & Maria - 2 mos. James Marshall is
         Hannah McCutchen's brother. Hannah died 9 Aug.
         1830. The negro slaves are now: Jack - 44 yrs.,
         Rose (she is now dead, but left 2 sons. They
         are Pleasant - 16 yrs., & King - 8 yrs.), Ben -
         37 yrs., Eliza - 29 yrs., Scintha - 25 yrs.,
         Harriet & Mariah (both are now dead), & Thomas -
         22 yrs.

P. 280   LEVIN CATOR - pl. vs JESSE COX - def.
              Oct. 1828
         Lewis Cator, one of the securities of Jesse Cox,
         Admr. of the estate of Charles Brown, deceased,
         wants to be released as a security as he thinks
         Cox will mismanage the estate.

P. 283   BENJAMIN W. BEDFORD - pl. vs THOMAS W. CASH - def.
              July 1830   Debt

P. 285   WILLIAM McKAY - pl. vs DANIEL McPHAIL & THOMAS
         W. CASH - def.
                           Debt

P. 288   JAMES C. HILL - pl. vs McCOY W. CAMPBELL - def.
                           Debt

P. 290   JOHN D. BENNETT, use & C - pl. vs JOHN NICHOLS -
         def.
              July 1830   Debt

P. 292   NANCY HILL - pl. vs BAILEY HARDEMAN, NICHOLAS
         SCALES, & JOHN PAGE - def.
                           Debt

P. 294   SAMUEL PRATT - pl. vs JAMES R. TISDALE - def.
                           Debt

P. 297   JAMES C. HILL - pl. vs THOMAS SIMMONS - def.
              July 1830   Debt

76

P. 299 STATE OF TENNESSEE - pl. vs ISHAM R. THWEATT -
def.
Indictment for Gaming

P. 303 STATE OF TENNESSEE - pl. vs JAMES G. JONES - def.
July 1830   Assault & Battery
Assault on John Turner.

P. 305 STATE OF TENNESSEE - pl. vs JOSHUA W. McCOWN -
def.
Indictment for Assault & Battery
Assault & battery on William B. McClellan.

P. 307 MARY DABNEY - pl. vs WILLIAM W. DABNEY, LUCY
W. DABNEY, PEGGY S. DABNEY, ANN DABNEY, JOHN
DABNEY, & MARY DABNEY, minor heirs of Charles
Dabney, deceased
Jan. 1830   Petition for Dower
Mary Dabney is the widow of Charles A. Dabney
who died May 1829 intestate. He had a tract
of land on the waters of the West Harpeth
River about 3 miles from Franklin adjoining
the lands of Samuel Glass & James Hughes.
The land contains about 400 to 500 acres.
Charles A. Dabney had children. They are:
William W., Lucy W., Peggy S., Ann, John,
& Mary. They are all minors & have no general
guardian. Mary Dabney, the widow, wants the
dower.

P. 310 MARY DABNEY, widow & relict of Charles A.
Dabney, deceased - pl. vs JOHN D. BENNETT,
Admr. of said Charles A. Dabney; WILLIAM W.
DABNEY; LUCY A. DABNEY; MARGARET S. DABNEY;
JOHN O. DABNEY; MARY E. DABNEY; & ANN P.
DABNEY, minor children of Charles A. Dabney
by their guardian, Mansfield House
Jan. 1831   Petition for Distribution
Charles A. Dabney died in 1828 intestate. He
left the following children: William W., Lucy
A., Margaret A., John O., Mary E., & Ann P.
Dabney. John D. Bennett was appointed Admr.
of the estate. Charles A. Dabney had slaves.
They are: George, Ben, Jack, Harry, Frank,
Jackson, Jim, Ben, Abner, Washington, Moses,
Charles, Rial, Aggy, Eliga, Mariah, Sophia,
Lucy, Celia, Betsy, Silah, Edy, Jane, Mary,
& Amanda (25 in all). Mary Dabney, the widow,
wants to sell the slaves to get the dower.

P. 312 NANCY BYRD; RICHARD BYRD; JOHN BYRD; ELIJAH
KING & SALLY, his wife; JAMES BYRD; JAMES T.
BROUGHTON; EDMUND BURCH & NANCY, his wife
      Jan. 1831   Exparte - Petition for
                      Distribution
Baylor Byrd died before last July term 1830 intestate.
His heirs are:. Nancy Byrd, Richard Byrd, John
Byrd, Elijah King & Sally, his wife, James Byrd,
James T. Broughton, Edmund Burch & Nancy, his wife.
James Byrd is appointed Adnr. Baylor Byrd left
slaves. They are: Clara, Peter, Oliver, Ned,
Ellick, Jefferson, Martin, & Daniel & her 7
children. The heirs want the slaves divided & not
to be sold as they were raised by the family.

P. 315 CAREY W. POPE; LEMUEL POPE; JOHN W. POPE; MARY
C. POPE; JANE O. POPE; METCALF DeGRAFFENREID &
CANDIS J., his wife; THOMAS J. PARHAM &
WINIFRED L., his wife; JOHN ANDREWS & ELIZABETH
A., his wife; WILLIAM BAUGH & AMARILLA T., his
wife; GUSTAVUS A. POPE & ANN L. POPE, minors who
petition by their guardian, Thomas J. Parham;
& ANN POPE, widow of John Pope, deceased
      Jan. 1830   Petition for Partition
John Pope died Jan. 1829 intestate. He owned tracts
of land on the head waters of Murfree's Fork of
the West Harpeth. Ann Pope, the widow, has
already had her dower laid out. John Pope, deceased,
left slaves. They are: Monday, Jerry, Easter,
Rosetta, Burrell, Dianna, Cherry, Eaton, Nelson,
Henry, Malvina, All ?___, Franklin, Bandy & her
child, & Fanny. John Pope, deceased, left heirs.
They are: William R. Pope, Thomas A. Pope,
Martha Crump (now a widow who has already received
her share of estate during her father's lifetime.),
Thomas J. Parham & Winifred L., his wife (They have
received their share of the land & only wish their
share of negroes.), Ann Pope, the widow (She only
wishes to have her share of negroes.), Cary W.
Pope (He had received his share of land & wishes
only his share of the slaves.), The other
petitioners want their share of land & slaves.

P. 323 WILLIAM A. BOYD; PRYOR HUGHES & MARTHA A., his
wife; PAULINE W. BOYD & ARMSTEAD BOYD, minors &
sue by their guardian, Margaret Boyd
      Jan. 1831   Petition for Partition
William I. Boyd died the latter part of 1828. He
left a Will. He left the following children:
Martha A., William A., Wilmoth, Pauline W., &
Armstead. He left them 50 acres of land each.
Margaret Boyd is his widow. Martha A. & her
husband received the place they now live on.
William A. Boyd received the Coon Spring. William
A. Boyd has purchased the share of Wilmoth & her
husband, Moses E. Farmer. The petitioners want
the land divided according to the Will.

P. 327 SEGAR McLEMORE & BETHENIA, his wife - pl. vs
ATKINSON J. McLEMORE; THOMAS G. MALLORY &
MARGARET, his wife, Exrs. of Robert McLemore,
deceased - def.
             Jan. 1831   Petition for Distribution
Robert McLemore died in 1823. He left a will.
His Exrs. were Atkins J. McLemore, Margaret
McLemore, & Charles A. Dabney. Robert McLemore
left a widow, Margaret. She has since married
Thomas Mallory. Segars McLemore & Bethinia, his
wife, now live in Madison County, Tennessee.
Robert McLemore owned a large real estate.
Charles A. Dabney has died. His survivors are:
Atkins J. McLemore & Thomas G. Mallory & his
wife, Margaret. The Exrs. want a division to
be made. (Copy of Will) April Term 1823 -
Dated April 14, 1822. Wife - Peggy - 220 acres
& 40 acre tract until youngest son, Robert W.,
reaches the age of 21. Robert W., son, receives
2 tracts of land 8 or 9 miles south of Franklin.
Atkins J., son, the tract of land he lives on
& negroes, Nathan & Epee & Nelson. John D.,
son, remainder of tract of land. Bethenia Ann
Gra_?_ McLemore, daughter, received the slaves,
John, Cleo & her child, Albert, Martha, & Anne.
Polly McLemore - daughter. Peggy S., daughter.

P. 338 STEPHEN WEST, Exr. of Thomas M. Childress
             Jan. 1831   Exparte - Petition for Sale
                                        of Land
Thomas M. Childress died. He left a will.
Stephen West is appointed Exr. in the July
Term 1829. Thomas M. Childress had a tract of
land containing about 55 acres. The land must
be sold to pay the debts.

P. 340 THOMAS OLD, JR. & SUSAN W., his wife; NICHOLAS
S. CRUNK, RICHARD CRUNK, & JOSEPH H. CRUNK, which
last three are minors & petition by their
guardian, Nicholas Scales.
             Oct. 1830   Petition for Distribution
The petitioners have negro slaves Bethel, Peggy,
Viney, & Mircy & their increases. They want
the slaves divided.

P. 342 JAMES H. HADLEY - pl. vs JOHN H. FAUIER (?) -
def.
           Jan. 1831   Convenant Broken

P. 345 GEORGE WHITE - pl. vs STEPHEN G. EUBANKS - def.
             Covenant Broken

P. 359 EDWARD G. CLOUSTON - pl. vs NICHOLAS T. PERKINS -
def.
Clouston wants the negro man, Landon, that Perkins has

P. 362   EDWARD G. CLOUSTON - pl. vs JOSEPH BURNETT - def.
            Jan. 1831   Trespass

P. 364   WILLIAM H. WELLS - pl. vs THOMAS WILSON - def.
                        Debt

P. 366   JAMES PATTON - pl. vs STEPHEN FRAZIER & JOHN
            S. RUSSWORM - def.
                        Debt

P. 368   JAMES PATTON - pl. vs JOHN P. IRION & ENNIS
            MURRAY - def.
                   Jan. 1831   Debt

P. 371   JAMES P. PETERS, Assignee & C - pl. vs JOHN P.
            IRION - def.
                        Debt

P. 373   BENJAMIN S. TAPPAN, PETER PERKINS, & EDMUND T.
            TAPPAN - pl. vs JAMES R. TISDALE - def.
                   Trespass & Damage
            Benjamin S. Tappan, Peter Perkins, & Edmund T.
            Tappan are merchants trading under the firm &
            style of Tappan, Perkins & Co.

P. 369   RICHARD H. EDMONDSON et al - pl. vs MARY A.
            McMURREY et al - def.
                   April 1857
            William McMurray died intestate in Davidson County,
            Tennessee. He left a widow, Polly McMurray,
            who is now Polly Farrow. William McMurray left
            the following children: Martha J., Mary A., &
            William McMurray. Martha J. married Richard
            H. Edmondson. She lives in Davidson County.
            She is a minor & her guardian is John M.
            Winstead. Mary A. McMurray & William McMurray
            are minors and their guardian is John M. Winstead.
            Polly Farrow has received her share of the estate.
            The children want a division of the negroes.

P. 376   PETER N. SMITH - pl. vs ABRAM M. WHITE - def.
            Jan. 1831   Debt

P. 378   EDWARD G. CLOUSTON - pl. vs NATHANIEL H. THOMAS -
            def.   Debt

P. 380   STATE OF TENNESSEE - pl. vs THOMAS MONTGOMERY -
            def.
                   Selling merchandise without a license

P. 383   THE PRESIDENT DIRECTORS & CO. of the BANK OF the
            STATE OF TENNESSEE - pl. vs JOHN C. SIMMONS,
            THOMAS SIMMONS, & JOHN P. IRION - def.
                   July 1830   Debt

P. 386   WILLIAM WEATHERLY - pl. vs EPAPHRODITUS W.
            BURGE - def.
            Weatherly rented a farm to David Barnwell, Sr.,
            & he made a crop of cotton on it & gathered &
            hauled it off to a gin where he sold it to Burge.
            Weatherly had a lien on the cotton.

P. 388 ROBERT SAYERS - pl. vs ROBERT RIDLEY - def.
July 1830   Debt

P. 390 SAMUEL PRATT - pl. vs JAMES R. TISDALE - def.
Debt

P. 393 ALFRED GEE, use of Joseph Wallace & HARTWELL H.
HOBBS - pl. vs HOLLAND L. WHITE, LEMUEL B.
McCONNICO & CAREY WHITE - def.
Debt
Joseph Wallace & Hartwell H. Hobbs are merchants
under the name of Wallace & Hobbs.

P. 396 JOHN W. ALLEN - pl. vs THOMAS B. GARRETT - def.
Oct. 1830   Trespass

P. 399 EPHRAIM BROWN - pl. vs WILLIAM M. WRIGHT - def.
Debt

P. 401 JAMES CAROTHERS - pl. vs JOHN NICHOLS - def.
Debt

P. 403 WILLIAM WALLACE & JOSEPH WALLACE - pl. vs SAMUEL
ATKINSON - def.
Oct. 1830   Debt
William Wallace & Joseph Wallace were merchants.

P. 406 HENRY WYNNE - pl. vs THOMAS MANEY - def.
Trespass

P. 408 DAVID DALTON, Assignee & C - pl. vs JOSHUA W.
McCOWN & JOHN NICHOLS - def.
Debt

P. 412 ELIZABETH FERGUSON, use of Ebbin B. Staggs - pl.
vs THOMAS WELLS - def.
Oct. 1830   Debt

P. 414 JAMES SWANSON, SR. - pl. vs ELIZABETH BROCK - def.
Elizabeth Brock is harboring a negro slave named
Nat.

P. 416 JAMES E. GALLOWAY - pl. vs NICHOLAS SCALES - def.
Debt

P. 419 JOHN HOUSE - pl. vs WILLIAM H. WELLS - def.
Oct. 1830   Trespass

P. 422 WILLIAM McKAY - pl. vs ANDREW S. HUDSON, JOHN
B. ANDERSON, & WILLIAM T. NORTH - def.
Debt

P. 424 ANDREW GAFF - pl. vs THOMAS MONTGOMERY, JOHN
MONTGOMERY, & HENRY VAN PELT - def.
Debt

P. 426 NICHOLAS WILBURN - pl. vs JAMES W. CURRY,
JULIUS HAM, & JAMES RICE - def.
Oct. 1830   Debt

P. 430 JAMES HUGHES & ROSANNA, his wife; NEWTON HOLLAND;
BYRD HOLLAND; JOHN M. HOLLAND; JANE HOLLAND; &
MARGARET HOLLAND
April 1831   Exparte - Petition for Partition
The Petitioners are the heirs of Kemp Holland & of
Jane Holland, his widow. Margaret Holland,
Newton Holland, & Bird Holland are minors & sue
by their guardian, John M. Holland. George B.
Holland's guardian is James Wilkins. Kemp Holland
left a tract of land (133 acres). It is that
part of the estate which was mentioned in the
division between the heirs of Holland & his first
wife & the above mentioned petitioners, who are
the children of Holland & his last wife. Jane
Holland's part is for her lifetime only.

P. 435 NICHOLAS PERKINS, guardian of Andrew W. Hunt
April 1831   Exparte - Petition for Sale
of Negro Slave, Anthony
Anthony is between the age of 20 & 30 yrs. & is
thought to be incorrigible. Perkins wants to
sell him.

P. 436 WILLIAM NICHOL - pl. vs ROBERT B. CROCKETT - def.
April 1831   Debt

P. 438 MATTHEW D. COOPER, MADISON CAROTHERS, & WILLIAM
McNEIL - pl. vs JOHN NICHOLS - def.
Trespass
Matthew D. Cooper, Madison Carothers, & William
McNeil are merchants & co-partners in trade
trading under the name & style of Cooper,
Carothers & Co.

P. 442 DANIEL DWYER - pl. vs JOHN P. IRION - def.
April 1831   Debt

P. 445 CAREY M. RATCLIFF - pl. vs STEPHEN G. EUBANKS -
def.   Debt

P. 448 WILLIAM NICHOLS - pl. vs THOMAS SIMMANS &
ALEXANDER Y. SIMMANS - def.
Trespass

P. 451 JOSEPH BURNETT - pl. vs ALEXANDER CLARK, SR. -
def.
April 1831   Debt

P. 454 EDWARD G. CLOUSTON - pl. vs JAMES SWANSON,
guardian of Louisa A. Word - def.
Debt

P. 456 HUGH McCABE - pl. vs MARK W. SMITH & WILLIAM
SMITH - def.
Debt

P. 459 STATE OF TENNESSEE - pl. vs WILLIAM SAWYER - def.
          April 1831
          William Sawyer maliciously & willfully threw
          down the fence of Levin Cator.
P. 461 JOHN L. WHEATON - pl. vs FERDINAND STITH - def.
               Covenant Broken

P. 464 SEYMOUR R. BONNER - pl. vs WILLIAM B. SWEENEY -
          def.   April 1831   Trespass

P. 467 NICHOLAS PERKINS, Assignee & C - pl. vs NEAL
          HAPKINS - def.
                         Debt

P. 470 THOMAS SIMMONS, Assignee & C - pl. vs JOHN B.
          ANDERSON - def.
                         Debt

P. 473 JAMES C. HILL - pl. vs WILLIAM MEBANE - def.
               July 1830   Debt

P. 475 JAMES C. HILL - pl. vs THOMAS SIMMONS - def.
               Debt

P. 477 ERASTUS T. COLLINS, use of Isaac Secrest -
          pl. vs JOHN NICHOLS - def.
               Debt

P. 479 THE PRESIDENT DIRECTORS & CO. of the BANK
          of the UNITED STATES - pl. vs JOHN C.
          SIMMONS, THOMAS SIMMONS, & JOHN P. IRICN - def.
               July 1830   Debt

P. 483 ROBERT P. CURRIN & CHARLES G. OLMSTED - pl.
          vs JOHN NICHOLS - def.
               Debt

P. 486 ROBERT P. CURRIN & CHARLES G. OLMSTED - pl.
          vs JOHN NICHOLS - def.
               July 1830   Trespass
          Currin & Olmstead are merchants.

P. 488 ANDREW CAMPBELL & WILLIAM P. CAMPBELL - pl.
          vs JOHN NICHOLS - def.
               Debt

P. 491 NANCY HILL - pl. vs BAILEY HARDEMAN, NICHOLAS
          SCALE & JOHN PAGE - def.
               July 1830   Debt

P. 494 MATTHEW D. COOPER, MADISON CARUTHERS, &
          WILLIAM McNEIL - pl. vs THOMAS MONTGOMERY,
          NATHANIEL H. THOMAS, & JOHN T. WHEATON - def.
               Debt
          Cooper, Caruthers, & McNeil are merchants
          & partners trading under the firm & style of
          Cooper, Caruthers, & Co.

P. 499 HENRY R. W. HILL, Endorsee of McAlister
Hill & Co. - pl. vs WILLIAM McCANNON &
Admr. of George Slicker, deceased - def.
July 1830   Debt

P. 505 DRURY SCRUGGS, use of John Graham - pl. vs JOSHUA
REAMS - def.
Debt
John Graham is Admr. of the estate of Keziah
Scruggs, deceased.

P. 507 JOSEPH CROCKETT - pl. vs WILLIAM E. ANDERSON - def.
July 1830   Debt

P. 510 DANIEL CRENSHAW - pl. vs WILLIAM ANTHONY - def.
Debt

P. 511 J. M. WINSTEAD - pl. vs JOSHUA W. McCOWN & JOHN
NICHOLS - def.
Debt

P. 515 STEPHEN NOLEN - pl. vs ALEXANDER ANDERSON, WILLIAM
C. ANDERSON, & WILLIAM E. ANDERSON - def.
Oct. 1830   Debt

P. 517 ELIJAH WILLIAMS - pl. vs THOMAS SIMMONS - def.
Debt

P. 520 ROBERT G. BAUGH - pl. vs JOSHUA FARRINGTON,
JACOB C. SMITH & JOHN C. CRITZ - def.
Debt

P. 522 STEPHEN TURNER, Assignee & C - pl. vs GEORGE
REDMOND & JOHN REDMOND - def.
Jan. 1831   Debt

P. 524 WILLIAM D. STEPHENS, by his next friend, Joel G.
Childress - pl. vs ELISHA DAVIS - def.
Elisha Davis became guardian of William B. Stephens
in 1817 - wants him removed.

P. 527 STEPHEN WEST & ELIZABETH, his wife; WILLIAM B.
SHEPPARD & MARGERY, his wife; CHARLES BOSLEY &
ELIZA, his wife; STEPHEN WEST, Exr. of Thomas
M. Childress & ELIZABETH WEST, by her guardian,
Stephen West
July 1831   Exparte - Petition for Sale
of Negroes & Distribution
Henry Childress died (no date). He left a
widow, Betsey West. She has since married Stephen
West. Henry Childress left the following
children: Margary (she married William B.
Sheppard), Eliza A. (she married Charles Bosley),
Thomas M. (he is now dead & without issue), &
Sarah C. (she is now dead & without issue).
Henry Childress left the following negroes: Perry &
Harriett. They are to go to Sarah C. Childress,
deceased.

84

P. 531 NOAH SCALES, Admr. of Fanny Scales
        July 1831   Exparte - Petition for
                                Sale of Negroes
        Noah Scales was appointed Admr. of Fanny Scales,
        deceased, in Oct. 1826. Fanny Scales left a
        negro woman, Judah, 25 yrs. old & her 2 small
        children. They were to be divided between
        Mary Downy, Sarah Scales, Jane Scales & the
        children of _______ Johnson.

P. 532 AARON A. WILSON, Admr. of Thomas Wilson
            July 1831   Exparte - Petition for Sale
        Thomas Wilson died intestate in   of Negroes
        1831. Margaret Wilson has since died. They
        left the negroes Nat & Rose to be divided. The
        heirs are: Aaron Wilson, Samuel Wilson,
        Thomas & Matilda Wilson, Robert Montgomery &
        Elizabeth, his wife; Jeremiah Morgan in right
        of John Tony & Elvy, his wife; & of Littlebury
        Tony in right of his wife, Mary.

P. 534 STATE OF TENNESSEE - pl. vs ELIJAH BROWN - def.
            Jan. 1831   Debt

RECORD BOOK

LAWSUITS

No. 6

1831 - 1836

This book was in the basement storage room of the
Court House. The last part of the book does not have
numbered pages and none of them are indexed.

P. 7   KEZIAH WOODDRIDGE & JOHN K. WOODDRIDGE - pl. -
        vs WILLIAM F. WOOLDRIDGE, ALFRED N. WOOLDRIDGE,
        SUSAN H. WOOLDRIDGE, JOSIAH WOOLDRIDGE,
        MANERVA E. WOOLDRIDGE, HENRY G. WOOLDRIDGE, by
        their guardian, Gilbert Marshall
                Oct. 1831
        The petition was filed in 1831. Josiah Wooldridge
        died Dec. 1824. He left the following heirs:
                1.   Keziah (his widow)
                2.   John K. Wooldridge
                3.   Narcissa C. (intermarried with William
                     I. Berryman)
                4.   William F. Wooldridge (minor)
                5.   Alfred N. Wooldridge (minor)
                6.   Susan H. Wooldridge (minor)
                7.   Josiah Wooldridge (minor)
                8.   Manerva E. Wooldridge (minor)
                9.   Henry G. Wooldridge (minor)
        Keziah, the widow, was Admrx. The Petitioners
        want a division made.

P. 9   DANIEL CRENSHAW & RUTH, his wife - pl. vs
        WILLIAM R. NUNN - def.
                Jan. 1832   Entered Petition 11 July 1831
        William R. Nunn was made guardian to Ruth Crenshaw
        then Ruth Anderson in 1819. Abraham Anderson,
        deceased, was the father of Ruth. In 1819 Nunn
        received $178 from Stephen Cantrell, pension
        agent for West Tennessee. In 1820, he received
        $24 from Cantrel. Ruth married Daniel
        Crenshaw June 20, 1829. She wants the money
        Cantrell paid that Nunn collected.

P. 10   THOMAS MERRITT & HENRY J. MERRITT & REBECCA,
        his wife - Admr. & Admrx. of Nathaniel Newson,
        deceased
                Jan. 1832   Petition for Sale of Negro
        Rebecca Merritt was formerly Rebecca Newson.
        The slave is now hired out to Allen Mabane.

86

P. 12   ELIZABETH HUNTER, MERRITT R. BROWN & MARY A., his
wife, CATHERINE A. HUNTER, JOSEPH R. HUNTER,
MARTHA S. HUNTER, JAMES A. HUNTER, NARCISSA R.
HUNTER & JUAN E. C. HUNTER
        Jan. 1832   Petition for Distribution
Catherine A., Joseph R., Martha S., James A.,
Narcissa R., & Juan E. C. Hunter are minors and
their guardian is Elizabeth Hunter. Elizabeth
is the widow of Elisha Hunter, who died intestate.
He owned 13 slaves which are to be distributed.
Elisha is the ancestor of 7 children (the petitioners
Henry Hunter is the Admr. 8 parts division.

_______   PATRICK McCUTCHEN & MARY, his wife - pl. vs
SPENCER BUFORD - def.
        April 1831   Entered Petition 22 June
                              1829
Mary is one of the children of Alexander Reid,
deceased. Alexander Reid died in 1816
intestate. He left a large estate. His
children are:
        1. Mary (She married Patrick McCutchen.
            She was 7 yrs. old when her father
            died.)
        2. Sarah (She married Leonard Dunnevant.)
        3. Priscilla (She married William
            Edmondson.)
        4. Catherine (She married German Lester,
            who died intestate & without issue.)
Spencer Buford was made Admr. in 1816. He was
also the guardian. Alexander Reid's estate
amounted to about $10,000. The Petition is for
a division to be made.

P. 14   GARNER McCONNICO, Admr. of Henry Walker
        Jan. 1832   .   Petition for Sale of
                              Negro Slave
Henry Walker, deceased, died in 1825.   John
Buchanan was appointed Exr. & he refused
execution. Henry Walker, deceased, left a
widow & children. Thomas H. Fletcher of
Nashville owes the estate $300 & he is insolvent.

P. 16   JOHN T. PURYEAR & JORDAN R. H. PURYEAR, by his
guardian, John Watson
        Oct. 1831   Petition for Distribution
John Tobe Puryear & Jordan R. H. Puryear, by his
guardian, John Watson. Hezekiah Puryear died
in 1816 intestate leaving Mordecia C. H.
Puryear & your Petitioners your only children.

P. 18   ELIZABETH BUGG, THOMAS A. CROW & LOUISA, his
wife - pl. vs MAHOLA BUGG, WILLIAM BUGG,
CATHARINE BUGG, MARY BUGG, ELIZABETH BUGG, &
MARK L. ANDREWS
        Oct. 1831   Petition for Partition &
                              Distribution
(CONT'D)

P. 18 Allen Bugg, deceased (CONT'D)
Allen Bugg, deceased, died in 1827. He left a
will. Mark L. Andrews was appointed Exr. Allen
Bugg left a widow, Elizabeth. He also left 5
children, who are all minors. The children are:
Mahola, William, Catharine, Mary, & Elizabeth Bugg.

P. 24 WILLIAM FARLGHAM - pl. vs LEWIS C. ALLEN - def.
July 1831   Debt

P. 25 STEPHEN NOLEN - pl. vs WILLIAM P. HAYS, NATHANIEL
H. THOMAS & JOHN PAGE - def.
July 1831   Debt

P. 30 THOMAS RYAN - pl. vs JAMES CRAIG - def.
July 1831   Debt

P. 32 FINIS W. SHANNON, use of Joshua Darden - pl. vs
JOSEPH BURNETT - def.
July 1831   Debt

P. 34 JOHN S. WOOD - pl. vs GEORGE B. MARK - def.
July 1831
George B. Mark, a tailor, would not make clothes
that John S. Wood paid for.

P. 38 JOHN W. WALKER - pl. vs THOMAS SIMMONS - def.
July 1831   Debt

P. 40 JOHN W. WALKER - pl. vs CAREY M. RATCLIFF &
JOHN B. ANDERSON - def.
July 1831   Debt

P. 43 LEMUEL SMITH, THOMAS H. PERKINS, JR., WILLIAM O.
PERKINS - pl. vs WILLIAM MEBANE & JOHN B. SCRUGGS -
def.   July 1831   Debt
Lemuel Smith, Thomas H. Perkins, Jr., William O.
Perkins are merchants & trading under the firm &
style of Smith, Perkins & Co.

P. 46 SMITH H. SAMPLE - pl. vs JOEL G. CHILDRESS - def.
July 1831   Covenant

P. 49 JOSEPH COWEN - pl. vs ORANGE HAM, LEMUEL SMITH &
WILLIAM B. McCLELLAN - def.
July 1831   Debt
Orange Ham's house has burnt & the neighbors
gave him household goods.

P. 52 HENRY COOK - pl. vs THOMAS H. PERKINS - def.
Case   Oct. 1831

P. 55 JOSEPH McEWEN - pl. vs THOMAS A. PANKEY - def.
Oct. 1831   Case

P. 61 THOMAS H. PERKINS - pl. vs HENRY COOK - def.
Debt

P. 63 JOHN B. BEECH - pl. vs THOMAS H. PERKINS - def.
Debt

88

P. 66   JOHN NICHOLS, use of Martha Wilson - pl. vs
         ELISHA DAVIS - def.
                   Oct. 1831   Debt

P. 67   Same as Above

P. 69   JOHN B. SCRUGGS - pl. vs JOHN GRAHAM, Admr. of
         Keziah Scruggs, deceased - def.
                   Oct. 1831   Debt

P. 72   MICHAEL KINNARD - pl. vs WILLIAM J. SHUMATE -
         def.   Oct. 1831   Debt

P. 74   JOSEPH WALLACE & HARTWELL H. HOBBS - pl. vs
         JOHN F. SMITH & ROBERT PEEBLES - def.
                   Oct. 1831   Debt
         Joseph Wallace & Hartwell H. Hobbs are
         merchants & partners trading under the firm of
         Wallace & Hobbs.

P. 78   WILLIAM NICHOL - pl. vs TILMAN F. ATKINSON - def.
                   Oct. 1831   Debt

P. 81   WILLIAM McGEE - pl. vs BENJAMIN KIDD - def.
                   Oct. 1831   Case
         Over water rights.

P. 86   LEMUEL B. McCONNICO, County Trustee of Williamson
         County - pl. vs JOHN FARRINGTON, late County
         Trustee of Williamson County - def.

P. 87   SAMUEL CROCKETT, Admr. of James C. Hill,
         deceased - pl. vs JOSHUA FARRINGTON, JACOB
         FARRINGTON, & WILLIAM B. McCLELLAN - def.
                   Jan. 1832   Debt

P. 90   HENRY WYNN & ANDREW MONTGOMERY - pl. vs ROBERT
         WHITE - def.
                   Case

P. 93   SAMUEL LEA - pl. vs JAMES CAPERTON - def.
                   Jan. 1832   Debt

P. 95   THOMAS H. BRADLEY - pl. vs WILLIAM G. CHILDRESS -
         def.   Jan. 1832
         Thomas Bradley, father of Thomas H., being
         seized of a certain tract of land. The tract of
         land contains 96 acres on the waters of the
         Little Harpeth River. Thomas was to convey
         the tract of land to his son for love &
         affection by deed of gift. Thomas H. Bradley
         promised to convey said tract of land by deed
         to William S. Childress.

P. 99   JOHN BARNES & JOSEPH H. MANGHAM - pl. vs
         THOMAS L. DOUGLASS - def.
                   Jan. 1832   Case
         Debt for work & labor.

P. 102 KEENEN & McCLUNG - pl. vs WILLIAM I. BERRYMAN -
        def.   Jan. 1832
        William I. Berryman held a note on Keziah
        Wooldridge. By deed of gift from John Nichols to
        Keziah Wooldridge & at her death to her children -
        2 negroes. William I. Berryman married the
        daughter of Keziah Wooldridge & the husband of
        said Wooldridge had some 10 years or more past
        sold the negro to "Wilson". The court refused to
        discharge the defendant.

P. 105 WILLIAM M. WRIGHT, Assignee of Isaac Stow - pl. vs
        JOSHUA McCOWN - def.
             Jan. 1832   Debt

P. 108 ASA JOHNSON - pl. vs JASON C. WILSON - def.
             Oct. 1831   Debt

P. 110 NICHOL HILL & CO. - pl. vs THOMAS HARDIN PERKINS,
        DANIEL P. PERKINS, & THOMAS H. PERKINS - def.
             Oct. 1832   Debt

P. 114 HENRY CHRISTMAS - pl. vs THOMAS H. PERKINS, JR. -
        def.
             Jan. 1832   Case
        Promised to pay a note.

P. 116 SAMUEL WHITE & NANCY, his wife; JAMES MEBANE, JR.;
        JAMES WOODS; MARGARET WOODS; MARY WOODS;
        ALEXANDER WOODS; ALEXANDER MEBANE; WILLIAM
        MEBANE; ROBERT MEBANE; NATHANIEL H. MEBANE; JANE
        ELLIOTT; MARY MEBANE; ALLEN MEBANE; JAMES TATE &
        MARGARET, his wife; & GEORGE ALLEN MEBANE
             April 1832   (To sell slaves & property)
        Margaret Woods, Mary Woods, & Alexander Woods
        petition by their guardian, James Mebane.
        George Allen Mebane, deviser of George Mebane,
        deceased, is an infant, who petitions by his next
        friend, Alexander Mebane. Samuel White & Nancy,
        his wife; James Mebane, Jr.; James Woods;
        Margaret Woods; Mary Woods; & Alexander Woods,
        which the last 3 petition by their guardian, James
        Mebane, are all of the state of North Carolina.
        James Mebane died in 1807 in North Carolina leaving
        a will: Give to my loving wife, Peggy, the
        plantation I now live on & the plantation known
        by the name of The Rosses place & certain slaves,
        etc. At my wife's death it is to be divided among
        all my children. Peggy Mebane died intestate in
        1830 in Williamson County, Tennessee. (Wants to
        sell slaves). Samuel White & Nancy are to receive
        1 share. James, Margaret, Mary, & Alexander
        Woods (children of Elizabeth Wood, deceased,
        daughter of James Mebane) are to receive one share.
        James Tate & Margaret, his wife, are to receive
        one share. George Allen Mebane being devisee of
        all of George Mebane's receives one share.
        (George was the son of James Mebane.)
                                      (CONT'D)

90

P. 116 Woods & Mebane (CONT'D)
        (According to Will: I give & bequeath to George
        Allen Mebane, all the money & property arising
        from my deceased father in North Carolina, after
        the decease of my mother.)

P. 119 WILLIAMSON JORDAN & ANN B., his wife & THOMAS
        S. SAPPINGTON, by his guardian, Nicholas T.
        Perkins & WILLIAM EDMISTON
                April 1832   Petition for Sale of Negroes
        Joseph H. Stockett died leaving a will. He left
        the major part of his estate to Nicholas T.
        Perkins, William Edmiston, & Susan Stockett, in
        trust for Susan Sappington, Rebecca Sappington,
        & Ann B. Sappington, & Thomas S. Sappington,
        to be given to them when they arrived of age.
        Susan Sappington has married James Shelburn &
        received her part. Rebecca Sappington has
        married Theopilus Gentry & received her part.
        Ann B. Sappington has married Williamson
        Jordan & she is to receive her part. Thomas
        Sappington is to receive his part.

P. 121 MARY TYRRILL; JOHN D. BENNETT & ELIZABETH,
        his wife; JOHN JOHNSON & MARY, his wife;
        JOEL TYRRILL; WILLIAM TYRRILL; TIMOTHY
        TYRRILL; HEZEKIAH, NANCY, MARTHA, & JAMES
        TYRRILL, infants by their guardian, John D.
        Bennett
                April 1832   Petition for Sale of Slaves
        James Tyrrill died intestate. He left a widow,
        Mary Tyrrill. He left the following
        children: Elizabeth Bennett, Mary Johnson,
        Joel, William, Timothy, Hezekiah, Nancy,
        Martha & James Tyrrill. John D. Bennett &
        Joel Tyrrill are the Admrs.

P. 124 CAREY A. HARRIS & MARTHA F., his wife - pl.
        vs ABRAM P. MAURY, JAMES P. MAURY, WILLIAM
        H. MAURY, & ZEBULON M. MAURY - def.
                April 1832   Petition for Partition
        Carey A. Harris & Martha F., his wife, are
        entitled to 1/6 part of a tract of land
        lying near Franklin, (about 600 acres), as one
        of the heirs of Abram Maury. The other heirs
        of Abram Maury are: Abram P., James P.,
        William H. (by their guardian, James P.), &
        Zebulon M. P. Maury (he is a minor & has no
        guardian). (Martha is the widow & her dower
        makes 6 parts).

P. 131 WILLIAM E. OWEN & FRANKLIN L. OWEN - pl. vs
        JOHN SWEENEY - def.
                April 1832   Debt
        William E. Owen & Franklin L. Owen were
        formerly merchants & partners in trade under
        the name of W. E. & F. L. Owen.

P. 133 JAMES BUFORD, Exr. of Francis Gidden, Sr.,
        deceased - pl. vs JOHN SWEENEY & MANSFIELD
        HOUSE - def.
                    April 1832   Debt

P. 136 WILLIAM B. McCLELLAN & CAREY A. HARRIS - pl. vs
        SMITH H. SAMPLE - def.
                    April 1832   Debt
        William B. McClellan & Carey A. Harris are merchants
        under the name of McClellan & Harris.

P. 138 ELISHA DAVIS, use of Thomas Holt - pl. vs JAMES
        C. IRVIN & JOHN PAGE - def.
                    April 1832   Debt

P. 141 WILLIAM PEEBLES - pl. vs JOHN SWEENEY - def.
                    April 1832   Case
        Bought sorrell stallion 16 years old for $700
        & found he was unsound & affected with diseases.

P. 144 THOMAS H. PERKINS, JR. - pl. vs RICHARD W.
        HYDE - def.   April 1832   Trespass

P. 146 JEREMIAH FIELD - pl. vs NATHANIEL H. THOMAS - def.
                    April 1832   Case
        Promised to pay by laying bricks.

P. 149 JEREMIAH FIELD - pl. vs WILLIAM P. HAYES - def.
                    April 1832   Case

P. 153 WILLIAM PARKER - pl. vs WILLIAM B. DULLEFIN &
        SEARCY D. SHARP - def.
                    April 1832   Debt

P. 155 JACOB EVERLY & LOUISA, his wife - pl. vs AMERICA
        WORD - def.
                    April 1832   Petition for Distribution
        Louisa Everly formerly Louisa Word & daughter of
        Thomas H. Word, is by deed of gift from said
        Thomas, entitled to 3 negroes & some money.
        Louisa & America are both daughters of Thomas H.
        Word. James Swanson, Sr. is the guardian of America.

P. 156 PEGGY S. MALLORY - pl. vs BENJAMIN MALLORY &
        OTHERS - def.
                    April 1832   Petition for Dower
        Peggy S. Mallory is the widow of Thomas G. Mallory,
        who died intestate Feb. 1832. He left no children.
        His heirs at law are:
                1. Benjamin Mallory of Robertson County
                    (Brother of Thomas G. Mallory.)
                2. Westley Mallory of Louisiana (Brother
                    of Thomas G. Mallory.)
                3. James Mallory of Montgomery County
                    (Brother of Thomas G. Mallory.)
                                        (CONT'D)

P. 156 Thomas G. Mallory, deceased (CONT'D)
      4. Rufus James Mallory of Montgomery County
        (He is the son of William Mallory,
        deceased. William Mallory was a brother
        to Thomas G. Mallory.)
Thomas G. Mallory had land in Williamson County.
(130 acres). His widow, Peggy S. Mallory, wants
1/3 part. She is entitled to 1/2 of the slave
estate. Frances Mallory, the mother of Thomas
G. Mallory, is entitled with others to the
other part.

P. 161 ZACHEUS H. GERMAN, guardian of James H. McEwen
      Petition for Sale of Negro Slave
James H. McEwen is an idiot or a lunatic.

P. 162 JAMES SWANSON, SR., Admr. of John House, deceased
      April 1832   Petition for Sale of Negroes
P. 164 GILBERT MARSHALL, Admr. of David H. Guthrie,
deceased
      April 1832   Petition for Sale of
                   Negroes
      P. 137 Cemetery Records - Williamson County
      David H. Guthrie
      B. Oct. 19, 1796
      D. July 23, 1832
P. 166 JEFFERSON MARTIN, Admr. of John G. Williamson,
deceased
      April 1832   Petition for Sale of
                   Negroes

P. 167 THOMAS HARDEMAN, Admr. & MARY O. SMITH, Admrx.
of Nicholas P. Smith, deceased
      April 1832   Petition for Sale of
                   Negroes

P. 169 RICHARD STEELE, JR., Admr. of Richard Graham,
deceased
      July 1833   Petition for Sale of Negroes

P. 171 JAMES H. F. ATKINS & LUCY, his wife - pl. vs
WILLIAM W. DABNEY, MARGARETT L. DABNEY, MARY
E. DABNEY, JOHN O. DABNEY, & NANCY P. DABNEY,
by their guardian, James Swanson, Sr.
      Jan. 1833   Petition for Distribution
Charles A. Dabney died 1830 intestate leaving
his widow, Lucy. Lucy has since intermarried
with James H. F. Atkins. Charles A. Dabney's
only heirs are: Lucy, his widow; William W.;
Margaret L; Mary E.; John O.; & Nancy P.
Dabney.

P. 173 SAMUEL FARNSWORTH - pl. vs JAMES COWSERT, JOHN
COWSERT, JAMES PATTON & POLLY, his wife - def.
Jan. 1833
Andrew Cowsert died April 1824. He left a will.
The land was divided into 3 parts. They are:
1. Jane (his wife) - Middle lot
2. James (son) - North lot
3. John (son) - South lot
At the death of his wife, Jane, it is to be
divided between the two sons, James & John.
Andrew Cowsert had 2 daughters. They were:
1. Polly (wife of James Patton)
2. Agatha Jane
Andrew Cowsert's wife, Jane, & his son, James, were
the Exrs. John Cowsert lives in Missouri. Polly
married James Patton in Missouri. Agatha Jane
married Samuel Farnsworth in 1826 & she is now
dead. The widow, Jane Cowsert died in 1831
leaving the said 4 children.

P. 176 FRANCES LANE - pl. vs ROBERT LANE, THOMAS LANE,
WILLIAM K. LANE, JOHN LANE, REUBEN LANE,
BENJAMIN LANE, & NANCY HOGAN - def.
July 1833   Petition for Dower
William Lane died Dec. 1832 intestate. He left a
widow, Frances Lane. Nancy Hogan was formerly
Nancy Lane. She married Josiah Hogan. Thomas
Lane was named Admr. William Lane, deceased, left
some land on the Big Harpeth River. (150 acres).

P. 180 WILLIAM DONNELSON, Admr. of Samuel Donnelson,
deceased
April 1834   Petition for Sale of Negro

P. 181 DONALD McGILVIRAY & ALEXANDER FORBES & WIFE - pl.
vs EDWARD G. CLOUSTON & JAMES PARK- def.
Oct. 1833   Petition
Donald McGilviray & Alexander Forbes & Catharine,
his wife, are all of the County of Columbia, Ohio.
William McGilviray, deceased, was of Williamson
County. He died Jan. 1831. He left a will.
The estate is to be divided between Donald
McGilviray & Catherine Forbes. James Parks &
Edward G. Clouston were named Exrs. William
McGilviray, deceased, left land in Williamson &
Maury Counties.

P. 195 WILLIAM F. WOLDRIDGE, ALFRED N. WOLDRIDGE, JAMES
H. NEELY & SUSAN, his wife - pl. vs JOSIAH
WOOLDRIDGE, MINERVA E. WOLDRIDGE, HENRY G.
WOLDRIDGE, infants by their guardian, Gilbert
Marshall
Jan. 1834   Petition for Sale of Slaves
The Petitioners want 1/6 part of the slaves.

94

P. 197 JOSEPH YATES & POLLY, his wife; DAWSON CLAXTON
& MICKEY, his wife; JACKSON MAYS, by his
guardian, Presley Dotson; NANCY JANE MAYS, by
her guardian, Joseph Yates
            Jan. 1834   Petition to Sale Negroes
Smith Mays died Feb. 1831 leaving his widow,
Polly. Micky Jackson & Nancy Jane are his
children. Obadiah Fitzgerald is the Adnr. The
Petitioners want 1/4 part.

P. 199 THOMAS MERRITT; HENRY J. MERRITT & REBECCA, his
wife; REBECCA NEWSOM & BENJAMIN S. NEWSOM, by
their guardian, Henry J. Merritt.
            Jan. 1834   Petition for Sale of Slaves
Thomas Merritt is the Adnr. of Nathaniel Newsom,
deceased. Rebecca Merritt, formerly Rebecca
Newsom, is the Adnrx. Rebecca Newsom &
Benjamin S. Newsom are infants. Their guardian
is Henry J. Merritt. Nathaniel Newsom died in
1830 intestate.

P. 201 WILLIAM O. PERKINS, JR. & POLLY M., his wife -
pl. vs ATKINS J. McLEMORE, PEGGY T. McLEMORE,
(now Peggy T. Mallory) & CHARLES A. DABNEY,
(now deceased) - def.
            April 1834   Petition to Sale Slaves
Robert McLemore died & left a will. He left
the following heirs: Peggy T., Polly M. (your
Petitioner), John D. McLemore, Robert W.
McLemore, & Peggy McLemore. Peggy, Robert W.,
& John D. McLemore are infants.

P. 204 ELIZA McFADDEN; JOHN ERWIN & ELIZABETH, his
wife; JAMES McCULLOCK & CATHERINE, his wife;
ROBERT W. McFADDEN; & MARY McFADDEN, by her
guardian, Robert W. McFadden
            April 1834   Petition for Dower
Candor McFadden died March 21, 1831. He
left the following: Jane McFadden (his widow),
Elizabeth, Eliza, Catharine, Robert W., & Mary
(his children). He left 297 acres of land on
Arrington Creek.

P. 209 WILLIAM NASH; JOHN NASH, by his guardian,
Thomas B. Garrett; & CHARLES W. CROUCH &
LUCRETIA, his wife
            Jan. 1834   Petition for Distribution
Dempsey Nash died intestate the first of Jan.
1833. He left the following children & heirs:
William, John, & Lucretia. Lucretia married
Charles W. Crouch.

P. 211 ALLEN N. McCORD; HARVEY B. McCORD; NEWTON McCORD,
by his guardian, Cowden McCord; & MARTHA JANE
McCORD & WILLIAM McCORD, by their guardian,
Mary McCord
Jan. 1834   Petition for Sale of Slaves
David McCord died in 1819 & he left a will. He
gave to Elizabeth McCord, the mother of the
Petitioners, a negro & at her death the negro is
to go to the Petitioners. Elizabeth died this
year intestate. She left the following heirs:
Cowden, Allen N., Harvey B., & Newton. Martha
J. & William are the children of Abner McCord,
deceased. Abner McCord, deceased, was a child
of David McCord & Jane McCord, who is now deceased.

P. 213 DAVID HILL, ROBERT HILL, MILUS W. HILL, &
THOMAS M. HILL
Jan. 1834
James S. Hill died in Iredell County, North Carolina.
He left a will. He left a tract of land in
Williamson County. The land contains 274 acres
& it is located on the Big Harpeth River. It is
to be divided as follows:
1/3 goes to David
1/3 goes to Robert
1/3 goes to Milus W. & Thomas M.

P. 216 JOHN ASHLIN - pl. vs DICY ASHLIN & OTHERS - def.
Jan. 1834
William Ashlin died intestate in 1821. He left
the following children & heirs:
1. Dicey Ashlin (his widow)
2. Francis (she married David Moore)
3. Mary (she married Carey H. Moore)
4. John Ashlin
5. Robert W. Ashlin
6. Martha Ashlin
7. William Ashlin
8. Ann Ashlin
9. Virginia Ashlin
William Ashlin, deceased, left a tract of land
on the West Harpeth River. (320 acres). He
also left a tract of land containing 235 acres.

P. 219 JOSEPH C. McDOWEL, Admr. & C
Jan. 1834   Petition for Distribution
John Hay died in 1826. He left a will. Balaam
Hay was named Exr. & he has since died intestate.
John Hay's will was annexed. His estate was to
be divided into the following 4 parts:
1. Jeremiah Hay - 1 part
2. Joseph C. McDowell & Patsey, his wife - 1 part
3. Nathan Bullock & Sarah, his wife - 1 part
4. Children of John Hay, Jr., deceased - 1 part
(The children are: Polly, Nancy, Franklin,
Garner, & Calvin Hay)

P. 221 THOMAS LANE, Admr. of William Lane
            Jan. 1834   Petition for Sale of Negroes
     William Lane died in 1832 intestate. He left
     a widow, Francis Lane. His children & heirs are:
     Robert Lane, Thomas Lane, William Lane, John
     Lane, Reuben Lane, Benjamin Lane, Nancy Hogan.
     Nancy married Josiah Hogan.

P. 222 DANIEL H. HAMER, Admr. of Hannah S. Roberts
            Jan. 1834   Petition for Sale of Negroes
     Hannah S. Roberts died 27 March 1833 intestate.
     She is a sister to Charlotte Hamer & Nancy Beard
     & William L. Roberts. Charlotte married Daniel
     H. Hamer. Nancy married Charles Beard. Hannah
     S. Roberts left the following heirs: Charlotte
     Hamer, Nancy Beard, Milton J. Hamer, & William
     L. Roberts.

P. 224 & P. 241
     THOMAS H. WILKINSON & MELVILLE WILKINSON, by
     his guardian, Thomas P. Carsey - pl. vs WILLIAM
     WILKINSON; STEPHEN WILKINSON; JAMES WILKINSON;
     SARAH ANN WILKINSON; ELIZA WILSON & GEORGE
     WILSON & JOHNSON B. WILKINSON, their infant- def.
            Oct. 1833   Distribution of Estate
     William Wilkinson, deceased, died Oct. 12, 1830 .
     intestate. He left the following heirs:
            1.   James Wilkinson (now residing in the
                 Republic of Mexico)
            2.   William Wilkinson now residing in Obion
                 County, Tennessee
            3.   Stephen Wilkinson (belonging to the U. S.
                 Navy & in active service on the high seas)
            4.   Sarah Ann Wilkinson (she is a minor
                 residing in Lincoln County, Tennessee)
            5.   Ann Eliza Wilson (she was formerly Ann
                 Eliza Wilkerson. She married George
                 Wilson) (She is of Lincoln County, Tenn.)
            6.   Johnson Blakely Wilkinson (infant & of
                 Lincoln County, Tennessee)

P. 241 Same as above
     The Petitioners want a division of the land
     to be made. William Wilkinson, deceased, had
     a tract of land granted to James Fergus by
     North Carolina. The grant was dated 14 March
     1787 & the tract contains 4800 acres. It is
     located on the head waters of Hays Creek &
     Mill Creek.

P. 238 MERRITT R. BROWN, guardian & C
            Oct. 1833   Petition for Sale of Negroes
     Merritt R. Brown is the guardian of Benjamin
     Brown.   (CONT'D)

P. 238 Merritt R. Brown (CONT'D)
Merritt R. Brown wants to sell the slaves for
support of Benjamin Brown & his family, namely his
mother & two brothers & sister.

P. 244 DELIA S. HIGHTOWER, Admr. of John Hightower
           Oct. 1833   Exparte - Petition for Sale
                                      of Negroes

P. 246 JOHN D. McALISTER - pl. vs HUMPHREY MARSHALL &
FRANCES, his wife; WILLIAM McALISTER & CHARLES
McALISTER, by their guardian, Charles G. Olmstead -
def.
        Oct. 1833   Petition for Partition
Charles McAlister died in 1818. He was the father
of the following: John, Frances, Charles,
William, Josiah, & James McAlister. James
McAlister is an infant. Frances married Humphrey
Marshall of Kentucky. Josiah McAlister is now
dead & left no issue. Charles McAlister, deceased,
left a tract of land in Williamson County about
1 mile from Franklin. He left a will & it was
probated 7 Oct. 1818.

P. 248 JAMES H. HERRON - pl. vs WILLIAM CRAIG - def.
           Oct. 1834
During the July Session 1827, the Court appointed
William Craig guardian to Lannes (?) B. Horton,
John F. Horton, Frances A. Horton, Bingham
Bloomfield Horton, John Horton, & Elizabeth
Horton, all of which are minor orphans. James H.
Herron & James Wilkins were appointed surities.
James H. Herron became apprehensive & asked to be
removed as his surity.

P. 249 JAMES MOTHERAL; JOSEPH MOTHERAL; SAMUEL SHANNON;
JOHN McCUTCHAN & ANN, his wife; JOEL WALKER &
MARY, his wife; JOHN C. KIRKPATRICK & WILLIAM A.
KIRKPATRICK, by their guardian, Joseph Kirkpatrick
        Oct. 1833   Petition for Sale of Negroes
Jane Motheral died March 1832 intestate. She left
the following heirs:
        1. Samuel Shannon in right of his wife, Catherine
        2. John McCutchen in right of his wife, Ann.
        3. Joel Walker in right of his wife, Mary.
        4. Joseph Kirkpatrick (guardian) in right
            of John C. & William A. Kirkpatrick.
        5. James Motheral (son)
        6. Joseph Motheral (son)

P. 251 JOHN GLENN & ELIZABETH, his wife; JAMES ELLIOTT &
        MARY, his wife; THOMAS BOBBETT, by his guardian,
        Joseph Bradley; NANCY BOBBETT, EMILY BOBBETT, &
        REBECCA BOBBETT, by their guardian, Benjamin
        W. Bradley; JOHN BOBBITT & his next friend,
        James Elliott
            July 1833   Petition for Distribution
        Stephen Bobbett, deceased, died intestate. He
        left the following heirs & children:
            1. Elizabeth (his widow who married John
                Glenn)
            2. Thomas
            3. Nancy
            4. Emily
            5. Rebecca
            6. John
            7. Mary Elliott (formerly Mary Bobbett)
        James Elliott is Admr. of the estate.

P. 254 MEREDITH P. GENTRY, Admr. of Thomas P. Gentry,
        deceased
            July 1833   Petition to Sell Slaves

P. 255 MARGARET S. HOUSE - pl. vs ROBERT HOUSE &
        OTHERS - def.
            July 1834   Petition for Dower
        John House died in 1832 intestate. He left
        a widow, Margaret & 5 children. The children
        are: Robert, Lemuel, Elizabeth, John, &
        Martha. They are all infants. Margaret, the
        widow, is the guardian for John & Martha.
        James Swanson, Sr. is the Admr. John House,
        deceased, left a tract of land in Williamson
        County on the Big Harpeth River containing
        260 acres. Mansfield House is guardian of
        Robert, Lemuel, & Elizabeth House.

P. 260 HUMPHREY MARSHALL & WIFE - pl. vs JOHN D.
        McALISTER, CHARLES McALISTER, JAMES McALISTER,
        WILLIAM McALISTER - def.
            Oct. 1833
        John D., Charles, James, William McAlister are
        under their guardian, Charles G. Olmstead.
        Humphrey Marshall's wife is Frances. Charles
        McAlister died in 1818. He left the following
        heirs:
            1. Frances Marshall
            2. John McAlister
            3. Charles McAlister (Charles Olmstead guardi
            4. William McAlister(Charles Olmstead guardia
            5. Josiah McAlister (now dead leaving no issu
            6. James McAlister (an infant)(Charles Olmste
                                        guardian)
                            (CONT'D)

P. 260 Charles McAlister, deceased (CONT'D)
Charles McAlister, deceased, left a tract
of land containing about 100 acres. He
left a will dated in 1818.

P. 261 THOMAS H. PERKINS - pl. vs JOHN WILLIAMS &
JOSEPH W. BAUGH - def.
July 1833   Debt

P. 265 JOHN BRANCH, HENRY R. W. HILL, & LAWRENCE O'BRYAN,
Exr. of Joseph Branch, deceased, use of Daniel
S. Donnelson - pl. vs PHILIP MAURY - def.
March 1833   Debt

P. 266 JOSEPH W. BAUGH, JOHN WILLIAMS & DANIEL
McCAULEY - pl. vs THOMAS H. PERKINS - def.
March 1833   Trespass

P. 268 JOHN BRANCH, H. R. W. HILL, & LAWRENCE O'BRYAN,
Exr. of Joseph Branch, deceased - pl. vs
PHILIP MAURY - def.
Oct. 1833   Debt

P. 271 JOHN NICHOLS, use & C - pl. vs LEMUEL DONELSON -
def.   Oct. 1833   Trespass

P. 273 ATKINS J. McLEMORE - pl. vs JOEL G. CHILDRESS &
DANIEL P. PERKINS - def.
Oct. 1833   Debt

P. 276 ATKINS J. McLEMORE - pl. vs DANIEL P. PERKINS &
JOEL G. CHILDRESS - def.
July 1833   Debt

P. 277 BENJAMIN S. TAPPAN - pl. vs BENJAMIN F. CROCKETT -
def.   July 1833   Debt

P. 279 MARY DOHERTY - pl. vs JAMES B. PORTER & NELLY,
his wife - def.
July 1834   Petition for Partition
Major George Doherty died in 1791 (Oct. 10) in
Orange County, North Carolina. He left a will
which was probated in 1793. His heirs are:
Mary (wife), Polly W. Burk (daughter), Francis
Doherty (daughter), & Nelly Doherty (daughter).
His estate consisted of a tract of land in what
is now Williamson County on the officers &
soldiers south boundary line (4800 acres).
Frances married William Yarbrough of Orange County.
Nelly married James B. Porter of Williamson
County. Mary Doherty, widow, gave about 1/2 of
her land to her grandson & granddaughter.

100

P. 121 & P. 286
MARY TYRRILL; JOHN D. BENNETT & ELIZABETH, his
wife; JOHN JOHNSON & MARY, his wife; JOEL TYRRILL;
WILLIAM TYRRILL; TIMOTHY TYRILL; & HEZEKIAH, NANCY,
MARTHA, & JAMES TYRRILL, the last 4 infants under
21 yrs. of age, by their guardian, John D. Bennett.
        April 1832   Petition for Sale of Slaves
James Tyrrill died intestate leaving Mary Tyrrill,
his widow. He left the following children: .
Elizabeth Bennett, Mary Johnson, Joel, William,
Timothy, Hezekiah, Nancy, Martha, & James. John D.
Bennett & Joel Tyrrill are the Admrs.

P. 288 JOHN McTHOMPSON - pl. vs MARTHA A. R. THOMPSON .&
al. - def.
        April 1835
Jason Thompson, deceased, died in Davidson
County, Tennessee. He gave for natural love   .
& affection a tract of land in Williamson County
on the Little Harpeth River & Mill Creek to
John McThompson. It contained 320 acres. The
land was granted by North Carolina to Jason
Thompson. It is Grant # 831.. The land was   .
conveyed June 28, 1824. The grant was for
640 acres. John McThompson got 1/2 of the
tract of land.

P. 291 ROSWELL BELKNAP & C - pl. vs JOHN B. BOYD - def.
        Oct. 1833   Debt
Roswell Belknap, Admr. of Lucy G. Belknap,
deceased.

P. 292 RICHARD REYNOLDS - pl. vs GILBERT MARSHALL,
Admr. - def.
        Oct. 1833   Debt
Gilbert Marshall, Admr. of D. H. Guthrie,
deceased.

P. 295 FRANCIS & ELIZABETH FLESHART - pl. vs JOHN
B. BOND - def.
        Jan. 1835   Debt

P. 297 STEPHEN G. EUBANK, use of Robert C. Foster &
JOHN W. MILLER - pl. vs PETER N. SMITH &
GENERAL LEE NOLEN - def.
        Jan. 1835   Debt

P. 308 JOHN JACKSON TURNER, by his guardian, William
Hunter - pl. vs ALLEN T. NOLEN - def..
        Jan. 1835
Has his slave.

P. 311 ENOCH ENSLEY, Admr. of Jason Thompson, deceased -
pl. vs ALLEN FIELDS - def.   Jan. 1835   Debt

P. 315 JAMES COLLINSWORTH - pl. vs JOSHUA K. SPEER - def.
                Jan. 1835   Trespass

P. 317 JAMES SWANSON - pl. vs INGRAM B. PEEBLES - def.
                Jan. 1835   Debt

P. 319 BENJAMIN J. BASS - pl. vs ELEAZAR HARDEMAN &
       THOMAS HARDEMAN - def.
                Jan. 1835   Debt

P. 320 JOHN PAGE - pl. vs JOSEPH KIMBRO - def.
                Jan. 1835   Debt

P. 323 MARY PETWAY, WILLIAM S. PETWAY, & JOHN C. PETWAY -
       pl. vs CURTIS STEVENS, Admr. of John Petway,
       deceased - def.
                April 1835   Petition for Partition
       William S. & John C. Petway are minors & their
       guardian is Henry Stevens. John Petway died
       in 1832 intestate. Mary Petway is his widow.

P. 325 MARY O. SMITH & THOMAS HARDEMAN, Admr. of
       Nicholas P. Smith, deceased
                Jan. 1835   Petition for Partition
       Nicholas P. Smith died intestate. Mary O. Smith
       & Thomas Hardeman, Admr., want to sell the
       slaves.

P. 327 MARTHA LEIGH, an infant who sues by her guardian,
       Martha Leigh; WILLIAM B. HULME & MARY, his wife;
       ELIZABETH LEIGH, an infant who sues by her
       guardian, William B. Hulme; AUGUSTUS D. FRAZIER &
       LAVINIA, his wife; GILBERT LEIGH, an infant who
       sues by his guardian, William B. Hulme
                Petition for Partition
       Benjamin Lee died many years past. He was the
       ancestor of the Petitioners & the husband of
       Martha Lee. Benjamin Lee left a will. Robert
       Hulme was appointed Admr. Benjamin Lee left
       some land (274 acres). He left 25 acres of
       land on the Big Harpeth River. He left one
       tract of land on the Big Harpeth.

P. 333 WILLIAM ARMSTRONG; ALLEN ARMSTRONG; JAMES L.
       ARMSTRONG; GEORGE ARMSTRONG; THOMAS ARMSTRONG;
       DAVID W. ARMSTRONG; & SARAH R. ARMSTRONG - pl.
       vs DANIEL BAUGH, Exr. of James Armstrong, deceased -
       def.
                Jan. 1835   Petition for Partition
       James L. Armstrong, George Armstrong, & Thomas A.
       Armstrong are infants who petition by their
       guardian, William Armstrong. David W. & Sarah R.
       Armstrong petition by their guardian, Allen
       Armstrong. The Petitioners father, James Armstrong
       departed this life Sept. 1833. He left a will.

P. 337 WILLIAM OGILVIE, Admr. of Henry Bailey,
        deceased
                    Jan. 1835   Petition for Sale of
                                        Slave

P. 338 EDWARD BREATHETT, Admr. of Henry Cook, deceased
                    Jan. 1835   Petition for Sale of
                                        Slave

P. 339 JOHN D. McLEMORE - pl. vs ROBERT W. McLEMORE,
        PEGGY S. McLEMORE, & ATKINS J. McLEMORE,
        their guardian - def.
                    Jan. 1835   Petition for Division
                                        of Slaves
        John D. McLemore petitions for 1/4 of the
        slaves.

P. 340 NANCY WATKINS & AL. - pl. vs HENRY KIRKPATRICK
        & AL. - def.
                    Jan. 1835   Petition for Partition
        Owen T. Watkins died in 1832 intestate.
        He left the following heirs & children:
                1. Nancy (widow)
                2. Mary T. (she married Curtis Stevens)
                3. Fanny G. (she married Green W. Hunt)
                4. William F. Watkins (minor)
                5. James D. Watkins (minor)
                6. Thomas O. Watkins (minor)
                7. Elizabeth H. Watkins (minor)
                8. Martha V. Watkins (minor)
        Guardian of the minor children is Gilbert
        Marshall. Nancy, Green W. & Henry Kirkpatrick
        are the Admrs.

        SARAH ANN WADE; JOHNSON BOXLEY & ELIZABETH,
        his wife; JARED BOXLEY; THOMAS BOXLEY; JOHN
        P. BOXLEY; HARRISON BOXLEY; WILLIAM J.
        BOXLEY; & TABITTA J. BOXLEY
                    April 1835   Petition for Partition
        Harrison Boxley is an infant who sues by his
        guardian, John W. Boxley. William J. Boxley
        is an infant who sues by his guardian, Thomas
        J. Boxley. Tabitta J. Boxley, infant, sues
        by her guardian, Jared Boxley. Benjamin
        Boxley, father of the Petitioners, died in 1819
        in Halifax County, Virginia. He left a will.
        Sarah Ann Boxley was left the slaves, etc.
        She has since died. The property was left to
        Benjamin Boxley's widow, Mildred. She has
        since released her claim to the items left.
        The family moved from Virginia to this County.
        Sarah Ann Boxley later intermarried, but it
        does not say who to.
                                        (CONT'D)

P. __ Benjamin Boxley, deceased (CONT'D)
This gives Benjamin Boxley's complete Will:
Halifax County, Virginia. Daughter - Sarah
Ann Boxley. Sons: Thomas, Jared, & John P.
Boxley. Daughter - Elizabeth Boxley. Sons:
Harrison J., & William J. Boxley. Daughter - ...
Tabitha J. Boxley. Wife. Brothers: Joseph
& George Boxley, Exrs. Will dated: 10 May
1819. Wit: Jacob Faulhner, Tilman Johnson, &
John E. Hart & Joseph Jones. Codicil: 1 acre ...
of land to Elisha Betts & James L. Blackwell
adjoining the Mill Dam. Will probated 27 Sept.
1819.

______ WILSON McCLELLAN, Admr. of William B. McClellan,
deceased - pl. vs WILLIAM BERSON - def.
                Debt

______ WILLIAM EDMISTON, Admr. of George W. Hulme,
deceased
                Sale of Slave

______ EDWARD BREATHITT - pl. vs REUBEN NICHOLS - def.
                Petition for Partition
Edward Breathitt owns 3/4 of a tract of land of
70 acres. It is located on Spencers Creek.
Reuben Nichols owns the other 1/4. Reuben
Nichols answers that he has been living on this
land 8 years & has cleared & made improvements
to the land.

______ CANTRELL & ALLEN, use of Edwin H. Ewing - pl.
vs ALEXANDER H. STOTHART - def.
                Oct. 1835   Case

______ PETER N. SMITH - pl. vs TILMAN F. ATKINSON = def.
                Oct. 1835   Trespass

______ CANTRELL & ALLEN, use of Edwin H. Ewing - pl. vs
GEORGE W. WHITFIELD - def.
                Oct. 1835   Trespass

______ ELI McGAN, Admr. of James Price, deceased - pl.
vs ANGUS McPHAIL - def.
                Oct. 1835   Case
James Price owed a debt.

______ RICHARD ASHMST (ASHURST?) & SONS - pl. vs THOMAS
S. ANTHONY - def.
                Oct. 1835   Debt
Richard Ashurst & his sons, John, Richard, &
Lewis are merchants.

DELIA S. HIGHTOWER - pl. vs WILLIAM C. ANDERSON,
Admr. of William E. Anderson, deceased - def.
            Oct. 1835   Debt

JAMES SANFORD - pl. vs JOHNSON WOOD & WILLIAMSON
JORDAN - def.
            Oct. 1835   Trespass

BURWELL G. LEWIS - pl. vs RICHARD VAUGHAN - def.
            Oct. 1835   Trespass
For rent of land.

DRURY NANCE - pl. vs THOMAS W. SHELTON - def.
            Oct. 1835   Trespass

DRURY P. HADLEY - pl. vs WILLIAM ALFORD, Exr.
of George W. Alford, deceased, & WILLIAM
HUGHES - def.
            Oct. 1835   Covenant

JARED BOXLEY - pl. vs THOMAS H. PERKINS, SR. -
def.   Oct. 1835   Covenant

MARY DAVIS; ALLEN T. NOLEN & FRANCES, his
wife; DRURY ROBERTSON & EMILY, his wife;
JAMES B. DAVIS; EVERETT DAVIS; ARTHUR J.
DENTON & MARY, his wife; & THOMAS DAVIS,
minor by his guardian, Allen T. Nolen
            Jan. 1836   Petition for Partition
Hollon Davis died July 1835 intestate. He
left a widow, Mary. He left the following
children: Frances, Emily, James B.,
Everett, Mary J., & Thomas.

MARY McCUTCHEN; CATHARINE E. McCUTCHEN;
MARY M. McCUTCHEN - pl. vs ROBERT McCUTCHEN
& WILLIAM EDMISTON - def.
            Jan. 1836   Petition for Partition
Catharine E. & Mary M. McCutchen are infants
& sue by their guardian, William Edmiston.
William McCutchen died intestate. He left
the following: Mary, his widow; 2 children,
Catharine E. & Mary M. McCutchen. William
Edmiston & Robert McCutchen are the Admrs.

NELSON ALLEN & SARAH ANN ALLEN, by her
guardian, James McCutchen
            Jan. 1836   Division of Slaves

WILLIAM S. MAYFIELD, Admr. & C of Robert C.
Thompson, deceased
            Jan. 1836   Petition for Sale of
                                        Slave
R. C. Thompson left a will.

ELIZABETH McGEE; MARY W. RUSSELL; SAMUEL S.
HAMMER & BLANCHE, his wife; THOMAS H. OLD;
CHARLES B. PORTER & MARTHA, his wife; ISHAM
R. TROTTER & SALLY, his wife; CHARLES W. OLD,
an infant who sues by his guardian, Samuel A.
Hanner; & ELIZABETH OLD - pl. vs JORDAN R. OLD;
WILLIAM A. OLD; THOMAS C. E. H. OLD; CORNELIA
F. OLD; MARY E. OLD; WILLIAM A. OLD, JR.; &
GILBERT MARSHALL, Admr. of Thomas Old, deceased -
def.

Jan. 1836   Petition for Partition
Elizabeth Old is the widow of Thomas Old, deceased.
Thomas H. Old died in 1830 intestate. John E.
Old, deceased, was the son of Thomas Old, deceased.
John E. Old left the following children: Thomas
C. E. H. Old, Cornelia F. Old, Mary E. Old, &
William A. Old, Jr. John E. Old, deceased, left
a widow, Elizabeth. The children of Thomas Old,
deceased, are: Elizabeth McGee, Mary W.
Russell, Blanche, wife of Samuel A. Hammer,
Thomas H. Old, Martha wife of Charles B. Porter,
Sally wife of Isham Trotter, Charles W. Old,
Jordan R. Old, & William A. Old. Thomas Old,
deceased, left a tract of land where he lived
for many years. It contained 150 acres. He
left another tract of land containing 12 acres.
He left another tract of land in Shelby County
containing 460 acres. He left 250 acres of
land in Obion County.

THOMAS L. DOUGLASS, Exr. of William McGee,
deceased
Jan. 1836   Petition for Sale
of Slaves

KITURA WILLIAMS, JAMES R. WILLIAMS, & FRANCIS
W. WILLIAMS
Jan. 1836   Petition to Sell Negroes
James R. Williams & Francis W. Williams by
their guardian, Archibald Lytle. Kitura Williams
is the widow.

JOHN JORDAN, Exr. of Johnson Wood
Sale of Slaves
A large debt due Johnson Wood estate in the
state of Mississippi & must employ someone to
collect it.

ALFRED N. WOOLDRIDGE & WILLIAM F. WOOLDRIDGE -
pl. vs JOSIAH WOOLDRIDGE, MINERVA E. WOOLDRIDGE,
& HENRY G. WOOLDRIDGE, & their guardian, GILBERT
MARSHALL - def.
Jan. 1836   Petition for Partition
(CONT'D)

106

Wooldridge (CONT'D)
    William F. Wooldridge - 1/7 part of slaves
    Alfred N. Wooldridge - 3/7 part of slaves
    Josiah Wooldridge - 1/7 part of slaves
    Henry G. Wooldridge - 1/7 part
    Minerva E. Wooldridge - 1/7 part

STEPHEN NOLEN & JOHNSON B. WILKINSON, by his guardian, Gilbert Marshall
    Jan. 1836   Petition for Partition
Stephen Nolen owns 4/7 of a tract of land & John B. Wilkinson owns 1/7. The tract contains 349 1/2 acres. The other 2/7 belongs to Thomas H. Wilkinson & Melvin Wilkinson, who have had their shares.

KEZIAH WOOLDRIDGE & ISAAC WILLINGHAM & NANCY, his wife - pl. vs JOHN NICHOLS & JAMES H. WILSON - def.
    Jan. 1836   Petition for Partition
Keziah & Nancy Willingham own 1/6 of a tract of land on the Big Harpeth River. It contains 228 acres. Other 2/3 of the land belongs to John Nichols, who has mortgaged his to James H. Wilson.

RANDAL EWING & WILLIAM B. EWING, Exr. of Alexander C. Ewing, deceased
    Jan. 1836   Petition for Sale of
                      Slaves
Alexander Ewing left a will. He wants the negro, Isham, sold as he is of a vicious nature.

MARY C. STANLEY - pl. vs AUSTIN C. STANLEY & AL. - def.
    Jan. 1836   Petition for Dower
Wright Stanley died 30 June 1833. He left a will. The will was probated in 1833. He left a widow, Mary C. Stanley. He left the following children: Austin C., Elizabeth C., Sarah Ann, Priscilla Amanda, & Wright Augustus Stanley. All of the children are minors & John Hodge is their guardian. Lemuel Farmer is the Exr. (Joseph Crockett & John Hodge renouned execution.) Wright Stanley, deceased, left a tract of land on Spencers Creek on the Turnpike Road. It contains 450 acres. The land was devised to Wright Stanley by Martin Stanley, deceased.

JOHN H. NEELLY & WIFE; SUSAN KEZIAH BERRYMAN;
JOSIAH WOOLDRIDGE; MINERVA E. WOOLDRIDGE; &
HENRY G. WOOLDRIDGE
      Jan. 1836   Petition for Division
Josiah, Minerva E., & Henry G. Wooldridge are
minors & their guardian is Gilbert Marshall.
They all own a tract of land on the Big Harpeth.
The land contains about 238 acres & it is now
occupied by Keziah Wooldridge. Josiah, Minerva
E., Henry, & Keziah each get 1/7 part & the
rest (3/7) goes to John H. Neelly & his wife.

THOMAS NEELLY & ELIZABETH, his wife - pl. vs
GREEN NEELLY & GEORGE NEELLY - def.
      Jan. 1836   Petition for Dower
Thomas Neelly died in 1832 intestate. He
left the following heirs: Elizabeth (his
widow), George (his child), & Green (his
child). The children are minors & their guardian
is Andrew Campbell. Tilman F. Atkinson is the
Admr. Thomas Neelly left a tract of land 2 miles
south of Franklin. It contains 260 acres.
Elizabeth, the widow, married Thomas Neelly.

DANIEL McPHAIL, Admr. of Joseph Phillips, deceased
      Jan. 1836   Petition for Sale of Slaves
4 legatees. Joseph Phillips left a will.

NELLY CATHEY - pl. vs THOMAS CATHEY & AL. - def.
      Jan. 1836   Petition for Dower
George Cathey died Jan. 1835 intestate. He left
a widow, Nelly. He left the following children:
Josiah, Thomas, James, John, George, Frances C.,
Rebecca B., William, & Henry Cathey. Josiah,
Thomas, James, & John Cathey are of age. George,
Frances C., Rebecca B., William, & Henry Cathey
are minors. William Glenn & Thomas Cathey
are the Admrs. George Cathey, deceased, left
2 tracts of land. One tract of land is located
at Flat Creek & it contains 200 acres. The
other tract of land also at Flat Creek contains
77 acres. George Cathey, deceased, lived on
the first tract of land.

RECORD BOOK

LAWSUITS

No. 7

1851 - 1859

P. 1   ADONIJAH GRAHAM, Et Als
            Dec. 1851   Exparte
John Graham died intestate July 1835. He
left the following heirs:
        1.   Jane Graham (his widow)
        2.   Abigail Brigance (then Abigail Henry,
             wife of Theophileus Henry, since
             deceased. Abigail is now married
             to Charles N. Brigance.)
        3.   George W. Graham
        4.   James C. Graham (he is an idiot
             who petitions by his guardian,
             Jane Dillon.)
        5.   Almedius Graham
        6.   Adonijah Graham
        7.   Naomi C. Graham (she is married to
             Jesse W. Johnson.)
        8.   John Graham
        9.   William A. Graham (he is married
             to Lucinda.)
George W. Graham, Adonijah Graham, Jesse W.
Johnson & his wife Naomi C. Johnson, William
A. Graham & his wife Lucinda Graham, Abigail
Brigance & her husband Charles N. Brigance,
& James C. Graham an idiot who petitions
by his guardian Jane Dillon, & of Robert
Blake Carothers. John Graham died possessing
a tract of land (111 acres) on Spencers
Creek. He owned other tracts of land on the
South Harpeth, but they were of little value.
John H. Graham purchased the others parts &
he died intestate in 1848. He was without
children. He left a widow, Lucinda Graham.
Aleuedius Graham died in 1850 intestate
having been unmarried. Lucinda is entitled
to her dower in that part of John H.
Graham's land (in his lifetime unincumbered
by the dower of siad Jane Dillon which has
never been assigned to her.) George W.
Graham, Adonijah Graham, & said Johnson &
wife, by deed dated 25 Nov. 1851 have sold
their share to your Petitioner. Jane
Graham has married ______ Dillon who has
since died.

P. 7   PHILIP CHAPMAN, Et Al
            Feb. 1852   Exparte
James B. Bond departed Feb. 1851 intestate.
Philip Chapman was named Admr. of James B. Bond.
James B. Bond, deceased, left a widow, Sarah
C. Bond. He left the following children:
John W., Catherine T., James W., & Margaret
L. Bond. James W. Bond is an infant & sues by
his guardian, Calvin C. Chapman. Margaret L.
Bond is the wife of Charles B. Morris. Philip
Chapman, the Petitioner, wants to sell the
slaves to pay the debts.

P. 11   OLLY SMITH - pl. vs SAMUEL SMITH, Et Al - def.
            Oct.
Samuel Smith died July 1850 intestate. James
Hughes is the Admr. Samuel Smith left a widow,
Olly Smith & the following children: Samuel
Smith, Daniel J. Smith, James S. Smith, Abram
Smith, Milly Ann Wright, Sally Jones, Nancy
Homel, & Hannah Homel. Samuel Smith, Daniel J.
Smith, James S. Smith, & Abram Smith are minors
& have no general guardian. Milly Ann married
Frederick M. Wright. Sally married Abner Jones.
Nancy married Henry Homel. Hannah married
Isaac Homel. Samuel Smith, deceased, owned the
tract of land where he resided at the time of
his death. This tract contained 230 acres. He
also owned several other small tracts of land
adjoining the above mentioned tract. These tracts
contain about 2000 acres, but are of little value.

P. 15   SERENA G. HULME, Et Al
            Dec. 1852   Exparte
Samuel E. McCutchan, Admr. of Mary Elizabeth
Hulme, deceased, & of Isaac Watson, Admr. of his
deceased wife, Sarah Jane Watson, & Serena G.
Hulme, & Nancy G. Hulme, a minor who sues by
her guardian, Serena G. Hulme. Mary Elizabeth
Hulme departed in 1851 leaving her 2 sisters.
Her sisters are: Sarah Jane Watson (the wife of
Isaac N. Watson. Sarah has since died without
issue & leaving her husband) & Nancy G. Hulme
(she is a minor. Her mother is Serena G. Hulme.)
The Petitioner wants to sell the negroes.

P. 18   ROBERT C. TULLOSS & WIFE
            Sept. 1852   Exparte
            1. Robert C. Tullos & Nancy P., his wife
            2. James H. Lampkins
            3. Sameul S. Starnes (minor by his guardian,
                James W. Starnes)
            4. John D. Starnes (minor by his guardian,
                James W. Starnes)
                            (CONT'D)

P. 18   Robert C. Tulloss   (CONT'D)
              5.   Ebenezer Starnes (minor by his guardian,
                   James W. Starnes)
A tract of land in Williamson County contained
about 400 acres. It is located on the Big
Harpeth River.

P. 20   ROBERT L. STEPHENS, Admr. & C
              May Term 1852   Exparte
Robert L. Stephens is the Admr. of James P.
Stephens, deceased. James P. Stephens died
29 April 1852 intestate. He was unmarried &
without children. He left the following
brothers & sisters:
              1.   Polly Jordan (she married Garner
                   M. Jordan)
              2.   Emily Oakley
              3.   Curtis Stephens
              4.   Charles Stephens
              5.   Sally Waggoner (deceased)
Sally Waggoner's children are named as part
of the heirs of James P. Stephens, deceased.
              6.   Children of Louis Stephens, brother.
              7.   Children of Henry C. Stevens, brother.

P. 23   HENRY TINDALL & WIFE, Et Al
              Sept. Session 1852   Exparte
              Petition to Sell Slaves
Alexander Holland is deceased. His children
are:
              1.   Henry Tindall & Mary, his wife
              2.   James Brooks & Elizabeth, his wife
              3.   Andrew Edministon & Jane, his wife
              4.   William S. Holland
              5.   James G. Holland (minor who petitions
                   by his guardian, Alexander Gray)
              6.   Gustavus Holland (minor who petitions
                   by his guardian, Alexander Gray)
              7.   Franklin A. Holland (minor who
                   petitions by his guardian, Alexander
                   Gray)
              8.   Richard A. Owen & Mary O., his wife

P. 24   EDMUND C. COOK, Et Al
              Oct. Term 1852   Exparte
John T. Cook died Feb. 1846 intestate. He
left the following heirs:
              1.   Gracy B. Cook (his widow)
              2.   Edmund C. Cook
              3.   Philip H. Cook
              4.   Richard D. Cook
              5.   Nicholas P. Cook
              6.   John T. Cook

(CONT'D)

P. 24   Edmund C. Cook (CONT'D)
John T. Cook's widow, Gracy B. Cook died Sept.
1850 intestate. Philip H., Richard D., Nicholas
P., & John T. Cook are minors & their guardian
is Gilbert Marshall. Edmund C. Cook arrived of
age July term court 1850. John T. Cook, deceased,
was over a tract of land at the time of his
death. It contains 75 acres. It is part of a
tract owned by him & Mary Perkins.

P. 27   WILLIAM L. POPE, Et Al
              Nov. 1852   Exparte
         Petition for the Sale of 2 Slaves
Lemuel Pope is deceased. He left the following
heirs:
         1. William L. Pope
         2. Gustavus A. Pope (minor)
         3. Lucy A. Pope (minor)
         4. James R. Pope (Minor)
         5. Mary R. Pope (minor)
Lucy J. Pope is guardian over the minor children.

P. 28   LUCY CRIDDLE, Et Al
              Nov. 1852   Exparte
Smith Criddle died Nov. 1845 in Henry County,
Tennessee. He left a widow, Lucy Criddle.
He left the following children:
         1. Mary E. Criddle (she married John Scruggs)
         2. Tennessee Criddle
         3. John H. Criddle
         4. Smith Criddle
Lucy Criddle, the widow, was guardian to the
children. Smith Criddle, deceased, left slaves.
He left the following tracts of land:
         1. 3 tracts of land in Henry County containing
             250 acres.
         2. 2 tracts of land in Dyer County. One
             tract contains 30 acres & the other tract
             contains 50 acres.
Lucy Criddle, widow, gives her dower to her children.

P. 34   JAMES G. HOLLAND, Et Al
              Dec. 1852   Exparte
The Petitioners are: James G. Holland, Sara J.
Edmondson & her husband Andrew Edmondson, Elizabeth
Brooks & her husband James Brooks, Gustavus A.
Holland, Franklin A. Holland, & Mary O. Owen.
Gustavus A. Holland, Franklin A. Holland, & Mary
O. Owen are minors & sue by their guardian,
Alexander M. Gray. A slave & a tract of land was
conveyed unto the late John A. Holland by
Franklin Hardeman & his wife. The deed was dated
Dec. 1840. About 20 acres of land was assigned
to Sarah Gray (formerly Holland) as her dower.
                              (CONT'D)

112

P. 34 James G. Holland   (CONT'D)
       One tract of land was conveyed to John A.
       Holland by Gustavus A. Holland. The deed was
       dated 3 July 1833. Elizabeth Brooks owns 2/7 of
       the said land. 1/7 by inheritance from her
       father, John A. Holland & 1/7 purchased from
       William S. Holland, an heir.

P. 38 CURTIS STEVENS, Et Al - pl. vs CHARLES STEVENS,
       Et Al - def.
              Feb. 1853
       The following are owners of a tract of land in
       Williamson County containing 62 1/2 acres.:
              1. Curtis Stevens (a citizen of Arkansas)
              2. Robert Oakley & Emily, his wife
              3. Garner M. Jordan & Mary Jordan, his
                  wife (of Williamson & Dickson Counties,
                  Tennessee)
              4. Lewis C. Waggoner
              5. Joseph H. Ladd & Emily, his wife
              6. Robert L. Stevens
              7. Robert L. Bateman & Catherine, his
                  wife
              8. ____ Harris & Mary M., his wife
                  (of Davidson County)
              9. Robert Bateman & Mary, his wife (of
                  Rutherford County)
             10. John H. Waggoner & William M. Waggoner
             11. Charles Stevens (of Louisiana)
             12. Sarah C. Waggoner (she is a minor in
                  the State of Arkansas & Curtis
                  Stevens is her guardian)
             13. Joel Stevens & Eliza C. Stevens (they
                  are minors & their guardian is
                  Ebanor C. Stevens)
             14. James M. Pickett & Louisa, his wife
                  (of Mississippi)
             15. Young Callaham & Eliza, his wife (of
                  Ovale (?) Parrish, Louisiana)
             16. Mary Ann Stevens (of Yazoo County,
                  Mississippi)
             17. Rufus Stevens (of Yazoo Co., Miss-
                  issippi. His guardian is Mirajah
                  Pickens)
             18. Lewis Stevens (of Yazoo Co.,
                  Mississippi. His guardian is Mirajah
                  Pickens)
             19. Clelia Stevens (of Ovale Parrish,
                  Louisiana. Young Callaham is her
                  guardian)
       Robert L. Stevens is to be appointed
       commissioner to make a sale of the land.

P. 41   SUSAN J. ANDERSON, Admrx. et al
         Feb. 1853   Exparte
         Petition to Sell Slaves
Joel Anderson died 30 Dec. 1853. He left a
widow, Susan J. Anderson & the following
distributees:
1.   William Anderson (his son)
2.   James Anderson (his son)
3.   Joel Anderson (his son)
4.   Catherine Kirkpatrick (daughter who married
     John Kirkpatrick)
5.   Frances Jackson (daughter who married
     John A. Jackson)
6.   Dorinda Samuel (daughter who married
     William Samuel)
7.   Children of Mary Amis, deceased (Mary
     Amis married William Amis & she's a
     daughter)
8.   Nancy Hughes (daughter who married
     Samuel Hughes. Nancy is deceased &
     she has children who survive her.)

P. 44   WILKINS WHITFIELD, Admr. - pl. vs THOMAS RIDLEY,
JR., Et Al
         March 1853
Wilkins Whitfield is the Admr. of William Ridley,
deceased. William Ridley died in 1851
intestate. He left the following heirs &
distributees:
1.   Thomas Ridley
2.   George Ridley, Jr.
3.   Sarah Ridley
4.   Elizabeth M. Whitfield
5.   George Ridley, Sr.
6.   George Alston (a minor)
William Ridley, deceased, left a tract of land
in the 14th District.

P. 47   THOMAS H. BOND & WIFE, Et Al
         Feb. 1853   Exparte
Thomas H. Bond & Mary M., his wife & Leonard
D. Banks, who petitions by his guardian,
Elijah Thompson are the Petitioners. Own a tract
of land containing about 425 acres. 2/5 of the
tract of land was owned by the late James Banks.
Also owned slaves. Mary M. has married Thomas
Bond & will be 21 years old in a short time.

P. 51   JOHN P. McKAY, Exr. & C
         March 1853   Exparte
Robert Hodge died. He left a will which was
probated in 1852. The Petitioner wants to sell
the slaves. The will names: Andrew Hodge (son),
Nancy Scott (daughter), & James Robert Green
(grandson & a minor)

114

P. 53   HENRY J. WALKER, Admr. & C
         March 1853   Exparte
Henry Walker died 11 March 1824 while most of
his children were under age. He left a will.
John Buchanan was named Exr., but he
renounced execution. Stephen Childress was
appointed Admr. Childress was removed as
Admr. & Garner McConnico was appointed Admr.
Garner McConnico departed this life. Stephen
Childress & John Buchanan were Admr. of Henry
Walker, deceased. Henry Walker, deceased,
left slaves. He left a widow, Mary Walker.
He left the following children:
         1.   Sarah
         2.   Elizabeth C.
         3.   Addison H.
         4.   Jason F.
         5.   Henry J.
         6.   William C.
         7.   Jonah J.
         8.   Mary A.
         9.   John S.   (he died in 1845 leaving a
              widow since dead & 4 children)
        10.   Tilman F. (he died in 1847 unmarried)
        11.   Nancy S. & Gideon B. (both died in
              infancy & unmarried)
Mary Walker, widow of Henry Walker, deceased,
died 18 Dec. 1852. (Copy of Will - complete)
The will was probated April Session 1824.
The will was dated 12 Feb. 1824. The will
does not give the names of wife or children.

P. 56   ROBERT W. McKNIGHT, Et Al
         March 1853   Exparte - Petition to
                             Sell Slave
The Petitioners are:
         1.   Robert W. McKnight & Martha A.,
              his wife
         2.   Ellen P. Roundtree (infant who
              petitions by her guardian, William
              T. A. Shaw)
         3.   Mary M. Roundtree (infant who
              petitions by her guardian,
              William T. A. Shaw)

P. 57   M. C. H. PURYEAR, Admr. & C
         April 1853   Exparte
Mordecai C. H. Puryear is the Admr. of John M
Currin, deceased, who died July 1852. He left
a widow, Elizabeth Currin & 3 children. The
Children are: Sally P., Eveline M., & Catherine
Currin. The Petitioner wants to sell the slaves
to help pay expenses. He also has a deed of
trust on a parcel of land near the city of Memphis.

P. 59   SAMUEL W. EDMISTON, Admr. & C
                April 1853   Exparte
Thomas J. Nolen died intestate July 1852.
He was unmarried. He left slaves. His heirs
are 4 sisters & the children of a deceased brother.

P. 61   JOHN B. CARSON & WIFE, Et Al - pl. vs HENRY B.
WALKER, Z All
                June 1853
The Petitioners are:
        1.   John B. Carson & Elizabeth C., his wife
        2.   Amos H. Rounsaville & Susan F., his wife
        3.   Henry J. Walker
        4.   Thomas K. Handy
        5.   Robert Chadwell
        6.   William L. Nance
        7.   Clem W. Nance
        8.   Henry B. Walker (a minor whose guardian
             is William C. Walker, his father)
To be divided where 2 tracts of land on the
Liberty Meeting House Road & 2 other tracts of
which one tract contained 137 1/2 acres & the
other tract contained 6 1/4 acres. It is to be
divided into 8 shares.

P. 65   JOHN H. ALLEN, Admr.
                Jan. 1853   Exparte
                Petition for Sale of Slaves
Anthony Gilliam departed this life Sept. 1851
intestate. He left the following heirs:
        1.   Thomas E. Gilliam
        2.   Elizabeth Shute
        3.   Lawson Allen & Martha A., his wife
        4.   Thomas B. Gilliam
        5.   John B. Gilliam
        6.   William A. Gilliam
        7.   James H. Taylor & Emily C., his wife
        8.   Harrison M. Short & Naomi, his wife
        9.   Alfred S. Redmon & Julia A., his wife
        10. James M. Gilliam
        11. Louisa Gilliam
        12. Martin R. Cayce & Rebecca J., his wife
The Petition is for the sale of 11 slaves.

P. 67   THOMAS GLYMP, Et Al
                Jan. 1853   Exparte
The Petitioners are:
        1.   Thomas Glymp
        2.   William Glymp
        3.   M. C. Haynes & Winney, his wife
        4.   Thomas, Berry, & Robert Griggs (minors who
             sue by their next friend, William Glymp)
        5.   Green, George, & Lewis Jenkins (minors who
             sue by their next friend, Thomas Glymp)
                                        (CONT' D)

116

P. 67   Thomas Glymp (CONT'D)
George Glymp died. He left a will. He left
land to his wife, Mildred, for her lifetime &
the remaining to his children (being 11 in
number). Thomas Glymp has purchased the shares
of Henry Glymp, Frances Taylor, John A. Glymp,
Elizabeth Griggs, & George Glymp. Thomas Glymp
owns 6 share out of the 11 in said land.
Frances Taylor is the daughter of the testator.
Her husband, James Taylor was dead when the
purchase was made. Elizabeth Griggs is the
daughter of George Glymp, deceased. She
married Wiley Griggs. Green, George, &
Lewis Jenkins are the sons of Sarah Jenkins,
deceased. Sarah is the daughter of the
testator & she married Jeremiah Jenkins.
John B. McEwen & A. C. Carter own the share
of land that was left to Jesse Glymp. The
entire tract of land contained about 189 acres.

P. 70   JAMES KING, Guard., Et Al
              Jan. 1853   Exparte
The Petitioners are: James King, John F.
King, Edward H. King, & Mary E. King. James
King is the guardian to Edward H. & Mary E.
King. Elizabeth King, wife of James King &
mother of Mary E., John F., & Edward H.
King, died intestate in the early part of the
year 1851. She owned slaves. She left a
will. She left 2 slaves to her husband &
the rest to her children.

P. 71   POLLY DAVIS, Et Al - pl. vs ALLEN NOLEN,
Et Al   July 1853
Thomas J. Nolen died July 1852 intestate.
He was unmarried. He owned 2 lots in
Nolensville (Lot # 21 & Lot # 24). His heirs
are:
         1. Polly Davis (sister)
         2. Dilly Gray (sister who married
             Henry H. Gray)
         3. Tabitha Taylor (sister who married
             John Taylor)
         4. Elizabeth Edmondson (sister)
         5. Harriet Karr (neice)
         6. Jane Hendley (neice)
         7. Caroline Elden (neice)
         8. Elizabeth Nolen (neice who is a
             minor & her guardian is William
             Brown)
         9. William Nolen (nephew)
        10. Allen Nolen (nephew who is a minor &
             his guardian is William Brown)
                                    (CONT'D)

P. 71   Polly Davis, Et Al (CONT'D)
        Samuel W. Edmondson & Elizabeth, his wife, are
        of Davidson County, Tennessee. Harriet Karr
        & ____ Karr are of Mississippi. James Henley
        & Jane, his wife, are of Maury County, Tennessee.
        Caroline Elden & ____ Elden are of Mississippi.
        Allen Nolen & Elizabeth Nolen are both of Maury
        County.

P. 73   ISAAC TWOOMEY - pl. vs CELIA SHEFFIELD, Et Al -
        def.   July 1853
        Isaac Twoomey is the Admr. of the estate of
        Robert C. Vaughn, deceased. Robert C. Vaughn
        died 17 Oct. 1845 intestate. He left a widow,
        Celia, who married John Stanfield. He left
        the following children: Franklin, John, Arch,
        James, & Tennessee. Robert C. Vaughn, deceased,
        owned a tract of land in District # 1 on the
        South Harpeth River. It contained 200 acres.
        No dower has been assigned & the estate is
        insolvent.

P. 77   ALFRED WALLIS, Et Al.
                July 1853   Exparte
        John Wallis of Rutherford County, Tennessee
        departed this life in 1840. He was unmarried &
        without issue. He left a will as follows:
        To John Wallis, son of Alfred Wallis, 100 acres
        of land on which his father now lives in
        Williamson County. At the time of his death,
        John Wallis held only a title bond for said land
        on William Wilson. John Wallis, deceased, left
        a father, Mother, brothers & sisters. They are:
        Mortimer R. Wallis, Catherine B. Wallis,
        Isabella A. Slate, Albert F. Wallis (deceased).
        Archibald Wilson, Exr. of William Wilson, conveyed
        100 acres of land to Mortimer R. Wallis,
        Catherine B. Wallis, & Isabella S. Slate in 1850.
        Isabella has since married Hiram Slate. She gets
        2/4 part. Mortimer Wallis gets 1/4 part &
        Catherine Wallis gets 1/4 part. Alfred Wallis &
        his wife are old & incapable of making support off
        of the said land. The land is located at
        Buffalo Lick. Alfred has agreed to sell his
        life estate. 29 March 1841 an agreement was made
        between Alfred Wallis & Isabella S. Wallis. Alfred
        is her father & John Wallis, deceased, was her
        brother. Deed Book G, Page 315 - 100 acres of land -
        Archibald Wilson, Exr. of William Wilson, deceased,
        of Henderson County, Tennessee. 7 July 1841 -
        Deed Book U, Page 247 - John Wallis, Sr., deceased,
        by his will to son John Wallis____________.

118

P. 81   JOHN W. MILLER - pl. vs LEWIS CORZINE & WIFE,
        Al. - def.
                Oct. 1853
        Lewis Corzine & Jane R., his wife, & Joel
        Anderson of Louisiana or Texas are the
        defendants. William Anderson, Franklin P.
        Anderson, & William S. Campbell are of
        Hardin County, Tennessee & they are also
        the defendants. They are all owners of a tract
        of land containing about 16 acres near Franklin.
        It has no house, trees or spring. It is part of
        a tract of land owned by Robert White,
        deceased, at the time of his death. Lewis
        Corzine & wife own 1/2 of the undivided interest.
        Joel, William Jr., & Franklin P. Anderson
        are minors & their guardian is William S.
        Campbell. They get 3/8 part & John P.
        Miller gets 1/8 interest.

P. 86   SUSAN J. ANDERSON - pl. vs JOEL ANDERSON,
        Et Al - def.
                Nov. 1853
        Joel Anderson died intestate. He left a
        widow, Susan J. Anderson. He left the
        following heirs:
                1.   William Anderson
                2.   James Anderson
                3.   Joel A. Anderson
                4.   William Samuels & Dorinda, his wife
                5.   John Kirkpatrick & Catherine, his wife
                6.   John A. Jackson & Frances M., his wife
                7.   _____ Evan & his wife
                8.   _____ Nicholson & his wife
                9.   Thomas Amis, John Amis, & _____ Amis
                     (children of the deceased daughter,
                        _____ Amis.)
                10. Robert J. McClelland & Sarah A.,
                     his wife
                11. Brice M. Hughes, Samuel H. Hughes, &
                     John L. Hughes (children of deceased
                     daughter, _____ Hughes)
        Joel Anderson, deceased, left a tract of land
        near the town of Franklin. It contained about
        11 acres. He also left 2 town lots in
        Chattanooga.
                Marriage Book 1800 - 1850
                Samuel C. Hughes married Nancy W.
                   Anderson Aug. 18, 1831.
                William Amis married Polly Anderson
                   March 26, 1822.

P. 88   JOHN S. WHITEHEAD, Et Al - Exparte
         ELIZA WHITEHEAD   Nov. 1853
         Milton Powell died intestate. He left a widow,
         Eliza, who married John S. Whitehead. He
         left the following children: Emily Jane &
         Sarah Powell. He left slaves. Eliza, his
         widow, wants her dower. Emily Jane & Sarah Powell
         are minors & John S. Whitehead is their guardian.
                   Williamson County Tennessee
                   Marriage Records 1800 - 1850
                   John S. Whitehead married Eliza Powell
                      Jan. 29, 1850.

P. 90   EDWARD B. CHANEY, Admr. - pl. vs RICHARD A.
         CHANEY, Et Al - def.
                   Dec. 1853
         Wilkins T. Chaney died intestate Sept. 1850.
         He left a widow, Letitia, who died a few days
         after her said husband. They left 3 children.
         The children are: Richard A. Chaney, Letitia
         M. Chaney, & Margaret Chaney. Richard A. &
         Letitia M. Chaney are minors & their guardian is
         Richard Steele. Margaret Chaney died intestate
         & unmarried a short while after her father.
         Wilkins T. Chaney, deceased, was guardian of his
         brothers & sisters. His brothers & sisters are:
         David S. Chaney, Ezekiel Chaney, Mary E. Chaney,
         & William T. Chaney. Wilkin T. Chaney, deceased,
         died owner of a tract of land in the 4th Civil
         District. The tract of land contains about
         75 acres.

P. 94   MOSES BEARD, Et Al
                   Dec. 1853   Exparte
         John Beard died in 1826. He left a will. He
         left 2 tracts of land each containing 50 acres.
         He left a widow, Mary Beard. He left her the
         land during her lifetime. He left the following
         children: Moses Beard, Nancy Hayes, Francis
         Beard, Katy Gwynn, Comfort Brown, Aaron Beard,
         Rody McGee, John Beard, Bird N. Beard, & Jane
         Beard. Mary Beard departed this life 5 Dec.
         1853 & the land left to her is to be divided
         between her children.

P. 95   THOMAS F. P. ALLISON, Et Al
                   Dec. 1853   Exparte
         Thomas F. P. & William Allison are minors & sue by
         their guardian, John S. Claybrook. Thomas F. P. &
         William Allison are owners of a tract of land on
         the waters of Grove Creek. The land contains
         about 792 acres. They also own slaves.

120

P. 99   SARAH V. BOYD, Et Al
                Jan. 1854   Exparte
         Sarah V. Boyd, Ann B. Boyd, George W. Boyd,
         & Abner Boyd are the Petitioners. Ann A.,
         George W., & Abner Boyd are minors & sue by
         their guardian, George Andrews. They are all
         the owners of slaves & they want a division
         made.

P. 100   WILLIAM BURNS, Admr. & C
                Jan. 1854   Exparte
         William Burns is Admr. of David A. Cowan, who
         died June 1853 intestate. David A. Cowan
         died unmarried. His survivors are:
              1. Jane Cowan (his mother)
              2. John Cowan (his brother)
              3. Richard G. Cowan (his brother)
              4. Rosa Meacham (his sister & she is the
                  widow of James Meacham)
              5. Nelly Baxter (sister, who is the widow
                  of William Baxter)
              6. Susan Burns (sister who is the wife
                  of William Burns)
              7. Mary Ann Meacham (sister who is the
                  wife of Matthew Meacheam)
              8. Virginia T. Robinson
              9. Elizabeth H. Robinson (Virginia T. &
                  Elizabeth H. Robinson are the children
                  of Jane Robinson, deceased. Jane is
                  the sister of David A. Cowan.)
             10. Neices & Nephews
             11. Mary A. Williams (sister)
             12. James & Sarah C. Meacham (children of
                  his deceased sister, Elizabeth Meacham)
         David A. Cowan, deceased, owned a negro man.

P. 102   PHILIP H. COOK, Et Al
                Jan. 1854   Exparte
         The heirs are:
              1. Philip H. Cook
              2. Richard D. Cook (minor whose guardian
                  is Edmund C. Cook)
              3. Nicholas P. Cook (minor whose guardian
                  is Edmund C. Cook)
              4. John T. Cook (minor whose guardian
                  is Edmund C. Cook)
         Philip H. Cook is now of age & he wishes his share
         the slaves.

P. 104 JOHN B. GRAY, Et Al
        Jan. 1854   Exparte
The heirs are:
    1. John B. Gray & Margaret B., his wife
    2. Susan J. McClelland (infant whose
        guardian is Constant W. Davis)
    3. Maria J. McClelland (infant whose
        guardian is Constant W. Davis)
    4. Sarah Elizabeth McClelland (infant
        whose guardian is Constant W. Davis)
Margaret B. is now of age & she wishes her share
of the slaves.

P. 105 ANN D. MERRITT - pl. vs SUSAN MERRITT, Et Al - def.
        Jan. 1854
John A. Merritt departed this life intestate
Aug. 1853. He left a widow, Ann D. Merritt.
He left the following children:
    1. Susan
    2. Rebecca
    3. Mary
    4. Frances
    5. Sarah
The children are all minors & have no guardian.
John A. Merritt, deceased, had a tract of land
where he resided. It was located in the 13th
District on the waters of Hurrican Creek. It
contains 262 acres. Ann D. Merritt, the widow,
wants her dower.

P. 108 HENRY R. SHERROD & Al.
        March 1854   Exparte
The Petitioners are:
    1. Henry R. Sherrod & Frances J., his wife
    2. Mary D. Scales (she petitions by her
        guardian, Absalom W. Scales)
Frances J. Scales married Henry R. Sherrod. The
Petitioners want a division of the slaves.

P. 110 LUCY CRIDDLE & Al.
        March 1854   Exparte
The Petitioners are: Lucy Criddle, Tennessee E.
Criddle, John H. Criddle, & William Smith
Criddle. Tennessee E., John H., & William Smith
Criddle are minors & petition by their guardian,
Lucy Criddle. They want a division of the slaves.

P. 113 THOMAS PATE
        March 1854   Exparte
Martha H. Pate died in 1848. She had an interest
in the real estate of Henry Beatty, deceased.
The real estate contained about 6 acres in one
tract & 10 acres in the dower of Mrs. Sarah
Beatty. Thomas Pate was appointed Admr. of the
                    (CONT'D)

P. 113 Thomas Pate (CONT'D)
estate of Martha H. Pate, his deceased wife.
Thomas Pate will apply to be appointed
guardian of the children of his deceased wife.
Thomas Pate wants the land sold.

P. 115 LUCY WILSON, Et Al
         March 1854   Exparte
The Petitioners are: Lucy Wilson, Lulie
Wilson, Samuella Wilson. Lulie Wilson &
Samuella Wilson are minors & their guardian
is Thomas Holt. Samuel L. Wilson is deceased.
He left an estate & the Petitioners want the
slaves divided.

P. 116 WILLIAM ANDERSON & OTHERS - pl. vs BRICE
HUGHES & OTHERS - def.
         March 1854
The Petitioners are:
    1. William Anderson of Hardin County,
        Tennessee
    2. James Anderson of Wayne County, Tenn.
    3. John Jackson & Frances, his wife
    4. William Samuel & Dorinda, his wife
        (of Giles County, Tennessee)
    5. John Kirkpatrick & his wife
    6. Joel A. Anderson & John W. Miller
The Defendants are:
    1. Brice Hughes
    2. Leander Hughes & Samuel Hughes
    3. Jesse Evans & Martha, his wife
    4. James Nicholson & Sally, his wife
    5. Henrietta Amis, John Amis, & Thomas
        Amis
    6. Cecil & Susan J., his wife (of
        Maury County, Tennessee)
Joel Anderson died in 1852 leaving a widow,
Susan J. She was appointed Admrx. She has
since married Cecil. Joel Anderson left the
following children: William Anderson, James
Anderson, Frances Jackson, Dorinda Samuels,
Catherine Kirkpatrick, & Joel A. Anderson.
Joel Anderson left the following grand-
children: Martha Evans, Sally Nicholson,
Henrietta Amis, John Amis, Thomas Amis,
Sally Ann McClellan, Brice Hughes, Leander
Hughes, Samuel Hughes. Henrietta Amis,
John & Thomas Amis are minors & have no
guardian. They are the children of Polly Amis.
Brice Hughes, Leander, & Samuel Hughes are
minors & their guardian is Brice Hughes. They
are the children of Nancy Hughes, deceased.
Nancy was the daughter of Joel Anderson.
                              (CONT'D)

P. 116 Joel Anderson, deceased (CONT'D)
        Joel Anderson, deceased, had 1 lot in town of
        Chattanooga in Hamilton County. (Lot # 36). He
        also had a tract of land in Williamson County
        near the town of Franklin containing 10 acres.
        This tract of land was on the Franklin &
        Columbia Turnpike. The Petitioners want the
        land sold for a division.

P. 120 GEORGE F. PLAXCO & JOHN L. McEWEN
                March 1854   Exparte
        The Petitioners are:
            1. George F. Plaxco of Franklin County,
                Alabama petitions by his guardian,
                Edward H. Plaxco
            2. John L. McEwen (a friend of George F.
                Plaxco's. John L. McEwen is of
                Williamson County.)
        The Petitioners own a tract of land in the 8th
        District. It is located on both sides of Spencers
        Creek. About 3 acres of the land is part of
        the original William McEwen tract of land & it
        was assigned to the great grandmother of the
        Petitioner, George F. Plaxco, as her dower. The
        great grandmother died & John L. McEwen has
        purchased all of the interests in the said 3
        acres. He also owns the surrounding land. They
        want to sell the land.

P. 122 JINCY ORUM - pl. vs STEEL BENNETT & Als.
                March 1854
        James Orum died in 1853 leaving a will. Moses
        Steele & William Y. Bennett were named Exrs.
        James Orum, deceased, left a tract of land near
        Bethesda. It contained 150 acres. He also left
        slaves. He left the following heirs:
            1. Jincy Orum (his widow)
            2. Jane Eliza Falkenberry (daughter)
            3. James H. Orum & Mary E. Orum (grandchildren.
                They are the children of his deceased son.)
            4. Children of his deceased daughter,
                Tabitha Curry (Cuny?) Giles of the State
                of Kentucky.
        Jincy Orum, the widow, wants her dower.
        (Complete copy of Will included in Lawsuits)
        Wife - Jincy Orum. Grandson - James Henry Orum,
        child of deceased son. Daughter - Tabitha Curry
        Giles. Daughter - Jane Eliza Falkenberry.
        Granddaughter - Mary Elizabeth Orum, child of
        deceased son. Obtain judgment against Paschall
        Giles by the Admr. of William Orum, deceased, &
        goes to daughter, Tabitha Cuny Giles. Dated -
        25 March 1850. Children of deceased daughter,
        Tabitha Cuny Giles are: Rebecca Ann Giles,
                                        (CONT'D)

P. 122 James Orum, deceased   (CONT'D)
         Martha Jane Giles, William Giles, Thomas Giles,
         John Giles, Meredith P. Giles, & Claibourne
         Giles, & an infant not named. John R. Roberts
         is their guardian.

P. 129 JANE E. FALKENBERRY, Et Al
                  March 1854   Exparte
         The Petitioners are: John A. Falkenberry &
         his wife, Jane Elizabeth. Cross Petition is:
         Rebecca Ann, Martha Jane, William, Thomas, John,
         Meredith P. Claiborne & _______ Giles, by their
         guardian, John R. Roberts. They are the
         children of Tabitha C. Giles, deceased. They
         are owners of a tract of land formerly owned
         by James Orum, deceased.

P. 134 ROBERT M. McDANIEL & Als.
                  Exparte
         The Petitioners are:
              1. Robert McDaniel & Margaret C.,
                  his wife
              2. Diana Maury
              3. Bethenia A. Maury & Nancy R. Maury
                  (These 2 are minors & their guardian
                  is William J. Boyd)
         Richard L. Maury died intestate. He left
         the following children: Margaret C., Diana,
         Bethenia A., & Nancy R., & Matthew F. Maury.
         His widow, Peggy A., has since married
         Harrison Boxley. Richard L. Maury owned land.
         The Petitioners want to divide the land & the
          slaves.

P. 132 MOSES STEELE, Admr., Et Al
                  Feb. 1854   Exparte
         Moses Steele is the Admr. of Sarah R. Steele,
         deceased. Rachel A. Steele petitions by
         her guardian, Moses Steele. Sarah R. Steele
         died 15 June 1853. They are the owners of
         slaves.

P. 139 JAMES M. SHELTON, Et Al
                  Feb. 1854   Exparte
         The Petitioners are: James M. Shelton, Thomas
         J. Shelton, & Sarah Ann Shelton. Thomas J. &
         Sarah Ann Shelton are minors & their
         guardian is Constant W. Davis. The Petitioners
         want the negroes sold.

P. 143 FRANCES SHEGOG - pl. vs JOHN ROBERTS, Et Als -
    def.   Feb. 1854
    Frances Shegog was the wife of James Shegog,
    who died intestate. He left the following
    children: James W., Fannie B., Mary E., &
    Arthur Shegog. They are all minors & have no
    guardian. James Shegog, deceased, left 2 lots
    in Nolensville. They are Lot # 14 & Lot # 15.

P. 140 DANIEL SLEDGE & WIFE & Als. - pl. vs NANCY
    PERKINS - def.
              Feb. 1854
    The Petitioners are:
        1. Daniel Sledge & Cely, his wife
        2. John Sledge & Mary Ann, his wife
        3. Elizabeth Corzine
        4. _____ Beard
        5. Rachel Kenneda
    Nancy Perkins is of North Carolina. William
    Kenneda died in 1853 intestate. He left heirs.
    He had a tract of land containing about 23
    acres. He had another tract of land containing
    2 1/2 or 3 acres & he had no deed on this tract.
    Octavius C. Hatcher is Admr. of the estate.
                Williamson County, Tennessee
                Marriage Records 1800 - 1850
                Bird Near Beard married Sarah Kennedy
                    Aug. 11, 1824.

P. 145 LEMUEL S. BOND, Et Al
              Feb. 1854   Exparte
    The Petitioners are: Lemuel S. Bond (of Illinois),
    Martha E. Bond (minor), Margaret L. Bond (minor).
    Sarah A. Bond (minor), Thomas J. Bond (minor),
    John B. Bond (minor), & Edward W. Bond (minor).
    Willis G. Jones is the guardian of the above
    mentioned minors. They are all owners of a tract
    of land (about 11 acres) derived from a deceased
    aunt's estate. The land was formerly owned by
    Nelson Lavender & others. The above named heirs
    are dependent on their weakly sickly mother for
    support. They want to sell the land.

P. 147 WILLIAM P. SMITH, Admr. & C
              Feb. 1854   Exparte
    William P. Smith is Admr. of the estate of Luke
    L. Smith. Luke L. Smith left a slave & he does
    not have sufficient funds to settle his estate.
    William P. Smith wants the slave sold.

126

P. 148 JOHN A. JORDAN & WIFE & Als
           Feb. 1854   Exparte
The Petitioners are: John A. Jordan, Myra P.
Jordan, Sophia A. Overall, & Mary J. Overall.
Sophia A. & Mary J. Overall's guardian is
John A. Jordan. Myra P. Jordan married
Jackson M. Overall. Jackson M. Overall
died leaving a widow, Myra P. & children.
He left the following children: Sophia A.
& Mary J. Overall. Myra P. Overall, his
widow, has now married John A. Jordan. The
Petitioners want a division of the slaves.

P. 150 REBECCA L. BOSTIC, Exrx. & C
           April 1854   Exparte
Richard W. H. Bostic died 14 Oct. 1853.
He left a will naming Rebecca L. Bostic,
Exrx. She wants to sell the slaves.
(Copy of Will - does not give the names
 of the children.)

P. 155 JAMES P. MAURY, Et Al
           June 1854   Exparte
The Petitioners are:
    1. James P. Maury
    2. Micajah G. L. Claiborne
    3. Nicholas E. Perkins & Martha T.,
        his wife
    4. William S. Reid & Sally C., his wife
    5. Abram P. Maury (infant)
    6. Septimia Maury (infant)
    7. Ferdinand C. Maury (infant)
Micajah G. L. Claiborne is guardian to the
above mentioned infants. Abram P. Maury
died July 1848. He left a widow, Mary E.
T. Maury. He left the following children:
Martha T., Sally C., Abram P., Septimia,
Ferdinand C., Josephine Maury, Octavia
Maury, & Elizabeth J. Maury. James P.
Maury is Exr. of the estate. Abram P. Maury,
deceased, left 775 acres of land. Josephine
Maury died June 1850 intestate. She was
unmarried & without issue. She left her
mother, brothers, & sisters. James P. Maury
was appointed Admr. Octavia Maury died Sept.
1851 intestate. She was unmarried & without
issue. She left her mother, brothers & sisters.
James P. Maury was appointed Admr. Mary E. T. Mar
died Aug. 1852 & she left a will. Elizabeth J.
Maury died in Jan. 1853 & she left a will.
The Petitioners want a division. (Copy of
Will of Abram P. Maury & Mary E. T. Maury.)

P. 185 JAMES P. MAURY & Als.
                May 1854   Exparte
Elizabeth J. Maury died in 1853. She left a
will naming James P. Maury, Exr. She left
the following heirs:
        1. James P. Maury
        2. Nicholas E. Perkins & Martha T.,
            his wife
        3. William S. Reid & Sarah C., his wife
        4. Abram P. Maury
        5. Septemia Maury
        6. Ferdinand C. Maury
Abram P. Maury, Septemia Maury, & Ferdinand C.
Maury petition by their guardian, Micajah G.
L. Claiborne.

P. 187 REBECCA L. BOSTICK, Exc.
                July 1854   Exparte
Rebecca L. Bostick is the Exr. of Richard W.
H. Bostick, deceased. She must sell the other
slaves to pay off the debts.

P. 189 HENRY B. BICKLE & Als.
                July 1854   Exparte
The Petitioners are:
        1. Henry B. Bickle & Elizabeth, his wife
        2. C. C. Cheatham & Bethenia, his wife
        3. Bettie Reid (infant whose guardian is
            William L. Reid)
The above mentioned are owners of a tract of
land on the waters of the West Harpeth River.
The land contains about 27 acres.

P. 191 THEOPHILUS MERRITT, Admr.
                Sept. 1854   Exparte
Theophilus Merritt is Admr. of Shimmy Merritt,
who died in 1854. Shimmy Merritt, deceased,
left the following children: Theophilus,
James, Lucinda, & Elizabeth York. Shimmy
Merritt, deceased, left a negro.

P. 193 SUSAN MONTGOMERY
                Nov. 1854   Exparte
Cyrus Montgomery died June 1854 intestate.
He left Susan Montgomery, his widow. He left
George Montgomery & Martha Montgomery, his
children. He left a tract of land containing
500 or 600 acres. Susan, his widow, wants
her dower.

128

P. 196 FRANCIS M. LAVENDER
            Nov. 1854   Exparte
Cyrup Montgomery died intestate. He left a widow,
Susan Montgomery. He left the following
children: Minerva, George, & Martha Montgomery.
Francis M. Lavender was appointed Admr. Lavender
feels that it is necessary to sell the land to
give the widow her dower & to settle the estate.

P. 198 JAMES W. STARNES & PARTHENIA N. TULLOSS
            Nov. 1854   Exparte
Robert C. Tulloss died intestate. He left a
widow, Parthenia N. Tulloss. She is his only
heir. James W. Starnes was appointed Admr.
They want to sell the slaves to pay off the
debts.

P. 200 PHILIP B. HALEY & Als.
            Nov. 1854   Exparte
The Petitioners are:
        1.   Philip B. Haley & Sallie N., his wife
             (both are minors. Philip's guardian
             is John Haley & Sallie's guardian is
             John D. Bennett.)
        2.   Josephus H. Conn & Mary, his wife
        3.   Nicholas G. Conn (minor whose guardian
             is Josephus Conn)
Theodrick Carter died in 1837 intestate. He
left a widow, Mary Carter. Mary married
Josephus H. Conn in 1840. Sallie N. Carter
married Philip B. Haley. Theodrick Carter,
deceased, left the following children:
        1.   Sallie N. Carter Haley
        2.   Newton Carter (a minor who died
             intestate in 1844)
Nicholas G. Conn was born in 1843. He is the
son of Mary & Josephus Conn. Theodrick Carter,
deceased, owned a tract of land 1 1/2 miles
west of Franklin on the public road to
Hillsborough.

P. 204 JOHN ROBERTS, Admr. & C - pl. vs FRANCES SHEGOG,
Et Al - def.   Nov. 1854
James Shegog died intestate in 1853. He left
a widow, Frances Shegog. He left the following
children: James W., Phoebe M., Heloise, &
Arthur Shegog. The children are all infants &
without guardian. John Roberts was appointed
Admr. The estate is insolvent. James Shegog,
deceased, owned 2 lots in Nolensville & 2 1/2
acre lots in Nolensville.

P. 207 HENRY KING, Et Al
                Nov. 1854   Exparte
Jeremiah Ezell died & left a will. He left a
widow, Rosanna D., who married Henry King.
Jeremiah Ezell, deceased, left the following
children: William, Nathan, Eliza, Ann,
Jeremiah, John E., & Mary Ezell. Charles
Sweeney is guardian to all of the children.
Jeremiah Ezell, deceased, had a tract of land
containing about 40 acres. Part of Will:
        Land that I bought from P. Cannon
        to my wife during her widowhood -
        also interest in my father's
        estate.
Rosanna D., the widow, wants her part of the land.

P. 209 CHARLES F. WALL, Admr. & C
                Dec. 1854   Exparte
John Wall died intestate May 1854. He left
the following heirs: Charles F. Wall, Christina
H. Boyd (wife of William A. Boyd), Braxton
J. Wall, & Sarah Wall. Charles F. Wall, Admr.
of John Wall's estate wants to sell the slaves.

P. 211 CHARLES W. SMITHSON, Admr. & C
                Dec. 1854   Exparte
Martha Smithson is deceased. Charles W. Smithson
was appointed Admr. of the estate. Martha
was his wife. Martha Smithson's heirs are:
        1. Moses G. Gocey & Mary, his wife
        2. John Nevils & Robert B. Beech, trustee
        3. Josiah W. Nevils (minor who has no guardian)
        4. Virginia Nevils (minor who has no guardian)
        5. Tennessee Nevils (minor who has no guardian)
Charles W. Smithson, Admr. & C wants to sell
  the slaves.

P. 215 JACOB J. MORTON & OTHERS
                Dec. 1854   Exparte
Susan Morton died 20 Aug. 1854 intestate. She
left the following children: Jacob J., Abram
W., William J. A. Morton, & Alexander S.
Strong & Lavinia E., his wife. Jacob J. Morton
is Admr. of the estate. They want to sell
the slaves.

P. 217 VIRGINIA F. BATEMAN, By & C
                Dec. 1854   Exparte
Virginia F. Bateman is an infant & petitions by
her next friend, Randal McEwing. John P.
McKay was appointed Virginia F. Bateman's
guardian & he has some of her property. She is
now 15 years old & wants to choose her
guardian. She now lives in Madison County,
                        (CONT'D)

130

P. 217 Virginia F. Bateman (CONT'D)
       Tennessee. She is living with her only sister
       & brother-in-law, William H. Mitchell. She
       plans to make that her permanent home.
       William H. Mitchell was appointed her guardian
       & John P. McKay was removed.

P. 220 HARRIET HENRY, By & C - pl. vs NATHAN OWEN - def.
                     Dec. 1854
       Harriet Henry is an infant & petitions by her
       next friend, Alexander C. Gower. William
       Henry, father of Harriet, died in 1850.
       Nathan Owen was appointed Admr. Harriet is now
       15 years old. She is now living with her
       full Aunt, who is her nearest relative in
       Tennessee. She is living with Orison Ellis &
       Mrs. Martha J. Ellis. Martha J. Ellis is her
       Aunt & they have been living in Davidson
       County for more than 1 year. Orison Ellis was
       appointed Harriet's guardian in April 1854.

P. 225 ALPHEUS TRUETT & WIFE, Et Al - pl. vs MARY
       C. MERRITT, Et Al - def.
                     Jan. 1855
       The Plaintiffs are:
            1.   Alpheus Truett & wife
            2.   Susan E. Smith
            3.   Rebecca Merritt
       The Defendants are:
            1.   Mary C. Merritt
            2.   Frances A. Merritt
            3.   Sarah Ann Merritt
       George W. Pollard is Admr. of John A. Merritt,
       deceased. The above mentioned are owners of a
       tract of land on the Hurrican Creek. It
       contains about 260 acres. John A. Merritt,
       deceased, was their father. He left slaves.

P. 222 LEANDER HUGHES, Et Al - pl. vs ARCHELUS HUGHES,
       Et Al - def.   Jan. 1855
       Leander Hughes, Letitia Dobson, Mary M.
       Buchanan, & Martha J. Nolen (all of Williamson
       County) vs. Nancy P. Dobson, William B. Dobson,
       Matthew H. Dobson, James M. Buchanan, William
       M. W. Nolen (all of Williamson County),
       Archelaus Hughes (of parts unknown), & William
       B. Dobson & wife. All of the above mentioned
       are owners of tracts of land. Letitia Dobson
       is the wife of Matthew H. Dobson. Martha J.
       Nolen is the wife of William M. W. Nolen.
       Mary M. Buchanan is the wife of James M.
       Buchanan. The tracts of land have been
       divided as follows:
                                      (CONT'D)

P. 222 Leander Hughes   (CONT'D)
     1. William B. Dobson - 1/7 part
     2. Leander Hughes - 1/7 part
     3. Matthew Dobson & wife - 1/7 part
     4. James M. Buchanan & Mary M. - 1/7 part
     5. Mary J. Nolen & William M. W. - 1/7 part
     6. Archelus Hughes - 1/7 part
     7. Letitia Dobson - 1/7 part

P. 231 GEORGE W. MORTON, Et Al
          Jan. 1855   Exparte
Sarah N. Morton is deceased. George Kidd is
the Admr. She left the following heirs:
Jane Morton, George W. Morton, Thomas K. Morton,
William S. Morton, & Sarah E. Whitsett.
George W. & Thomas K. Morton are infants &
their guardian is James C. Copeland. William S.
Morton is an infant & his guardian is William
H. Hogan. Sarah E. Whitsett is an infant & her
guardian is William A. Whitsett. The heirs
want to divide the slaves.

P. 234 RICHARD M. MATTHEWS
          Jan. 1855   Exparte
Richard M. Matthews purchased the interest of
his brother, John L. Matthews, which was in the
estate of Cornelius Matthews, deceased, Feb.
1853. George Andrews is Admr. of the estate.
John L. Matthews has moved from Tennessee & is
believed to be in Illinois.

P. 235 WILLIAM A. BAUGH, Et Al
          Jan. 1855   Exparte
The Petitioners are:
     1. William A. Baugh & Mary E., his wife
     2. Edward H. King (by his guardian,
          James King)
Elizabeth King died in 1851. She left a will
which is in Vol. 10 of Will Book. Elizabeth King,
deceased, gave to James King, her husband, 2
slaves & the remaining was to be divided among
her children. Her children are: John F. King,
Edward H. King, & Mary E. King. Mary E. King
has married William A. Baugh.

P. 237 COPELAND, OLIPHANT, & HOLMES - pl. vs JOHN B.
McEWEN - def.   Nov. 1854
Nelly (Eleanor) Pryor died in 1854. She left a
will naming James C. Copeland, Exr. The will
was contested. There was a trial as to the
validity of the will. It was appealed to the
Supreme Court. James C. Copeland wants to be
removed as the Exr., so he can be a wittness
at the trial & he wants John D. Oliphant named
in his place.   (CONT'D)

132

P. 237 Copeland, Oliphant, & Holmes   (CONT'D)
John Holmes became his security. John M. Rodgers,
one of the next of kin of Eleanor Pryor, deceased,
was the one who contested the will. The jury ruled
against the validity of the will.

P. 241 MARY T. BOSTICK, Exr.
               Feb. 1855   Exparte
John Bostick, Jr. died Feb. 1850. He left
a will. Richard W. H. Bostick was named Exr.
& he has died in Oct. 1853. Mary T. Bostick was
named Exrx. John Bostick, Jr., deceased, has
3 young children. The estate has some large
debts & some slaves must be sold.

P. 244 BARBARA INMAN - pl. vs ADELINE PEWITT, Et Al -
       def.   Feb. 1854
Barbara Inman was the wife of Joseph Pewitt
who died Sept. 184_ intestate. Wiley B. White
was named Admr. Joseph Pewitt left a widow &
following children as his heirs:
          1.   Barbara (widow)
          2.   Catherine (she married Givens)
          3.   Adeline
          4.   William M. Pewitt
          5.   Minerva Pewitt
          6.   Polly Pewitt
Joseph Pewitt, deceased, left 2 tracts of
land on the waters of the South Harpeth. One
tract contains 195 acres & the other tract
50 acres. Barbara, the widow, wants her dower.

P. 246 JOSEPH H. HAMPTON
               Feb. 1855   Exparte
Rufus S. Hampton died in 1853 intestate. He
was unmarried. Joseph H. Hampton was appointed
Admr. Rufus S. Hampton, deceased, left as his
heirs his brothers, sisters, nephews & neices,
who are entitled to his estate. Rufus S.,
deceased, left a slave.

P. 248 DANIEL BAUGH, Admr. & C - pl. vs WILLIAM E.
       McGEE, Et Al - def.
               March 1855
Anthony H. McGee died in 1853 intestate in
the state of Louisiana. He left the following
heirs:
          1.   William E. McGee
          2.   John R. McGee of Hickman County, Tenn.
          3.   James Wood & Mary A. C., his wife
          4.   Newman L. Bennett & Cena O. F., his wife
          5.   Joseph A. Bennett & Martha S., his wife
          6.   Thomas S. Watkins & Henry C. Watkins
               (They are the children of   (CONT'D)

P. 248   Anthony H. McGee, deceased   (CONT'D)
         Sally J. Watkins, who is deceased.)
Anthony H. McGee, deceased, owned 1/7 part of
a tract of land containing 250 acres. The land
must be sold to pay the debts.

P. 251 DAVID C. KINNARD, Et Al
              March 1855   Exparte
Richard Ogilvie died July 1822. He left a will.
William S. Webb & William Allison, Jr. are the
Exrs. Richard Ogilvie, deceased, left a
widow, Cynthia M., who died 18 Nov. 1853.
They left the following children: Sarah T.
Kinnard, Richard H. Ogilvie, William H. Ogilvie,
James S. Ogilvie, Jason W. Ogilvie (he has since
died intestate), Elizabeth Ogilvie (she married
Ephraim H. McLeon & she has died), & Mary
Ogilvie (she died unmarried more than 20 years
ago). The Petitioners want to divide the slaves.

P. 253 GUSTAVUS HOLLAND, Et Al
              March 1855   Exparte
The Petitioners are: Gustavus Holland, Franklin
A. Holland, & Mary O. Owen. Franklin A. Holland
& Mary O. Owen are minors & their guardian is
Alexander M. Gray. They are all the owners of
slaves & 2 tracts of land. One tract of land
was conveyed to the late John A. Holland by
deed by Frank Hardeman & his wife. It was
dated Dec. 1840 & contained 110 3/4 acres of
land. The other tract of land is located on
Mill Creek. Gustavus is of age & wants his
1/3 part of the property.

P. 257 ANDREW ERVIN & WIFE, Et Al - pl. vs PARTHENIA
        GILES - def.
              April 1855
The heirs are:
    1. ANDREW ERVIN & ELIZABETH, his wife
    2. James Robinson & Parthenia, his wife
    3. David Evans of the state of Mississippi
    4. Duncel Evans of the state of Mississippi
    5. Jonathan Evans of the state of Kentucky
Parthenia Giles is a minor & Edward E. J.
Giles is her guardian. The above mentioned
are owners of a tract of land containing 110
acres in the 22nd District on Flat Creek.
They want to sell the land for a division.

134

P. 259 JAMES H. W. JONES, Et Al
                April 1855   Exparte
The Petitioners are: James H. W. Jones, John
H. Jones, Thomas G. Jones, William R. Jones,
& Andrew J. Jones. Thomas G., William R.,
& Andrew J. Jones are minors & William M.
Nunn is their guardian. The Petitioners are
owners of a tract of land containing 318
acres. They want to sell the land so they
can each have their share.

P. 263 WILLIAM C. BIZZELL, Admr. & NANCY BIZZELL -
pl. vs SARAH JANE BIZZELL - def.
James Bizzell died (last) 6 Feb. 1855
intestate. He left a widow, Nancy. He
left the following children: William C.,
Sarah Jane, Elisha A., Alfred G., Susan S.,
Ann E., Nancy A., Ardella, Eveline, & James
O. Bizzell. William C. Bizzell is the Admr.
James Bizzell, deceased, owned 2 tracts of
land. One tract contained about 48 1/2
acres on Grove Creek. The other tract
contained about 162 acres on Duck River
Ridge. The widow, Nancy, wants a dower &
the remainder must be sold to pay the debts.

P. 268 JOSEPH A. C. SCALES - pl. vs WILLIAM T. &
ROBERT S. SCALES - def.
William G. Scales died. His widow, Elizabeth
Scales married _____ Jackson. William G.
Scales, deceased, left the following
children: Joseph A. C. Scales, William T.
Scales (a minor without a guardian), &
Robert S. Scales (a minor without a
guardian). William G. Scales, deceased, had
2 lots in Eagleville. The Petitioner wants
the lots sold. Elizabeth, the widow,
relinquished her right.

P. 270 BRICE M. HUGHES, Et Al
                Aug. 1855   Exparte
Samuel A. Hughes, deceased, was joint owner
of some slaves. He had children. They are:
Brice M., John L., & Samuel H. Hughes. John
L. & Samuel H. Hughes are minors. Brice M.
Hughes, Sr. is their guardian.

P. 274 JOHN R. CARTER, Et Al - pl. vs COLEMAN F.
CARTER, Et Al - def.
                Sept. 1855
Sarah Carter died Jan. 1852. She left a
non-cupative will. John R. Carter was
made Admr.   (CONT'D)

P. 274 Sarah Carter, deceased (CONT'D)
Sarah Carter, deceased, left the following heirs:
1. John R. Carter
2. James G. Carter
3. William F. Carter
4. Mary (she married Thomas Polmore)
5. Sarah (she married Pleasant R. Brin)
6. Coleman F. Carter
7. Ruth (she married James H. Glenn)
Sarah Brin & Ruth Glenn are the daughters of Jane
Christopher who was the daughter of Sarah
Carter, deceased. Sarah Ann Elizabeth Glenn
was the only heir of Sarah Elizabeth Glenn
who was another deceased daughter of Sarah Carter,
deceased. The estate of Sarah Carter, deceased,
was to be divided into 7 shares. Sarah Carter,
deceased, was the Admrx. of Richard Carter,
deceased. Richard Carter died in 1815 or 1816.
He left a widow & 8 children. He died
intestate. His children were: John R. Carter,
William F. Carter, Richard D. Carter, James G.
Carter, Coleman F. Carter, Sarah Ann Elizabeth
Carter, Mary R. Carter, & Jane Carter. Sarah
Christopher & Ruth Christopher are minor
children of Jane Christopher, deceased. Jane
Christopher was formerly Jane Carter. Sarah &
Ruth Christopher's guardian is Richard D. Carter.
Sarah Carter, deceased, being old & somewhat
infirm gave her rights in property to her
children. (Copy of Nuncupative Will). Article
of Agreement executed 24 July 1838 by Sarah
Carter & her children then living. Sarah Carter
left a tract of land in the 14th District. The
tract contained 120 acres.

P. 287 MARGARET PROWELL
            Nov. 1855   Petition for Dower
Thomas Prowell died & left a widow, Margaret.
He left the following children: Andrew, Jan,
Elizabeth, Thomas, Eleanor R., Mary Agnes, &
Kissa Prowell. He left a tract of land on Lick
Creek containing 100 acres.

P. 289 SARAH J. RASH
            Nov. 1855   Petition for Dower
Stephen H. Rash died Aug. 1855 intestate. He left
a widow, Sarah J. He left the following children:
Samuel Robert, Mary Scales, Sarah Morton, &
Gustavus Henry Rash. He left a tract of land on
Mill Creek in the 16th District containing 167
acres. He also left a tract of land on Mill Creek
in the 7th & 8th District of Davidson County which
contains about 15 acres. Thomas Holt is the Admr.

P. 294 JULIA COLEMAN & C
           Dec. 1855   Exparte
The Petitioners are: ____ Coleman & Julia,
his wife, John Jones, J. H. W. Jones, Thomas
Jones (minor), William Jones (minor), &
Jackson Jones (minor). William M. Nunn is
guardian of the above mentioned children who
are minors. Oratrix is the widow of ____
Jones. ____ Jones left the following
children: John, J. H. W., Thomas, William,
& Jackson Jones. He also left a tract of
land containing 70 acres. The Petitioners
want a dower.

P. 296 TILMAN F. ATKINSON, Et Al
           Dec. 1855   Exparte
Franklin B. Haynes died intestate in 1854.
He left a widow, Nancy J. Haynes. He
left a child, Tilman Haynes. They want
to sell the slave.

P. 297 SAMUEL SPRATT & JAMES S. WILLIAMS, Admrs. -
       pl. v.s PARALLEE LAVENDER & OTHERS - def.
               Nov. 1855
Anthony Lavender died intestate. He left
a widow, Parallee. He left the following
children: Poindexter, Virginia, Delilah,
Richard, Gustavus, Tennessee, Anthony C.,
& Emaline Lavender. Anthony Lavender,
deceased, left a tract of land containing
17 acres. It is located about 1 mile
from the home tract. The Petitioners
want to sell this tract of land & the
negroes to pay off the debts of the estate.

P. 300 JOHN W. ALEXANDER, Et Al
           June 1856   Exparte
The Petitioners are: James W. Williams,
John W. Alexander, & Price Williams.
Price Williams is an idiot & petitions
by his guardian, James S. Williams. They
own land in the 11th District containing
207 acres. John W. Alexander is entitled
to 1/2 of the land. James W. & Price
Williams are entitled to 1/4 of the land
each.

P. 303 THOMAS P. DITTO
           July 1856   Exparte
Thomas P. Ditto is guardian to Martha A.
E. Vaughan, an orphan who resides with him.
Thomas P. Ditto has moved to Madison
County & Martha has moved there to. He
has his bond in Madison County.

P. 304 RACHEL BROWN - pl. vs JOHN T. HARRIS - def.
           April 1856
        Rachel Brown is the widow of William Brown, who
        died March 1856 intestate. He left the following
        heirs:
             1. Margaret Nolen of Maury County
             2. John Brown of Lauderdale County
             3. Ann Homer of Alabama
             4. Sophronia Ann
             5. Melissa E.
             6. Nancy T.
             7. Margaret
             8. William J.
             9. Frances Black
            10. John Brown Harris
        The last 6 are minors without a guardian & they
        live in Marshall County, Tennessee.
            11. James Brown of Kentucky
            12. Elizabeth P. Neal of Marshall County,
                 Tennessee.
        William Brown, deceased, left land on Mill Creek
        containing 120 acres. Rachel Brown, the widow,
        wants her dower.

P. 307 THE STATE OF TENNESSEE - pl. vs ALBERT LOFTIN - def.
           Aug. 1856
        Albert Lofton, a free boy of color was bound
        as an apprentice some years ago by the Williamson
        County Court. He is now 21 years old. From
        imbecility of mind he is unable to manage his
        affairs & he is entitled to an estate of $25. He
        is indebted to William A. Rodgers.

P. 308 REBECCA T. DAVIS - pl. vs THOMAS B. BOND, Et Al -
        def.   June 1856
        Rebecca T. Davis vs Thomas B. Bond, Thomas Oden
        & Rebecca, his wife, Robert McAlister &
        Caledonia, his wife, Martin T. Chairs of Maury
        County, Tennessee, & _____ Sutton & Virginia, his
        wife of Mississippi. Sterling Davis died 15 April
        1856. He left a will. He left a widow, Rebecca
        T. Davis. He left the following children:
        Virginia Sutton & Caledonia A. He left a
        grandchild, Rebecca Oden. Thomas B. Bond is the
        Exr. Sterling Davis, deceased, left several
        tracts of land. One tract contained 150 acres.
        One tract contained 50 acres. One tract contained
        140 acres. Rebecca T. Davis, his widow, wants
        a dower of the land.

138

P. 313 MINERVA T. JOHNSON - pl. vs WILLIAM T. JOHNSON &
OTHERS - def.
Oct. 1856
Joshua Johnson died in 1856 intestate. He left a
widow, Minerva T. Johnson. He left the following
children: William S., James M., Martha E. R.,
John F., Joshua M., & Alabama M. Johnson. Chesley
Williams was appointed Admr. The children are
minors & have no guardian. Joshua Johnson,
deceased, left a tract of land containing
about 112 acres. He purchased the land from
Peter C. Scales dated 11 May 1842. He also owned
a tract of land containing 148 acres which was
conveyed by David C. Kinnard dated 10 May 1842.
He had another tract of land containing 72
acres which was purchased from R. W.
Calhoun & Cathy. He had another tract of land
that contained 50 acres which was purchased
from William R. Nunn. Joshua Johnson, deceased,
also had the following:
1. Tract of land purchased under a decree
of the Chancery Court of Franklin in
the case of Johnson Jordan & others vs
William Cathey, Admr., et al, dated
1845. This tract contained 216 acres.
2. Tract of land containing about 30
acres purchased from A. Waller.
3. Tract containing 80 acres purchased
from James J. Neal.
4. Tract containing 39 acres purchased
from John W. Crafton.
5. Tract containing 35 acres purchased
from John H. Haley & D. W. Haley.
Minerva T. Johnson, the widow, wants her dower.

P. 319 ESTHER FLOYD - pl. vs JOHN H. FLOYD - def.
Sept. 1856
Jones Floyd died 22 July 1856 intestate. He
left a widow, Esther Floyd. He left the
following children: John H. Floyd, William
W. Floyd, Sarah Jane Kelly, Jones T. Floyd,
Charles A. Floyd, Drury A. Floyd, Richard N.
Floyd, Lundy H. Floyd, Nancy L. Floyd, &
Zachary T. Floyd. He left the following
grandchildren: John M. Floyd, William Floyd,
& James Floyd. They are the children of his
deceased son, James H. Floyd. John H.
Floyd is the Admr. Jones Floyd, deceased,
had a tract of land containing about 314 acres.
He also had 2 tracts of land in Bedford County
containing about 207 acres. His widow,
Esther Floyd, wants her dower.

P. 324 WILLIAM PARRISH, Admr. & Et Al
        Oct. 1856   Exparte
Gabriel H. Kinnard a minor orphan died 15 April
1856. William Parrish was named Admr. Gabriel
H. Kinnard, deceased, was part owner of some
slaves with Newton C., Adeline E., & Frances V.
Kinnard, who are minors & William Parrish is
their guardian.

P. 327 SAMUEL HENDERSON & B. F. ROBERTS - pl. vs
FRANKLIN HARDEMAN - def.
        Dec. 1856
Samuel Henderson & B. F. Roberts are securities
of Franklin Hardeman in the bond given by him
as the guardian of Thomasella Hardeman. They
wish to be removed as securities.

P. 328 GEORGE M. MORTON & OTHERS
        Nov. 1856   Exparte
George Morton & Thomas Morton are minors & their
guardian is James C. Copeland. Samuel C. Morton
died. He left a will. George wants his share
of the property since he has reached the age of
19 as stated in the will.

P. 331 MINERVA T. JOHNSON, Et Al - pl. vs CHESLEY
WILLIAMS - def.
        Dec. 1856
Joshua Johnson died in 1856 intestate. He left
a widow, Minerva T. Johnson. He left the
following children: William F., James M.,
Joshua M., Martha E., Alabama M., & John F.
Johnson. The children are all minors & their
 guardian is Minos C. Jordan. Joshua Johnson,
deceased, left slaves & the land descended to
his said children.

P. 339 MARY W. BUFORD, Et Als
        Dec. 1856   Exparte
Robert W. Buford died July 1852. He left a widow,
Mary W. Buford. He left an only child, Henrietta
A. Samuel F. Glass, Jr. was appointed Admr.
Henrietta A. married James C. Morton. The
Petitioners want to divide the slaves.

P. 342 EDWARD C. COOK & OTHERS
        Dec. 1856   Exparte
Richard D. Cook died intestate as a minor on
3 Jan. 1855. He left the following brothers:
Edmund C., Philip H., Nicholas P., & John T.
Cook. Philip H. Cook is the Admr. The
brothers want a division of the slaves.

140

P. 346 REBECCA WARREN, By & C
              Jan. 1857   Exparte
       Rebecca Warren, a minor child of Drury Warren,
       deceased, is now living in Maury County with
       her uncle, Franklin A. Polk, who is now her
       guardian. She wants Beverly B. Toon removed
       as her guardian & her money to go to Polk.

P. 349 ABRAM P. MAURY, Et Al - pl. vs JAMES P. MAURY,
       Et Al - def.   Dec. 1856
       Abram P. Maury died 22 July 1848. He left a
       will. Mary E. T. Maury & James P. Maury
       were named Exrs. Mary E. T. Maury has died.
        He left the following children: Martha T.,
       Sally C., Josephine, Elizabeth J., Octavia,
       Abram P. (infant whose guardian is Micajah
       G. T. Claiborne), Septimia (infant whose
       guardian is Micajah G. T. Claiborne), &
       Ferdinand C. Maury (infant whose guardian
       is Micajah.G. T. Claiborne). Elizabeth
       J. Maury, sister, is dead. Abram P. Maury,
       deceased, left 384 acres of land. He
       left slaves & property.

P. 366 CLEMENT W. WADE, Et Al
              Nov. 1856   Exparte
       The Petitioners are: Clement W., Thomas B.,
       Lucy D., Martha A., & John F. Wade. Their
       guardian is Henry P. Wade. They are joint
       owners of a tract of land containing about
       275 acres. They are also owners of slaves.
       Clement W. Wade has reached 21 years of age
       & wants a division.

P. 373 BENJAMIN F. GLEAVES, Et Als - pl. vs ROBERT
       J. WILSON - def.   April 1857
       Richard Herbert died in 1834. He left a
       will. Will stated: to my grandson, Charles
       Casson Wilson & my granddaughter, Rebecca
       Wilson, children of my daughter Eliza Wilson.
       Son, Robert N. Herbert - land on Lick Creek
       of Duck River. Ruth Gleaves had her name
       changed from Rebecca Wilson (Rebecca to
       Ruth) & she has married Benjamin F. Gleaves
       in 1855. Charles Casson Wilson died 10
       Oct. 1842 in the Republic of Texas leaving
       surviving him his father, Samuel D. Wilson,
       & his sisters, Ruth Gleaves & Catherine M.
       Wilson. Brothers - Robert J. Wilson. Eliza
       Wilson, his mother, died 1 Sept. 1842. The
       Petitioners want a division of the negroes &
       400 acres of land. Samuel D. Wilson died
       in 1855. He left a will. (Will of Samuel
       D. Wilson) Daughter - Ruth.   (CONT'D)

P. 373   Richard Herbert, deceased   (CONT'D)
         Father-in-law - Richard Herbert. Ruth's
         grandfather, James H. Wilson, deceased.

P. 385   WILLIAM L. BUFORD & WIFE - pl. vs HEIRS OF
         ELDRIDGE CLAUD - def.
                   April 1857
         Philip Claud died in 184_. He left a will.
         Eldridge Claud was an heir of Philip Claud,
         deceased. Eldridge Claud died intestate in
         Arkansas. Nancy K. Buford, widow of Eldridge
         Claud, deceased, was appointed Admr. Francis
         Claud is the Exr. of Philip Cloud. The clerk
         made a mistake in the settlement of Philip
         Claud's estate as he thought Eldridge Cloud
         died before Philip Cloud.

P. 388   BENJAMIN F. GLEAVES, Et Al - pl. vs ROBERT
         JAMES WILSON, Et Al - def.
                   March 1857
         Samuel D. Wilson died in 1855. He left a will.
         He left 3 children: Ruth Gleaves, Catherine M.
         Wilson, & Robert James Wilson. Robert James
         Wilson is a minor & he has no guardian. James
         H. Wilson & Robert N. Herbert were named Exrs.
         They renounded the execution. Thomas Holt is now
         the Exr. Ruth Wilson married Benjamin F. Gleaves
         in 1855. Charles C. Wilson died intestate &
         he was the grandson of Richard Herbert & also
         the grandfather of Ruth. He left land & slaves
         to them. (Copy of Will of Samuel D. Wilson)
         Father-in-law - Richard Herbert. Father gave
         slave Harriet to his daughter, Ruth. Brother -
         James H. Wilson, Exr. The will was dated 22
         Nov. 1846. Codicil - Having sold the land in
         Texas - Gaudaloupe County - to Mildred T.
         Littlefield. Exr. to sell remainder of land
         in Texas.

P. 392   JOSEPH T. MANSON, Et Al - pl. vs ANN E. ORGAN,
         Et Al - def.   May 1857
         Joseph T. Manson of Wilson County, Tennessee.
         James E. Manson of Rutherford County, Tennessee.
         vs ANN E. Organ, Virginia A. Organ, Mary C.
         Organ, James M. Organ, Edward M. Neal, James
         Neal, Nancy M. Neal, Elizabeth Neal, Lucy B.
         Owen. Ann E. Organ is a non-resident. Edward
         M., James, Nancy M., & Elizabeth Neal are of
         Wilson County. Lucy B. Owen is of Williamson
         County. All of the above mentioned are minors
         & have no guardian. Nancy W. Manson died Jan.
         1857. She left a will. She left slaves. The
         Petitioners want a division made. Randal M.
         Ewing was appointed guardian of the minors.

142

P. 396 MATTHEW WILSON
              Nov. 1857   Exparte
     Matthew Wilson bought 38 1/2 acres of land
     sold by William C. Bizzell, Admr. of James
     Bizzell, deceased. The land was sold at
     a public sale in 1855. William C. Bizzell,
     Admr. & Nancy Bizzell vs Sarah Jane Bizzell.
     The clerk figured the price wrong.

P. 398 SAMUEL S. STARNES, Et Al
              Jan. 1858   Exparte
     Samuel S. Starnes, John D. Starnes, &
     Ebenezer Starnes are owners of slaves.
     Samuel S. Starnes has reached the age of 21
     & he wants his part of the slaves. J. W.
     Starnes is guardian of the minors.

P. 401 FRANK A. HOLLAND - pl. vs MARY O. PRICE,
     Als - def.   Jan. 1858
     James T. Price & his wife, Mary O. Price,
     are both minors. His guardian is James
     H. Tompkins. Her guardian is Alexander M.
     Gray. The Petitioner wants a division of
     the slaves.

P. 403 LEANDER HUGHES & OTHERS
              Feb. 1857   Exparte - Petition
     Leander Hughes & Samuel C. Hughes are owners
     of 2 slaves. Leander has reached the age
     of 21.

P. 405 JAMES E. OWEN, Et Al
              Jan. 1858   Exparte
     James E. Owen, Littleberry R. Owen, & Susan
     F. Owen own slaves & they want a division.
     Littleberry R. & Susan F. Owen are minors
     & their guardian is Franklin A. Burke. James
     E. has reached the age of 21.

P. 406 JAMES T. SHANNON, Petitioner
              Sept. 1857   Exparte
     John Roberts, Ad & C vs Francis Shegog
     Case: A tract of land was sold. Cyrus S.
            Bittick & Benjamin H. Saddler purchased
            the land. It was ordered that the title
            to said lots be vested in the said
            Bittick & Saddler & deeds be executed
            to them upon the payment of purchase
            money.
     The Petitioner became the purchaser at second
     hand from them of said land. He had paid the
     clerk of this Court the entire purchase money
     & he holds the written assignment of Bittick
     & Saddler to him of all right & claim. (CONT'D)

P. 406 James T. Shannon (CONT'D)
        The Petitioner wants the deed to them be set
        aside & made directly to him.

P. 409 JOHN W. EVANS & OTHERS
                Oct. 1858   Exparte
        John W. Evans, Henry D. Evans, Fannie H. Evans,
        Thomas Evans, Alley Evans, & George Evans are
        residents of the state of Missouri (Saline
        County). George Evans is an infant & he sues
        by his friend, Randal M. Ewing. The above mentioned
        moved to Missouri after the death of their
        father, John W. Evans, who died in Williamson
        County intestate. Thomas Brown was appointed
        Admr. Their grandfather also has died & he left
        the estate that they are heirs to. Their mother
        has married John Demoss, who they live with.

P. 411 THE STATE OF TENNESSEE - pl. vs HENRY S.
        BATEMAN - def.   Feb. 1857
        Henry S. Bateman is an idiot. He is the owner
        of an estate & is not capable of managing it.
        He owns 5 or 6 lots in Franklin & one building
        formerly occupied by Bateman's Grocery on
        Main St. He also owns land in the 14th District.
        He has a small interest in it. Isaac L.
        Vaughn was appointed his guardian. Witnesses
        have declared Henry S. Bateman has fully restored
        to his right mind & they want the guardian
        removed.

P. 414 GEORGE W. BOYD, Et Al
                Jan. 1858   Exparte
        George W. Boyd & Abner Boyd are minors & their
        guardian is George Andrews. They are owners of
        slaves. George W. Boyd became 21 on 29 April
        next & he will be home on or by the 1st day of
        Jan. 1858. He does not want the slaves hired
        out for the following year so he may have his
        share.

P. 416 MINERVA O. RALSTON - pl. vs RICHARD C. OWENS,
        Et Al - def.   Nov. 1857
        Robert Ralston died 1 Aug. 1857 intestate. He
        left a widow, Minerva. He left the following
        children: William, Josephus, Mary C., David
        J., & Susannah L. Ralston. They are all minors
        & have no guardian. Richard C. Owens is the
        Admr. Robert Ralston, deceased, left 2 tracts
        of land on the waters of the Big Harpeth in
        the 23rd District. One tract contains 58 acres
        & the other tract contains about 27 acres.
        The widow, Minerva, wants her dower.

144

P. 420 BETHENIA J. McLEMORE & OTHERS
                Jan. 1858   Exparte
        Bethenia J. McLemore, Elizabeth M., & Lemuel
        P. McLemore are owners of slaves. Elizabeth
        M. & Lemuel P. McLemore are minors & their
        guardian is Robert A. McLemore. Bethenia has
        reached the age of 21 & she wants her share.

P. 423 HENRY P. FOWLKES - pl. vs WILLIAM CUMMINS,
        Et Al - def.   Jan. 1858
        Henry P. Fowlkes is a minor & he sues by his
        guardian, Gabriel B. Fowlkes of Maury County,
        Tennessee. William Cummins is Admr. of the
        estate of Nancy J. Fowlkes, deceased. Henry
        P. Fowlkes, William Cummins & Susan A., his
        wife, are owners of slaves. Each get 1/3
        part & they want a division made.

P. 426 VIRGINIA C. JORDAN, By & C - pl. vs WILLIAM
        A. MARSHALL, Admr. - def.
                Jan. 1858
        Virginia C. Jordan is a minor & sues by her
        friend, John E. Drongoole. William A.
        Marshall is Admr. of Gilbert Marshall's
        estate. Gilbert Marshall was the guardian
        of Virginia C. Jordan. She is now living
        in Rutherford County & has been under her
        new guardian, John E. Drongoole.

P. 430 JAMES T. BOYD, Et Al
                Feb. 1858   Exparte
        James T. Boyd, Washington T. Boyd, & Mary
        V. Boyd are owners of 4 slaves. They are
        all minors & their guardian is D. R. Crutcher.

P. 432 WILKINS WHITFIELD & WIFE - pl. vs THOMAS M.
        RIDLEY & OTHERS - def.
                Feb. 1858
        William B. Ridley died intestate. Wilkins
        Whitfield & Elizabeth, his wife, of Cheatham
        County vs Thomas M. Ridley, George R. Ridley,
        Francis M. Williams & Sarah, his wife, &
        George Alston, a minor with no guardian.
        They are all joint owners of a tract of land on
        the waters of Hays Creek bounded by Frederick
        Davis. The land contains 100 acres. William
        B. Ridley has departed this life intestate
        & his interest was sold to George B. Ridley.
        The Petitioners want sale of the land & a
        division made.

P. 438   JOHN W. JACKSON, By & C - pl. vs ISAAC IVY - def.
              Dec. 1857
John W. Jackson a minor, sues by his friend,
Washington G. Smith. Westly Jackson died 14
Oct. 1854. He left a will. He was the father
of John W. Jackson, who is now 16 years old
& wants to select his own guardian. Isaac Ivy
is now his guardian & he is not John W.'s choice.
John W. Jackson wants Washington G. Smith made
his guardian.

P. 443   DAVID SAYERS, Admr. & C.
              April 1857   Exparte
David Sayers is the Admr. of Robert A. Sayers
estate. He finds the estate insolvent. There
is 1 slave belonging to the estate named Peter.
David Sayers wants to sell him to help pay the
expenses.

P. 444   MARGARET WATSON - pl. vs JOHN L. HOUSE, Admr.
& Et Al - def.   Jan. 1858
Beverly O. Watson died 17 May 1857 intestate.
He left a widow, Margaret Watson. He left the
following children: Augustus, Elizabeth A.,
Marietta S., Eva, Laura, Maggie Oscar, John,
Jennie, Ida, Starneton, & Florence Watson.
The children are infants & their guardian is
William M. Wright. John L. House is the Admr.
Beverly O. Watson, deceased, left a tract of land
containing 640 acres. Margaret, his widow,
wants her dower.

P. 449   THE STATE OF TENNESSEE - pl. vs FRANCIS M.
CARSEY - def.   June 1857
Francis M. Carsey is of unsound mind & not
capable of managing his own affairs. Eli A.
Walters is his guardian.

P. 451   JOHN W. BUFORD, Et Al
              Dec. 1857   Exparte
The Petitioners are: John W. Buford, James A.
Buford, Thomas S. Buford, Spencer Buford, &
Sarah E. Buford. The last 4 are minors & their
guardian is Obadiah Fitzgerald. Spencer Buford,
their father, died in 1845. He left a will.
He left his widow, Mary Buford & 8 children.
The children are: William C., Susan T., Mary W.,
John W., James A., Thomas S., Sarah E., & Spencer
Buford. The will was probated July 1845. A
Bill of Complaint was filed in Chancery Court
for a dower & division of the 3 older children
who are: William C., Susan T., & Mary W. Buford.
The division was made. A part was set aside for
the 5 youngest children. They want a division
between them. (copy of Will)

146

P. 464 MARY CHRISWELL - pl. vs NOAH CHRISWELL, Et
Al - def.   Petition   March 1858
Laban Chriswell died in 1857. He left a will.
He left a widow, Mary Chriswell. He left the
following children: Noah, Nancy, Samuel,
Sarah, Laban, Jane, George, Emaline, Phereby,
& Joseph Chriswell. Laban Chriswell, deceased,
owned a tract of land containing 185 acres.
Mary Chriswell, his widow, wants her dower.

P. 467 WILLIAM Y. BENNETT, Et Al
          Oct. 1858   Exparte - Petition
Elizabeth Campbell died intestate. Her heirs
are the owners of slaves which is to be divided
into 9 parts. Her heirs are:
          1. William Y. Bennett
          2. Edward B. Bennett
          3. Mary W. Bennett
          4. Newman L. Bennett
          5. Marcany Carson & Thomas Carson, her
              husband
          6. Nancy D. Bennett
          7. Joseph A. Bennett
          8. Rebecca A. Steward & Andrew K.
              Stewart, her husband
William Y. Bennett is Admr. of Elizabeth
Campbell, deceased. The Petitioners want to
sell the slaves.

P. 470 JOHN H. CARMICHAEL, Admr. & C - pl. vs
       MARY J. WISENER & OTHERS - def.
          Oct. 1858   Petition
James Wisener died 17 April 1856 intestate.
John H. Carmichael is Admr. of James Wisener,
deceased. Mary Jane Wisener is the widow of
James Wisener, deceased. His children are
Margaret & James H. Wisener, both infants &
without a guardian. The Petitioner feels
  that he must sell a slave to pay the debts
& also a land warrant issue under the Act of
Congress of 3rd March 1855 for 120 acres of
land for services rendered as a soldier in
the War of 1812.

P. 475 ESTHER FLOYD, Et Als
          Oct. 1858   Exparte - Petition
Jones Floyd died 22 July 1856 intestate.
He left a widow, Esther Floyd. He left
the following children:
          1. John H. Floyd
          2. Enoch B. Kelly & Sarah Jane, his wife
          3. William W. Floyd
          4. Jones T. Floyd
          5. Charles A. Floyd   (CONT'D)

P. 475 Jones Floyd, deceased (CONT'D)
          6.   Drury A. Floyd
          7.   Richard M. Floyd
          8.   Lundy H. Floyd
          9.   Nancy T. Floyd
         10.   Zachary T. Floyd
The last 5 children are minors & their guardian
is William W. Floyd. Jones Floyd, deceased, left
3 grandchildren, who are the children of his
deceased son, James H. Floyd. The grandchildren
are: John M., William, & Jones Floyd. Their
guardian is John H. Floyd. John H. Floyd is
the Admr. of the estate. Jones Floyd, deceased,
left slaves & 304 acres of land. The Petitioners
want a division made.

P. 482 MARY RAGSDALE & OTHERS - pl. vs GEORGE W. RAGSDALE
       & OTHERS - def.   Oct. 1858
       Mary Ragsdale, Jane Ragsdale, Thomas Ragsdale &
       wife Dicy Ragsdale, William Ragsdale, & Henry
       H. Ragsdale vs George W. Ragsdale (minor), Sarah
       Jane, Martha E., & Charles W. Robinson (minors
       whose guardian is William Skelley). The above
       mentioned are children & grandchildren of Daniel
       Ragsdale. They are all owners of slaves &
       they want a division made.

P. 487 WILLIAM PARRISH, Admr. & C, Et Al
              Oct. 1858   Exparte
       The following are all owners of slaves & they
       want a division made. They are:
          1.   William Parrish, Admr. of Gabriel H.
               Kinnard
          2.   William Parrish & Susan C., his wife
          3.   Gomen G. Kinnard
          4.   Newton C. Kinnard (Minor whose guardian is
               William Parrish)
          5.   Adaline E. Kinnard (minor whose guardian
               is William Parrish)
          6.   Francis V. Kinnard (minor whose guardian
               is William Parrish)
          7.   David M. Kinnard of Maury County, Tennessee
          8.   Mercer M. Kinnard of Christian County,
               Kentucky
          9.   Mary & Michael (they are the children of
               Christopher Kinnard, deceased. Their
               guardian is William Parrish & they are
               residents of Arkansas).

148

P. 490 GILLEY M. LEWIS & WIFE, Et Al
                Feb. 1859   Exparte
        The Petitioners are:
                1. Gilly M. Lewis & Martha Jane, his wife
                2. John Osburne Crump (infant)
                3. George R. Crump (infant)
                4. Ann Maria Crump (infant)
                5. Romelia Crump (infant)
        Claiborne H. Kinnard is the guardian of the
        infants. Martha Jane will be 21 years old in
        the next year & she wants a division of the
        slaves.

P. 492 JOHN H. WILLIAMSON & MARTHA JANE WILLIAMSON -
        pl. vs RICHARD W. WILLIAMSON - def.
                Oct. 1858   Petition
        John H. & Martha Jane Williamson are minors &
        sue by their next friend, J. R. Marable.
        Richard W. Williamson was appointed guardian
        in 1851 or 1852 when they were living in
        Williamson County. They are now in Rutherford
        County & Richard W. Williamson is their
        guardian. It states that he is also their
        father. They are the heirs of Absan Glenn,
        deceased.

P. 496 LOUISA J. & WILLIAM G. HOUSE - pl. vs
        WILLIAM RAINEY - def.
                Oct. 1858   Petition
        Louisa Jane House & William G. House are
        minors & sue by their next friend, Richard
        W. Williamson. They are the heirs of George
        H. House, deceased. William Rainey was
        appointed their guardian in 1840 in
        Williamson County & in Rutherford County
        in 1858.

P. 500 WILLIAM R. STILL & WIFE - pl. vs WILLIAM
        McMURRY - def.
                March 1859   Petition
        William R. Still & wife, Mary A. Still vs
        William McMurry (minor of the state of
        Kentucky) & John M. Winstead (his general
        guardian). They are the owners of negroes
        & want a division made.

P. 502 F. G. McGAVOCK, Trustee & C, Et Al
                March 1859   Exparte - Petition
        F. Grundy McGavock is trustee for Mary
        Manoah McGavock, who is formerly Mary M.
        Bostick. John C. Bostick is trustee of
        Lucy J. Bostick, now Lucy Jordan, wife of
        Thomas Watson Jordan. R. W. H. Bostick,
                                        (CONT'D)

P. 502 F. G. McGavock (CONT'D)
former trustee for Mary M. McGavock is now deceased.
John Bostick, Jr. died leaving a will. He left
a wife, Mary T. Bostick, a tract of land
containing 753 acres & at her death it is to be
divided between his daughters, Mary M., Lucy J.
Mary T. Bostick relinquishes her claim to the
land & her daughters want a division of the land
made.

P. 508 SARAH E. ELLIS, Et Al
              March 1859   Exparte - Petition
The following are owners of a tract of land
descended to them from their ancestor, Wyatt
Ellis, deceased. The land contains about 150
acres. They want a division made of the land.
They are:
    1. Sarah E. Ellis
    2. James B. Ellis
    3. Virginia L. Ellis
    4. David S. Ellis
    5. William W. Morris(only child of Ann E.
        Morris, deceased. She was formerly Ann
        E. Ellis.)
The last 4 are minors & William C. Hunt is their
guardian.
    6. Martha J. Rash (formerly Martha J. Ellis.
        She is the wife of J. W. C. Rash. She
        is also a minor under 21 years of age
        & she petitions by her husband, J. W. C.
        Rash.)

RECORD BOOK

LAWSUITS

No. 8

1860 - 1872

P. 1   JOHN O. KIRKPATRICK, By & C - pl. vs D. M.
CRAFTON, Guardian - def.
April 1860
John O. Kirkpatrick is a minor & sues by his
next friend, Thomas H. Priest. The Petitioner
is of Maury County, Tennessee. He has
always lived with his mother who is now married
to Thomas H. Priest. He is also a resident
of Maury County. John O. Kirkpatrick wants
Thomas H. Priest to be named as his guardian.

P. 3   SANFORD G. ALLEN, Trustee & C - pl. vs SARAH
R. REAMS, Et Al - def.   May 1860
William R. Reams executed a deed of assignment
on 18 Aug. 1859, for certain real & personal
estate in trust for the benefit of Sarah F.
Reams & her 3 children, Henrietta T., Sarah
A. N., & James W. Sanford G. Allen asks
that he be permitted to resign his trusteeship. The deed of assignment stated that
it deeds Sanford G. Allen a tract of land
containing 56 acres. It also deeds him a
negro man Billy who is 35 yrs. old, a woman
Lucy Ann who is 25 yrs. old. Interest in the
undivided estate of my father, William Reams,
deceased, (which is 1/7 part), my livestock,
crops, book of accounts for blacksmith work
done. Allen is to pay all of William R.
Reams, deceased, debts. After the debts are
paid, he is to use the balance for the
benefit of my wife, Sarah T. Reams & her
3 children & anymore which may be born to us.
Francis M. Lavender has been appointed trustee.

P. 8   HANNAH WAGGONER - pl. vs JAMES WAGGONER, Et
Al - def.   May 1860
Valentine Waggoner died 8 Nov. 1852 intestate.
He left a widow, Hannah Waggoner & the heirs,
James Waggoner & Samuel Waggoner, the only
children of his deceased son, James M.
Waggoner. James & Samuel are minors & Hannah
is their guardian. James C. Copeland was
appointed Admr. Valentine Waggoner, deceased,
had a tract of land containing 72 acres

(CONT'D)

P. 8   Valentine Waggoner, deceased (CONT'D)
         adjoining the land of Joseph Wilson, James H.
         Wilson, & John B. Crockett. (Hannah wants
         her dower.) Valentine Waggoner, deceased, left
         slaves: Emily - 40 yrs., Marilla - 20 yrs.,
         Minerva - 18 yrs., Martha Ann - 16 yrs., Anderson -
         7 yrs., Louisa - 7 yrs., John - 6 yrs., Susan -
         4 yrs., Sarah - 3 yrs., Lark - 2 yrs. 1/2 of the
         slaves are owned by Hannah.

P. 12   JOHN O. BOYD, Extr. & Et Al - pl. vs MARY V.
         BOYD - def.   May 1860
         Washington L. Boyd died 8 Jan. 1860. He left a
         will. John O. Boyd was named Exr. Washington
         L. Boyd & his sister, Mary V. Boyd, a minor, were
         joint owners of 3 slaves. The slaves were:
         Julia - 34 yrs., Violet - 17 yrs., & Dee - 11 yrs.
         Washington L. Boyd directed by will that his
         slaves were to be divided between his sisters &
         his estate & that his portion of said negroes
         be sold & the proceeds be used for the support
         of his mother. Samuel S. House is guardian for
         Mary V. Boyd.

P. 16   JAMES W. OWEN, Guardian & C - pl. vs ISABELLA
         OWEN - def.   May 1860
         James W. Owen has attended to the business &
         made settlement of his ward, Isabella Owen. He
         wants to resign the guardianship. James W. Owen
         has sold his land & is going to leave the state.
         Isabella is now 14 years old & she has a
         valuable tract of land containing 110 acres &
         it rents for $300 per year.

P. 17   SYNTHIA WILSON, By & C
                 May 1860   Exparte
         Synthia Wilson is a resident of Calloway County,
         Kentucky. She is a married woman who sues by
         her husband, James R. Wilson. She is under the
         decree of Chancery Court in the case of Joseph
         B. Dwyer. She wants John Wall appointed her
         trustee so he can receive her share & she can
         benefit from it.

P. 18   SARAH C. HARTLEY - pl. vs ANDREW IRVIN - def.
                 May 1860
         Laban Hartley, deceased, named Andrew Irvin,
         the trustee for Sarah C. Hartley & her children.
         Laban Hartley, the husband of Sarah Caroline
         Hartley, is appointed trustee. Sarah C. Hartley
         is the daughter of Laban Hartley, deceased.
         (Sr.?). The will was probated Sept. 1856.

P. 19   FRANCIS M. LAVENDER, Admr.
              May 1860   Exparte
         Charles A. Merrill & James Hughes purchased
         some land sold in this cause & have paid the
         money to L. B. McConnico, former clerk of the
         County, but no deed has been made to purchasers.
         They sold the land to Eli Montgomery & executed
         their title bond to him & bind themselves to
         convey said deed to him. James Hughes has
         died & Barrett R. Hughes is the Exr. of his
         will. He wants the court to give Eli
         Montgomery his deed.

P. 20   LUKE CRICK, Admr. & C - pl. vs MARY M. HOOD,
         Et Al - def.   June 1860
         Gilly J. Skinner died Aug. 1858 intestate.
         Luke Crick was appointed Andr. Oct. 1858.
         The estate is insolvent. Gilly J. Skinner,
         deceased, left a widow, Mary Matilda who has
         since married Jefferson Hood. He left the
         following children: Mary, Ann, Susan E.,
         Lucy J., & Tennessee Skinner. Gilly J.
         Skinner, deceased, left a tract of land in
         the 22nd District containing about 13 acres.
         His widow wants her dower & the remainder
         must be sold to pay the expenses. (The
         land bounded as follows: north side of
         the Duck River Ridge --- to Luke Crick ---
         Edward J. Giles.) The land was bought from
         Robert Pate in 1844. Isaac Ivy is the
         guardian of the above mentioned children.

P. 23   JOHN EDMONDSON, Trustee & C - pl. vs J. B.
         OWEN - def.   June 1860
         In March 1859, J. B. Owen executed a deed of
         assignment for the benefit of himself to
         John Edmondson. Edmondson accepted the
         said trusteeship & sold the property & paid
         all of the debts. The remainder of the
         property was conveyed in said trust & is
         ready to be delivered to his successor.
         Edmondson wants to resign his trusteeship.
         John Edmondson, Sr. is appointed trustee.

P. 27   MARY WARREN, By & C - pl. vs B. B. TOON,
         Guardian & C - def.   June 1860
         Mary Warren is a minor & she petitions by
         her next friend, Franklin Polk. Mary is
         14 years old & a resident of Maury County
         & she lives with her aunt & uncle. She
         selected her uncle, F. A. Polk, as her
         guardian. Her previous guardian, Beverly
         B. Toon, is willing for F. A. Polk to be
         her guardian.

P. 29   WASHINGTON HARTLEY - pl. vs ANDREW IRVIN - def.
                    June 1860
        Labon Hartley died & left a will. He appointed
        Andrew Irvin as trustee for Washington Hartley
        & his children. Andrew Irvin declined & Jackson
        C. Biggers will be appointed. Washington Hartley
        is the son of Labon Hartley.

P. 30   THOMAS SHORT - pl. vs CATHERINE VAUGHAN - def.
                    June 1860
        Catherine Vaughan, 40 years old, is an idiot &
        lunatic & she is in the poor house. She has been
        in this shape some 8 or 10 years & she has no
        husband or children. She is entitled to an
        inheritance from her brother's estate, who died
        in Memphis, Tennessee. The estate requires
        some attendance.

P. 32   LAADOCIA WHEELER, Et Al - pl. vs ISSACHER
        ROBERTS, Et Al - def.   July 1860
        Laadocia Wheeler is a citizen of Mississippi.
        John Roberts died in 1859. He left a will.
        Isaac Ivy was appointed Exr. of the estate.
        John Roberts left the following heirs:
            1. Issacher Roberts of China
            2. The Board of Home Missions located at
                Marion, Alabama
            3. Lenadia Wheeler of Mississippi
        John Roberts, deceased, owned a tract of land
        containing 134 3/4 acres. Isaacher Roberts
        is the principal legatee of the will. (Will
        included: Brother - Issacher J. Roberts,
        missionary in China. Sister - Laodicia
        Wheeler - during her lifetime & to her
        daughter, Anadia. To the Board of Home Missions
        in Marion, Alabama. Will made in Shelby
        County, Tennessee, April Term 1859.)

P. 36   J. C. HELM, Admr. - pl. vs HEIRS OF JOHN WILLIAMS
        (NEWTON WILLIAMS, Et Al) - def.
                    Dec. 1859
        There is not sufficient funds to pay off the
        debts of the estate of John Williams. They must
        sell the slaves, John & Sam, to pay the debts.
        John C. Helm is Exr. of the will. Sarah Williams
        is the widow of John Williams.

P. 38   CATHERINE BROWN & SARAH W. FITZGERALD
                    Aug. 1860   Exparte
        Catherine Brown & Sarah W. Fitzgerald are entitled
        to certain legacys under the will of their
        father, Solomon Oden. The will asks that a
        trustee be appointed & they have selected
        Hezekiah Oden, their brother.

154

P. 39   SMITHSON & JOHNSON - pl. vs WILLIAM J. JONES -
        def.   Sept. 1860
        Sylvanus W. Smithson & Jesse Johnson show that
        William Jones was appointed guardian of James
        C. Jones, Sarah A. E. Jones, Martilia L.
        Jones, Martha J. Jones, John W. Jones, &
        Samuel J. Jones on 4 April 1859. Smithson &
        Johnson gave bond for William Jones & they now
        want to be released. William Jones is removed
        & George Andrews is appointed guardian.

P. 40   SUSAN A. WILSON, Et Al - pl. vs ANDREW IRVIN -
        def.   Oct. 1860
        Upon motion of Benjamin T. Wilson, by attorney,
        Andrew Irvin was appointed trustee for
        Susan A. Wilson & her children by the will of
        Labourn Hartley. Andrew Irvin declined
        the trusteeship. Benjamin T. Wilson is the
        husband of Susan A. Wilson. She was the
        daughter of Labourn Hartley. Benjamin T.
        Wilson is appointed trustee.

P. 42   W. W. BURNETT, Et Al - pl. vs JOHN J.
        BURNETT, Et Al - def.   Nov. 1860
        William W. Burnett, Bird F. Dodson & his
        wife Elizabeth A. Dodson, John J. Burnett,
        William Atkinson & his wife Emily J., &
        James T. Burnett are joint owners of a tract
        of land containing 26 acres & lying in the
        2nd District. (Bounded by William W.
        Burnett, Bird F. Dodson & others). They are
        also joint owners of slaves. The slaves are:
        Harvey - 45 yrs., Dicey - 45 yrs., George -
        23 yrs., & Catherine - 8 yrs. John J.
        Burnett is a minor & William W. Burnett is
        his guardian. William Atkinson & his wife
        & James T. Burnett are non-residents of
        Tennessee. They all want the land & slaves
        sold & a division made.

P. 45   MARY DAVIS & JAMES W. DAVIS - pl. vs
        SETH L. DAVIS, Et Al - def.
                    Nov. 1860
        Seth L. Davis died 5th day July last intestate.
        He left a widow, Mary. He left the following
        children: James W., Seth L., David M.,
        Stokely A., Francis H., & John W. Davis.
        Seth L. Davis, deceased, left 4 tracts of
        land. Tract # 1 - about 114 acres. Tract
        # 2 - on the Harpeth River - about 89 acres.
        Tract # 3 - 70 acres. Tract # 4 - 293 acres.
        Seth L. Davis, deceased, left the following
        slaves: Cela - 44 yrs., Anna - 15 yrs.,
        Harry - 14 yrs., Rutha - 12 yrs.,   (CONT'D)

P. 45   Seth L. Davis, deceased (CONT'D)
         Judd - 17 yrs., Jefferson - 14 yrs., Larry - 13
         yrs., George - 10 yrs., Cherry - 9 yrs., Willis -
         7 yrs., Joseph - 6 yrs., Sarah - 4 yrs.,
         Amanda - 4 yrs., Nancy - 3 yrs., & Sophronia -
         9 months. James W. Davis is the Admr. of the
         estate. Mary Davis wants her dower & a division made.

P. 53   ELIZABETH HAMPTON - pl. vs WILLIAM H. HAMPTON,
         Et Al - def.   Aug. 1860
         Henry Hampton died in 1858 intestate. He left a
         widow, Elizabeth Hampton. He left the following
         children: William, Jeremiah, Sarah Ann, Jane,
         & Mary Ann Hampton. The children are all minors
         & the judge of the County Court is their
         guardian. Henry Hampton, deceased, had a tract
         of land in the 16th District. It contains about
         54 acres. (Bounded by James Sayers, John D.
         Stanfield, & Edward Stevens). Henry Hampton's
         widow wants her dower.

P. 56   WILLIAM HARTLEY - pl. vs ANDREW IRVIN - def.
                     Dec. 1860
         Andrew Irvin was named trustee for William
         Hartley in the will of Laborn Hartley, Sr., deceased.
         Andrew Irvin declined to act. Stanfield
         Anderson is appointed trustee.

P. 57   JAMES W. CRAWFORD, Exr. & C
                     Nov. 1860   Exparte
         George W. Barker died 8 May 1860. He left a will.
         James W. Crawford & William B. Barker were named
         Exrs. George W. Barker, deceased, left the
         following children: William B. Barker, Martha
         Jane Loften, Eliza Coleman, Matilda C. Barker, &
         Emily A. Barker. He left the following
         grandchildren by his deceased daughter, Mary
         Ann Loften: Mary Jane Smithson, Augustus M.
         Loften, William H. H. Loften, Joseph Loften,
         Frances Loften, & Benjamin F. Loften. The
         grandchildren are minors & their guardian is Herbert
         C. Loften. George W. Barker left the following
         slaves: Aggy - 71 yrs., Anica - 38 yrs., Sarah -
         24 yrs., Polly - 17 yrs., Dony - 12 yrs., Elizabeth -
         10 yrs., Susan Jane - 8 yrs., Ester - 5 yrs.,
         Catherine - 3 yrs., Jones - 26 yrs., Jack - 21 yrs.
         (Jack has died since the death of the testator),
         Anderson - 19 yrs., Calvin - 17 yrs., Bill - 15
         yrs., Harvey - 7 yrs., & Andrew - 1 yr.

P. 62   LYCURGUS. McCALL, Admr. & C - pl. vs MARY
         MARTIN, Et Al - def.   Sept. 1860
         Hudson Martin died intestate in 1858. He
         left a widow, Mary M. Martin. He left the
         following heirs:
              1.   Hudson J. Martin (son)
              2.   William C. Martin (son)
              3.   Jefferson P. Martin (son)
              4.   Louis Martin (son)
              5.   William Martin & Mary Jane Martin
                   (grandchildren. They are the
                   children of James T. Martin, deceased.)
              6.   Sallie Ann, Mary, & John D.
                   Martin (children of Daniel G.
                   Martin, deceased. Daniel G. is
                   the son of Hudson Martin, deceased.)
         Lycurgus McCall was appointed Admr. of the
         estate in 1858. Littleton Fuller, Elizabeth
         A. Hartley & her husband, Washington
         Hartley, are also petitioners. George W.,
         Jefferson P., & Lewis Martin are of
         Kentucky. They are minor children & have
         no guardian. Hudson Martin owned a tract
         of land on Flat Creek. It contains about 70
         acres & is bounded by Thomas White, Emanuel
         Sampson, Stanfield Anderson, & others.
         Fuller sets up a claim by right of purchase
         of the interest of Hudson J. Martin.
         Hartley & wife set up a claim to 1 share in
         the tract of land. A portion of the land
         must be sold to pay the debts. The Admr.
         thinks all of the tract should be sold as
         selling only part of the tract would hurt
         the value of the rest of it & there would
         be no way to divide it & lay off a dower.

P. 71   F. A. POLK & WIFE - pl. vs MARY WARREN, Et
         Al - def.   Nov. 1860
         The following are all owners of a tract of
         land on the waters of Hayes Creek containing
         100 acres. They are:
              1.   Franklin A. Polk & Mary E., his wife
                   (of Maury County)
              2.   Richard N. Herbert & Sarah, his wife
              3.   John Burge & Nancy, his wife
              4.   Edward Stevens
              5.   Mary Warren (a minor of Maury County
                   for whom F. A. Polk is her
                   guardian.)
              6.   Sarah Warren (a minor of Williamson
                   County for whom Beverly B. Toon is
                   her guardian.)
                                  (CONT'D)

P. 71 F. A. Polk   (CONT'D)
Edward Stevens owns 3/7 part of the said tract of
land. One part is in his name & the other two
parts are in the right of William & Hines
Stevens. Burge & wife receive 1 share. Herbert
& wife receive 1 share. Polk & wife receive 1
share. Mary & Sarah Warren receive 1 share.
23 Aug. 1834 - Indenture between Joel Stevens of
1 part & William D. Stevens, Edward Stevens,
Mary E. Poke, Charles H. Stevens, Nancy Stevens,
Sally Stevens & Ann Stevens, children of Charles
& Rebecca Stevens, of the other part. For the
sum of $500 paid by William D.,Edward, Mary E.,
Charles H., Nancy, Sally & Ann have conveyed &
sold a tract of land on the waters of Hays
Creek. To Joel Stevens the tract that Charles
now lives on. In trust, nevertheless, during the
lifetime of their mother, Rebecca. She shall be
able to occupy & use the land. If Charles should
survive his wife, Rebecca, William D., Edward,
Mary E., Charles H., Nancy, Sally & Ann shall
support their father, Charles, during his
lifetime from the profits of the land. Mary Warren
is 15 years old. Dec. 1860.

P. 77 THOMAS B. McGAHEY, Trustee & C - pl. vs JOHN B.
BARNES, Et Al - def.   .Jan. 1861
Thomas B. McGahey appeared in court & asked to
resign the trusteeship of John B. Barnes, under
a deed of assignment executed by Barnes to McGahey
4 Jan. 1861. John B. Barnes & Thomas Holt were
beneficiaries under the deed of assignment.
McGahey, as trustee, has not discharged his duties
as such trustee & none of the funds had come to
his hands & he had not entered bond. Thomas Holt
is appointed trustee instead of McGahey.

P. 79 H. HELM, Exr. & C, Et Als - pl. vs BIRD TERRILL,
Et Als - def.   Nov. 1860
Petition of Henderson Helm, Exr. of Timothy
Terrill. Timothy Terrill died in 1859. He left
a will. He left the following children: Mary
(she married William Akin), Bird (minor), Sallie
(minor), Nancy (minor), Sufrona (minor), & John
(minor). The minors mentioned above have no
guardian. Timothy Terrill, deceased, left slaves.
They are: Matilda - 45 yrs., Tom - 30 yrs., Jeff -
18 yrs., Jane - 26 yrs., Alice - 24 yrs., Martha -
16 yrs., Providence - 16 yrs., Eliza - 13 yrs.,
Judith - 11 yrs., Malinda - 10 yrs., Ellen - 8 yrs.,
Ann - 8 yrs., Jo - 6 yrs., Jordan - 5 yrs., Aggy -
3 yrs., Charles - 1 yr., Fannie - 5 yrs., Jennie -
4 yrs., & Frank - 2 yrs. Terrill died indebted.
The Exr. has exhausted all funds & will have to
(CONT'D)

P. 79   Timothy Terrill, deceased (CONT'D)
         sell 2 of the slaves to pay the debts. Akin
         & his wife are entitled to their share.
         Sallie Terrill states that she is 21 years of
         age - in an order made the same day. 3 Dec.
         1860 - statement by James B. Terrill says he
         will attain his full age in July 1861 - says
         the death of his father - are as stated in
         bill - (James B. Also called Bird.) Sam
         J. Cook was appointed guardian.

P. 84   CORTNEY SAWYER - pl. vs COSTEN SAWYER - def.
                    Nov. 1860
         Courtney Sawyer is the widow of Dempsey Sawyer,
         deceased. Dempsey Sawyer died Oct. 1860
         intestate. He left the following heirs:
                 1.   Costen Sawyers
                 2.   James Sawyers
                 3.   Sarah, wife of James Knight
                 4.   Elisha D. Sawyer
                 5.   John S. Sawyer
                 6.   Charles Sawyer
                 7.   Dempsey R. Sawyer
                 8.   William H. Sawyer
                 9.   Sterling B. Sawyer
                10.   Levin E. Sawyer
         Sterling B. & Levin E. Sawyer are non-residents
         of Tennessee. Dempsey Sawyer, deceased,
         left a tract of land containing about 368
         acres. bounded by John Evans, Hay, & Big
         Harpeth River. The widow wants her dower.

P. 87   ELIZABETH M. McLEMORE & L. P. McLEMORE, By
         & C   Dec. 1860   Exparte - Petition
         Elizabeth M. McLemore & Lemuel P. McLemore
         are joint owners of slaves: Tom - 31,
         Green - 24, Jim - 16, Louisa - 40 & her
         children, Martha - 12, Atkins - 10, Isabella -
         8, Eunice - 5, Ben - 3, & Mary - 8 months.
         R. A. McLemore is guardian of Lemuel P.
         McLemore. Elizabeth has reached the age of 21.

P. 88   JAMES P. OGILVIE, Et Al
                    Dec. 1860   Exparte
         James P. & William H. Ogilvie are owners of
         slaves: Charlotte - 40, Hannah - 38, Bill -
         26, Bob - 19, Harriet - 16, Lark - 13, Jeff -
         6, & John - 3. James P. Ogilvie has reached
         the age of 21. James P. Allison is guardian
         of William H. Ogilvie.

P. 90   NEWTON C. KINNARD, Et Al
                Nov. 1860   Exparte
        Newton C. Kinnard, Addie E. Kinnard, & Fannie
        V. Kinnard are owners of slaves. The slaves are:
        Philip, Hannah, James, Bettie, Daniel, Betsy,
        Eliza, Margaret, Miles, Jack, Peter, Thomas,
        Adam, Ellen, Mary, James, Susan, & Wesley.
        William Parrish is guardian of Addie E. & Fannie
        V. Kinnard. Newton Carmon Kinnard has reached
        the age of 21.

P. 91   SOPHIA & MARY J. OVERALL, By & C - pl. vs
        JONATHAN BOSTICK - def.   Jan. 1861
        Sophia & Mary J. Overall are minors & they sue by
        their next friend, William LaFayette McConnico.
        They have moved to Rutherford County. Jonathan
        Bostic has been their guardian for several
        years. He has also moved to Rutherford County.
        Their mother lives there too. They want the
        guardianship moved to Rutherford County. They
        are the minor heirs of Jackson Overall, deceased.

P. 94   ADAM WHITE, Exr. & C, Et Al - pl. vs ROBERT
        ANDREWS - def.   Dec. 1860
        Jones Andrews died Nov. 1848. He left a will.
        He named Lucy Andrews & Adam White, Exrs. He
        left a widow, Lucy Andrews. He left the following
        children: Mary Ann White, Newton L. Andrews,
        Lucy B. Floyd, William Andrews, Horace G. Andrews,
        & Robert Andrews. He left the following slaves:
        Buck - 54, Merritt - 32, William Spraggin - 28,
        Adaline - 34, Elijah - 25, Ruth - 23, Arthur -
        44, Lucy - 24, Will - 6, Elisha - 4, Lucy's
        youngest child's name not given, but it is 3
        months, Phebe - 8, Thomas - 7, Peggy - 6, Martha -
        2, & Mira - 1. Lucy Andrews died Sept. 1860.
        She left no will. Jones Andrews left a large
        tract of land. Robert Andrews, a minor, has no
        guardian. Adam White married Mary Ann before the
        death of her father. Lucy B. has since married
        Drury Floyd. Martha Andrews married Rollins White
        & has since died, leaving no issue. (Will included)
        Leaves land, negroes, stock, & possessions to
        wife (not named). At wife's death all is to be
        divided between the children (not named). The
        will was dated 13 Nov. 1843.

P. 99   CEPHUS SHELBOURNE, By & C - pl. vs JOSEPH
        TENNISEN, Et Al - def.   Jan. 1861
        The Petition of Cephus Shelbourne, an idiot, by
        his guardian, Samuel T. Thomas vs Joseph Tennison
        of Williamson County, Shelbourne Tennison, &
        Elizabeth Armstrong & her husband, _____
        Armstrong of Davidson County, Tennessee.   (CONT'D)

P. 99   Cephus Shelbourne   (CONT'D)
They are all owners of a tract of land in the
4th Civil District. The land contains about
100 acres (bounded by Wiley B. Carothers,
Henry Jackson, William Regen, Joel Regen, &
W. M. Nolen). Joseph Tennison is entitled to
1/5 of the tract of land during his life & it
then descends to his children, Shelbourn Tennison
& Elizabeth Armstrong. <u>Cephus</u> Shelbourne owns
4/5 of the tract of land.

P. 102 JOHN H. FLOYD & WIFE, Fannie E. Floyd - pl.
vs JOSEPH McPEAK & FRANCES, his wife; JAMES
W. GARRETT & NANCY G. GARRETT of Williamson
County, minors by their guardian, Presley
Jones of Marshall County, Tennessee - def.
                Feb. 1861
The above named are owners of slaves: Harriet -
30, Mary - 12, Sarah Yoke - 8, Martha - 6,
Matilda - 3, & Minerva - 8 mos. The slaves
were left from the estate of the father of
the Petitioner, Fannie E. & late husband
of Frances McPeak & father of minor
defendant. Fannie has been married to John
H. Floyd about 2 years. The Petitioners
want a division made.

P. 104 NANCY DAVIS
            Feb. 1861   Exparte
Turner Davis died intestate in Jan. 1861.
In Feb. 1861, Washington G. Smith was appointed
Admr. Turner Davis, deceased, left a widow,
Nancy Davis & children & heirs: William
Davis, James T. Davis, N. J. Davis, Fannie Davis,
Vina Moss (Mays?), Elizabeth C. Smith; Grand-
children: Adda Jackson, Lovy Jackson, Sarah Jackson,
Charles Jackson, Nancy Jackson, James Jackson,
& John Jackson. Washington G. Smith, Elizabeth
C. Smith, George G. Moss (Mays?), & Vina Moss
(Mays?), his wife, Adda Jackson, Lovy Jackson
are all citizens of Davidson County. James
Jackson of Kentucky is a minor & Washington G.
Smith is his guardian. John Jackson of
Kentucky is a minor & Isaac Ivy is his guardian.
Adda Jackson & Lovy Jackson are minors & their
guardian is Washington G. Smith. Sara, Charles,
& Nancy Jackson are minors & their guardian
is Washington G. Smith. Turner Davis, deceased,
owned a tract of land containing 400 acres on
the east fork of the south Harpeth in the 1st
District. It was bounded by Jo McPherson,
Enoch Brown, Silas Linton, Lucinda Anderson,
& John Pritchett. This is where Turner
Davis lived. His widow wants her dower.

P. 109 MARY E. WALTER - pl. vs JAMES A. WALTERS,
Et Al - def.   Feb. 1861
Eli A. Waters died in 1861 intestate. He left
a widow, Mary E. & children. His children are:
James A., William C., Dora P., Thomas, &
Florence Waters. Eli A. Waters, deceased, owned
a tract of land containing 150 acres bounded by
Robert Buchanan, the heirs of B. C. Watson,
James Carothers, the estate of John Hodge, Freeman
Jordan, & the heirs of Stephen Bradley. Daniel
B. Cliffe was appointed guardian of the
children who were minors.

P. 113 HARVEY E. PARRISH & WIFE, Et Al
            Dec. 1861   Exparte
Harvey E. Parrish & his wife Eudora, Rosanna
Patton & Septunia O. J. Patton are all owners of
the following slaves: Jack - 65, Jenny - 68,
John - 18, Edmond - 26, Melissa - 40, Lewis -
44. Rosanna Patton & Septunia O. J. Patton are
minors & J. C. Crawford & W. B. Patton are their
guardians & trustees. Eudora has now married &
she wants her share. The slaves are being held by
the will of Tristram Pratton, deceased.

P. 114 LOUISA HINSON - pl. vs HENRY WALKER & TENNESSEE
his wife (of Marshall County, Tennessee), JARVIS
C. HINSON, WARREN HINSON, JAMES H. HINSON,
CINTHIA C. HINSON, MILTON HINSON, & THOMAS
HINSON (the last 5 are minors & William L. Pate
is their guardian) - def.
            Dec. 1861
Tilman D. Hinson died 19 Nov. 1861. He left a
will. He left a widow & children who were named
as defendants. Edward W. Eggleston was named
Exr. Louisa, the widow of Tilman D. Hinson.
Tilman D. Hinson, deceased, owned a tract of land
containing about 112 acres bounded by Edward
W. Eggleston, David Comstock, Pettus S. Hay,
Edward Smithson, & William Spratt.

P. 118 COURTNEY SAWYERS, Et Al - pl. vs LEVIN E. SAWYERS,
Et Al - def.
            Oct. 1861   Division
Dempsey Sawyers died 10 Oct. 1860 intestate. He
left a widow, Courtney Sawyers & the following
children: Costin Sawyers, James R. Sawyers,
Dempsey R., Sarah wife of James Knight, Elisha
D., John S., Charles M., William H., Levin E.,
& Sterling B. Sawyers. Levin E. lives in
California & Sterling B. lives in Texas. Costin
Sawyers was appointed Admr. Dempsey Sawyers owned
a tract of land containing about 380 acres
bounded by James Knight, Lavinia Craw, James S.
Demoss, John Gray & others.   (CONT'D)

P. 118 Dempsey Sawyers, deceased (CONT'D)
157 acres of the land was set aside for the
dower. Dempsey Sawyers also left the following
slaves: Lineus - 35, Celia - 40, America & her
child about 5 mos, Marice - 11. Sterling B.
Sawyers sold his share of the estate to Costin
Sawyer.

P. 123 MARY JANE FLEMING - pl. vs ROBERT J. FLEMING,
Et Al - def.
           Nov. 1861   Division .
Mary Jane, Robert J., Helen Ann, James S. &
William P. Fleming are owners of the following
slaves: Hannah - 75, Faney - 26, Albert - 24,
Polly - 22, Joanna - 16, Samuel - 14, Benjamin -
13, Husyfort - 12, Nelly - 30, Charles - 12,
Thomas - 10, William - 8, Samuel - 4, John -
18 mos., John Watson - 2, Mary Jane - 1,
Catherine - 26. Mary Jane Fleming has reached
the age of 21 & she wants her share. The
other Petitioners are minors & their guardian
is William L. Pate.

P. 125 JAMES W. OWEN - pl. vs E. BROWN, Et Al - def.
            April 1862
Benjamin Owen, Enoch Brown, & L. F. Beech
are the Exrs. of John Beech, deceased.
Thomas Holt, James Crockett, & A. J.
Crockett were the beneficaries named in the
deed of trust of said Benjamin Owen to James
W. Owen. Benjamin Owen executed a deed of
trust for the benefit of the creditors &
James W. Owen qualified as trustee. James
W. Owen wants to resign as trustee.

P. 128 REBECCA PENNINGTON - pl. vs WILLIAM JONES,
Admr. & Et Al - def.
            May 1864   Division
Clement S. Pennington died 21 Dec. 1861.
He left the following children & grandchildren:
Rebecca Pennington, Charles W., William P.,
Martha Haley wife of Dabney Haley, John
Pennington & David Pennington. David lives in
Hickman County, Tennessee. William W. Jones
presented the will of Clement S. Pennington
& he was named Admr. Clement S. Pennington,
deceased, had a tract of land in the 13th
District containing about 260 acres bounded by
E. Maxwell, G. A. Nichols, G. Lowe, & William
Rucker. Clement S. Pennington owned the
following slaves: Fred - 60, Reuben - 30,
Mary Ann - 14, Hustin - 13, Tila - 12, Martha -
9, Winny - 7, Dennis - 10, Mary Jane - 13, &
Bett, who is serving the said Jones. The last of th
case is not recorded.

P. 129 - 149 Blank

P. 150 OUILLA M. WARREN, Admr. & C - pl. vs ELIZABETH
HAMER - def.
            Sept. 1870   Insol Bill
Ouilla M. Warren is the Admr. of Fielden Warren.
Ouilla M. Warren brings an insolvent Bill
against Elizabeth Warren, the widow of Fielding
Warren, John Hughes & wife Jane, Joseph Faught
& wife America, ____ Ginger & his wife Caroline.
The last 4 mentioned are residents of Missouri.
L. S. Rowlett & wife Mary E., William Rowlett
& wife M. A. are of Rutherford County, Tennessee.
John Glenn & wife Virginia are of Williamson
County, Tennessee. M. F. Warren is of Arkansas.
Oliver Warren & wife Rachel of Williamson County.
Emma Jean & Lilly Warren (who are minors & have
no guardian) are of Mississippi. Alener Sayers,
John King., J. Murry & all other creditors of
Fielding Warren. Fielding Warren died intestate.
He left a widow, Elizabeth & the defendants
except the creditors named, as his children,
grandchildren, & heirs at law. There is no
personal estate with which to pay the debts.
Fielding Warren, deceased, owned a tract of land
containing 61 acres in the 19th District on the
headwaters of Huges Creek bounded by G. H. Lamb,
William Johnson, Matthew McCallum, & J. C.
Neelly estate. The widow of Fielding Warren,
deceased, is entitled to her dower & the remainder
must be sold to pay the expenses.

P. 160 P. D. SCALES - pl. vs MARY A. HARTLEY, Et Al -
def.   March 1871   Petition
P. D. Scales was appointed Admr. of N. B. Hartley
Jan. 1869. Mary A. Hartley is the widow of
N. B. Hartley. Alice, Ophelia B., & Oliver C.
Hartley are minors & their guardian is Mary A.
Hartley. N. B. Hartley died Dec. 1868. He left
an insolvent estate. He owned a small lot &
house in Bethesda bounded by C. C. Bond, E. R.
Waddey, & R. F. McCaul. N. B. Hartley paid
$90 for the property & there is a lien on it.
His widow is entitled to a dower. The lot & house
must be sold to pay the debts.

P. 165 A. T. MORGAN & WIFE, Et Al - pl. vs T. H.
ODEN & WIFE - def.
            March 1871
The Petitioners are:
    1. Absolom T. Morgan & Mary C., his wife
        (of Marshall County, Mississippi)
    2. William T. Wells & Virginia, his wife
        (of Coahoma, Mississippi)   (CONT'D)

164

P. 165 A. T. Morgan (CONT'D)
        3. James Lockridge (of Marshall County,
            Mississippi)
        4. James W. Wells & Elizabeth, his wife
            (of Marshall County, Mississippi)
        5. Logan Sutton (of Marshall County,
            Mississippi)
        6. Ella Sutton (of Marshall Co., Miss.)
        7. Ada Sutton (of Marshall Co., Miss.)
        8. William Sutton (of Marshall Co., Miss.)
The last 4 mentioned above are minors & have no
guardian. They sue by their next friend,
Absolom T. Morgan.)
        9. Aurelina Joplin & Rebecca, his wife
            (of Panola County, Texas)
The Petitioners petition against Thomas H.
Oden & Rebecca H., his wife (of Williamson
County). They are all owners of a tract of
land in the 10th District of Williamson
County. The land is bounded by M. H. Page,
Gideon & Wesley Ratcliff, Fleming, Tom
Graham, & James P. Johnson. The tract of
land contains about 115 acres being bequeathed
to Elizabeth Sutton & Rebecca H. Oden by
their father, the late Sterling Davis whose
will was probated. Elizabeth Sutton died
15 March 1870 in Mississippi & left
surviving her are: Mary C. Morgan, Virginia
Wells, James Lockeridge, Elizabeth Wells,
Logan Sutton, Ella Sutton, Adda Sutton,
William Sutton, & Rebecca Joplin. The
Petitioners want a division made.

P. 172 S. W. COLE & MARY S., his wife - pl. vs
SAMUEL R. RASH, Et Al - def.
            (No date)
Henry Rash died in 1855 intestate. He left
the following children & heirs:
        1. Samuel R. Rash
        2. Sarah M. Rash
        3. G. H. Rash
        4. Mary S. Rash (she married S. W. Cole)
        5. Sarah & Gustavus H. (minors whose
            guardian is Hezekiah Hill)
Henry Rash, deceased, left his children &
heirs a tract of land in the 16th District
adjoining the lands of Elizabeth Vaughn,
Mary McMurry, Samuel H. Barnes, & the heirs
of John P. Hill. The land contains about
191 acres. The heirs of Henry Rash, deceased,
want a division made.

P. 178 ALEXANDER C. BROWN, Guardian - pl. vs ROBERT P.
MOSS, Admr.   Jan. 1871
Joseph T. Brown died in 186_ intestate. He left
a widow, Mattie J. Brown & the following children:
Callie, Bertie, Mattie, & Mary. Robert P.
Moss was appointed Admr. & he declared the estate
insolvent. The widow, Mattie J. died intestate
& Moss was her Admr. She owned a house & lot in
Franklin purchased from John B. McEwen & adjoining his property. The paternal uncle of the
children, Alexander C. Brown, took them to his
house to live with him where they are now. They
live in McCrocken County, Kentucky. They have no
near relatives in Tennessee. Alexander C. Brown
was appointed guardian for the children. He
wants the money from the estate for the use of
the children.

P. 182 WILLIAM GIVENS - pl. vs SARAH J. HARPENDING,
Et Al - def.   Aug. 1870
Henrietta Harpending died intestate in 1865.   She
owned 2 tracts of land in the 18th District
containing 108 acres. Her heirs are:
    1. Henry C. Harpending
    2. James C. Harpending
    3. Sarah Jane Harpending of Johnson County,
        Illinois
    4. Emily Harpending of Union County, Illinois
        (she is a minor & has no guardian)
William Givens has purchased the interest of
Henry C. & James C. Harpending. These tracts of
land are very poor & cannot be redivided
without a sale. The land is bounded by land
that was purchased by William Givens from L.
H. Woldrage, G. W. Givens, & Hargrove.

P. 188 MARGARET S. BROWN - pl. vs J. T. BROWN, Et Al -
def.   (No Date)
Thomas Brown, Sr. died intestate in Jan. 1870.
He left his widow, Margaret S. Brown, John Thomas
Brown, Betthenia A. wife of John A. Miller,
Jennie E. wife of Joseph H. Bowman & Maggie S.
Brown, his heirs. John Thomas Brown is of
Davidson County. Bethenia A. Miller is of Maury
County. Maggie S. Brown is a minor & has no
guardian. Thomas Brown, Sr., deceased, owned a
tract of land he lived on at the time of his
death. It contains about 500 acres & is bounded
by John Hill, James B. Hill, Philip Brown &
Enoch Brown, Mrs. Elizabeth Bradley by the
Franklin & Tank Road & Harpeth River. Thomas
Brown, Sr., also had a tract of land containing
about 50 acres. Both tracts of land where in
the 6th District. The Petitioner wants to
set apart her dower.

166

P. 193 ISAAC IVY, Admr. & C - pl. vs MARGARET
GREER, Et Al - def.
Isaac Greer died in 1863 intestate. He left
his widow, Margaret Greer & the following
heirs:
1. Henry Greer
2. Mary Ferby
3. Charlotte McClarin
4. Susan Marchbanks
5. Nancy Inman
6. Tennessee Haly
7. Leanorah Greer
8. Isaac, Thomas, & Tabitha Stewart
(children of his deceased daughter,
Sarah Stewart)
9. William H. Greer (son of his deceased
son, William Greer)
Isaac Ivy was appointed Admr. Isaac Greer,
deceased, left a tract of land in the 1st
District. It contains about 113 acres.
Henry Greer is in Perry County, Tennessee.
Mary Ferby is in Kentucky. Susan Marchbanks
& her husband, John & Charlotte McClarin &
her husband, William are of Humphreys County,
Tennessee. Nancy Inman is of Missouri.
Isaac & Thomas Stewart, Andrew Jackson & his
wife, Tabitha are of parts unknown. William
H. Greer is of Dickson County, Tennessee.
The land must be sold to pay the debts.

P. 201 HENRY B. NORTH, Et Al - pl. vs ATHA THOMAS,
Et Al - def.   Petition for Partition
Henry B. North, trustee of Robert H. North;
James A. North; Margaret North; & Willie
North, & also of the said Robert, James;
Margaret; & Willie North in their own name
vs Sallie P. Watson, Jane Watson, Letitia
Watson, Martha Watson, Thomas J. Watson, Jr.,
& Kittie Watson, all minors without general
guardian, but having Atha Thomas Esq. as
their trustee. Patrick Reese died in Dec. 1865
& he left a will. James, Robert, Margaret &
Willie North, Sallie P., Jane, Letitia,
Marietta, Thomas Jr., & Kittie Watson became
the joint owners of certain real estate
bequeathed to them by Patrick Reese. The
first tract of land is in the 4th & 5th
Districts on the waters of the West Harpeth
bounded by Claiborn Kinnard (deceased), Young
Scruggs, Sidney B. Smith, Richard S. Boxley,
Thomas J. Watson, A. J. Puryear, C. C. Crump,
& J. D. DeGraffenried. The tract of land
contains about 602 acres. Patrick Reese,
deceased, left another tract of land in the   (CONT'D

P. 201 Patrick Reese, deceased (CONT'D)
4th District bounded by Thomas A. Pope, Bird
Dodson's estate, Z. M. Drake, Drury Lamb,
Watson & others. This tract contains about 285
acres of land. These 2 tracts of land were
bequeathed by the 2nd Item of the Will of
Patrick Reese.

P. 212 JOHN COWLES - pl. vs WILLIAM B. KING - def.
Oct. 1871
The Petitioner makes this statement:
William B. King is badly paralised &
perfectly helpless in consequence of
which he has lost his mind & is totally
unfit to attend to his business.
William B. King has been of unsound mind & not
able to attend to his business for 2 years. He
has about 400 acres of land, $2,200, personal
property, livestock, furniture, & rents of land.
He has a wife, Jane, aged 45 & 3 children
living. Mary Bostick aged 23. Sallie Roberts
aged 23 & Lucy King aged 20. He also has 2
grandchildren. They are: Willie, son of James
King, deceased, & Emma Flippen, daughter of Irene
Flippin. Thomas H. Roberts is appointed
guardian of William B. King.

P. 215 OPHELIA BITTICK - pl. vs JO J. GREEN, Exr.,
Et Al - def.
Aug. 1871   Petition for Dower
C. S. Bittick died 28 Aug. 1871. He left a will.
Jo J. Green & James T. Shannon were named Exrs.
C. S. Bittick left a widow, Ophelia Bittick.
He left the following children: John, Elizabeth,
Samuel, Emmet, & Rolie Bittick. The children are
minors. C. S. Bittick left a house & lot in
Nolensville & land in the vicinity of Nolensville
containing about 622 acres. C. S. Bittick directed
in his will for 120 acres to be sold to pay the
debts. The land is bounded by the lands of Mary
Nolen, William M. Clark, the estate of Thomas
J. Seals & others.

P. 222 NATILLA SEALS - pl. vs JO J. GREEN, Admr. -
def.   Sept. 1871   Dower
Thomas J. Seals died intestate. He left a widow,
Natilla & the following children: John,
Mollie, Sandy, Isaac, Davy, & Kitty Seals. They
are minors who have no guardian. Joseph J.
Green was appointed Admr. Thomas J. Seals,
deceased, owned a tract of land in the 17th
District containing about 230 acres bounded by
the estate of C. S. Bittick & others.

168

P. 226 FARRY (FANY?) JONES - pl. vs W. L. JOHNSON,
        Et Al - def.
        Farry Jones of Davidson County, Tennessee
        against Joseph Cruse & Sminy, his wife (they
        are supposed to be living in Iowa), 2 sons &
        2 daughters of McCalpin Oscar Johnson (who is
        deceased) (they are supposed to be living
        in Johnson County, Missouri. The names of
        the children is unknown except Charles
        McCalpin Johnson.), William L. Johnson
        (who is supposed to be living in Calhoune
        County, Georgia.), Ruth Ann Johnson & John
        McCalpin Johnson (they are minor children
        of John D. Johnson, deceased, who have
        no guardian & they live in Hickman
        County, Kentucky). John J. Johnson died 6 May
        1847 intestate. Statement by Farry Jones &
        she states he is her father. John J.
        Johnson, deceased, left a widow, Jane, who
        died 19 June 1863. He left the following
        children:
            1. Sminy Cruse
            2. Farry Jones
            3. McCalpin O. Johnson (he has since died
                & left surviving him is one son
                named Charles McCalpin Johnson. Another
                son & 2 daughters whose names are not
                known & they are suppose to be living
                in Johnson County, Missouri.)
            4. William L. Johnson & John D. Johnson
                (John D. has since died & left children.
                His children are Ruth Ann & John
                McCalpin who have no guardian & they
                live in Hickman County, Kentucky.)
            5. Nancy Jane Hobbs (she has since died
                & left no issue)
        Farry Jones was appointed Admr. of John J.
        Johnson. He owned a tract of land in the
        2nd District containing about 80 acres.
        The land is bounded by Alexander Dodd, Seth
        Sparkman, John Sparkman, & others.
        Petition for Partition.

P. 231 ELIZABETH J. POLLARD - pl. vs SAMUEL H.
        POLLARD, Et Al - def.
        Elizabeth J. Pollard is the widow of Robert
        L. Pollard who died 19 Sept. 1863. He left
        surviving him, his widow & 1 child, Samuel
        H. Pollard, an infant without a guardian.
        Robert L. Pollard left a very small personal
        estate that was all consumed by the debts.
        He left a tract of land containing about
        80 acres bounded by John W. Tulloss, George
        W. Pollard, Mrs. Thomas Carsey,   (CONT'D)

P. 231 Elizabeth J. Pollard   (CONT'D)
Lampkins, John MacPherson, & John Starnes heirs.
The income from the land is not enough to
support them & the widow wants to sell it.

P. 236 THOMAS P. BARNES, Admr., Et Al - pl. vs SAMUEL
L. WILLIAMS, Et Al - def.
Thomas P. Barnes is the Admr. of the estate of
Peter Barnes, deceased. Peter Barnes died 7 Nov.
1871 intestate. He left the following sons:
John B., William, Thomas P., & Samuel R. Barnes.
He left the following daughters: Martha Owen
(now a widow), Sarah Ann Pomeroy (wife of
Thomas Pomeroy), the only surviving child of
Mary A. Robinson (Mary A. being the daughter
of said Barnes), William Williams, Thomas L.
& Samuel L. Williams (children of Tabitha
Williams, deceased), James V. Barnes & Martha
A. E. Barnes (minor children of Aurelus Barnes,
deceased). Peter Barnes, deceased, owned land
in the 16th District containing about 46 acres
bounded by Sterling B. Fly, James H. Allen,
Mrs. Dorsey & Miss Mary Sayers. Petition for
Partition.

P. 244 LAURA E. COOK - pl. vs RICHARD R. COOK, Et Al - def.
Phillip H. Cook died Feb. 1872. He left a
will. He left a widow, Laura E. Cook & family
(no names given). He left a tract of land
bounded by John Reese, Sanford Allen's heirs,
Stevenson, Hawks, Reams, & others. He left another
tract of land bounded by Richard Reams, Mrs.
Allen, William Cartwright, & others. The
Plaintiff has given the Defendant Richard Reese
Cook (heir of said deceased), N. P. Fowlkes, &
John T. Cook, his Exrs. notice of application.
One tract of land contains 66 acres & Ed J. B.
Smith now lives there. The other is a small
tract of land where Abijah Smith lives & it
contains 66 acres. Another tract of land known
as the home place where the deceased lived
before he died. It contained 115 acres.

P. 247 GEORGE NICHOLS & WIFE - pl. vs ORLANDO McPHAIL,
Et Al - def.
George Nichols & wife, Alice Nichols against
Orlando McPhail, Marcus McPhail & Angus
McPhail (minors who have no guardian). Fountain
B. Carter died & left a will. He left a parcel of
land to Alice McPhail, Orlando, Marcus & Angus
McPhail. (Fountain & Ruth Carter had a share
according to section of will.). The tract of land
contains 46 acres. Alice McPhail has since married
George Nichols. She wants a division of the
land.

INDEX

CHAFFIN, Edward H. 67
CHAIRS, Martin T. 137
CHANEY, David S. 119; Edward
E. 119; Ezekiel 68, 119;
Letitia 119; Letitia M.
119; Margaret 119; Mary E.
119; Richard A. 119;
Wilkins T. 119; William
T. 119
CHAPMAN, Calvin C. 109;
Philip 109
CHARLTON, Edmund 10
CHARTER, John N. 18, 38, 54,
68, 69, 70
CHEATHAM, Bethenia 127; C.
C. 127; Fanny 14, 15;
Thomas 14, 15; Thomas
M. 78
CHILDRESS, Eliza 73, 74;
Henry 73, 74, 83; James
12; Joel 56; Joel G. 27, 31,
83, 87, 99; John Sr. 73;
Margery 73, 74; Polly 56;
Sarah C. 73, 74, 83; Stephen
31, 114; Thomas J. 35;
Thomas M. 73, 74, 83;
William G. 88; William S.
88
CHRISMAN, David 57
CHRISTMAS, Henry 89; Richard 62
CHRISTOPHER, Jane 135; Ruth
135; Sarah 135
CHRISWELL, Emaline 146; George
146; Jane 146; Joseph 146;
Labon 146; Mary 146;
Nancy 146; Noah 146; Phereby
146; Samuel 146; Sarah 146
CHUNN, James S. 21
CLAIBORNE, Micajah G. L. 126,
127; Micajah G. T. 140
CLARK, Alexander Sr. 81;
Andrew 37; Samuel 30;
William 30, 38; William M.
167
CLAUD, Eldridge 141; Francis
141; Philip 141
CLAXTON, Dawson 94; Micky 94
CLAYBROOK, John S. 119
CLIFFE, Daniel B. 161
CLOUD, Joshua D. 11, 32, 39
CLOUSTON, Edward G. 3, 4, 10,
13, 17, 27, 28, 59, 70,
78, 79, 81, 93
COBLER, Harris 56; Sally 56

COCKRILL, James 3; John 30
CODINGTON, John 17
COHORN, Aaron D. 13
COLE, Mary S. 164; S. W.
164
COLEMAN, Eliza 155; Eliza-
beth 19; Fanny 19;
Joshua 19; Julia 136;
Nancy 19; Thomas 19
COLLINS, Erastus T. 25, 82
COLLINSWORTH, James 101
COMSTOCK, David 161
CONN, Josephus H. 128; Mary
128; Nicholas 128
CONNER, Elenor 8; William 8
COOK, Edmund 111; Edmund
C. 110, 120; Edward C.
139; George E. 28, 42,
60; Gracy 110, 111;
Gracy B. 111; Henry 2, 3,
11, 87, 102; Henry Sr.
6, 17; John T. 23, 28,
110, 111, 120, 139,
169; Laura E. 169;
Nicholas P. 110, 111, 120,
139; Philip H. 110, 111,
120, 139, 169; Richard
D. 110, 111, 120, 139;
Richard R. 169; Richard
Reese 169; Sam J. 148
COOPER, Matthew D. 38, 81,
82; Thomas 70; William
Sr. 4
COPELAND, James C. 131, 150
COPERTON, James 61
CORZINE, Elizabeth 125;
Jane R. 118; Lewis 118
COUNCELLE, William H. 21
COWAN, David A. 120; Jane
120; John 120; Richard
G. 120
COWEN, Joseph 87
COWLES, John 167
COWSERT, Agatha Jane 93;
Andrew 93; James 93;
Jane 93; John 93
COX, Elizabeth 24; Jesse
9, 24, 75, 68
CROSBY, Levi 66
CRAFTON, Daniel 15; Dennis
M. 15, 41; D. M. 150;
George F. 15; John 15;
John W. 138; Mary A. 41;
Richard L. 15

DAWSON, Hudson 42; John. M. 50;
  Phebe 50
DEAN, Francis M. 18
DEGRAFFENREID, Abram M. 31;
  Candes J. 77; Christopher
  39; J. D. 166; Mary Ann
  31; Metcalf 2, 6, 22, 77
DEMOSS, James S. 161; John
  143
DENTON, Arthur J. 104; Mary
  104
DICKINSON, William G. 54, 68
DILLIHUNTY, Lewis 7
DILLON, Jane 108
DITTO, Thomas P. 136
DOBBINS, Hugh 6
DOBSON, Letitia 130, 131;
  Matthew 131; Matthew H.
  130; Nancy P. 130; William
  E. 130, 131
DODD, Alexander 168; Samuel
  69
DODSON, Bird 25, 167; Bird
  F. 154; Elias 6; Elizabeth
  A. 154; Ellis 62; Judith 25
DOE, John 28
DOHERTY, Francis 99; George
  99; Mary 99; Nelly 99
DONALSON, John 7; John Jr. 34
DONELSON, Daniel S. 99; John
  Jr. 32; Lemuel 32, 99
DONNELSON, Samuel 93;
  William 93
DOOLIN (DOOLM), Nathaniel 31
DORSEY, _______ 169
DOTSON, Bird 64, 65; Judith
  64, 65; Presley 94
DOUGLASS, Thomas L. 88, 105
DOUNING, William H. 18
DOWNY, Mary 84
DOYLE, Michael 68, 69, 70
DRAKE, James L. 12; John 11;
  John N. 12; Lila 11;
  Lilah T. 12; Rhoda 11,12;
  Zachariah 11, 12
DRENNEN, John 71
DROMGOOLE, John E. 144
DUDLEY, Ranson 57
DUFF, Ennis 30
DUKE, William P. 3, 5, 16
DUNLAP, Hugh M. 21; Nancy
  16; Samuel 16
DUNAVANT, Leonard 4, 17,
  43, 66

DUNNEVANT, Leonard 86;
  Sarah 86
DUPREE, James 2, 14; John 2;
  Nancy 2
DURHAM, John 47; Matilda 47;
  Millage 47
DUSHAM, Clarisa 31
DUVAL, Samuel H. 66
DWYER, Daniel 40, 81; John
  8; Joseph 8, 32; Joseph
  B. 151
EASTEP, Samuel 45
EDLIN, James H. B. 1; Mary
  1; Oswald 1; T. 1
EDMISTON, Alice 22; Andrew
  110; Jane 110; John 22;
  Samuel 63, 115; William
  24, 27, 54, 63, 90, 103,
  104
EDMONDSON, Andrew 111; Charles
  37; Charles H. 44;
  Elizabeth 15, 116, 117;
  John 2, 37, 44, 152;
  John Sr. 36, 37, 152;
  Levi 20; Mary 44; Mary
  W. 37; Priscilla 86;
  Richard H. 79; Robert B.
  28; Samuel 36; Samuel
  W. 117; Sara J. 111;
  William 15, 37, 44, 86
EDMONSTON, John 44; Robert
  B. 27
EDNEY, Alford A. 56; Alfred
  A. 56; Alson 51, 56;
  Charlotte 56; Emily 56;
  John 41; John D. 51, 56;
  Harry 56; Levin 56;
  Milton 56; Nancy 56;
  Polly 56; Winson 24, 44
EDWARDS, William 38
EELBECK, Henry 23
EGGLESTON, Edward W. 161
ELBECK, Henry 48
ELLIOTT, Elizabeth 8;
  Hugh 33; James 8, 98;
  Jane 89; Mary 98
ELDEN, Caroline 116, 117
ELLIS, Ann E. 149; David S.
  149; James B. 149; Martha
  J. 130, 149; Orison 130;
  Richard 7; Sarah E. 149;
  Virginia L. 149; Wyatt
  149
ELLISON, Joseph T. 39
ELMORE, Henry 44

192

SWANSON, Edward Jr. 20; James
    30, 46, 63, 64, 69, 81,
    91, 92, 101; James Sr. 46,
    69, 80, 92, 98; Richard 10
SWEENEY, Charles 129; Henry
    68; John 39, 46, 90, 91;
    William B. 82
SWINNEY, John 11
SWISHER, Elizabeth 49; Henry
    H. 49; James G. 49; Samuel
    42; Sinai 49
TAIT, Bacon 68; Netherland
    6, 68
TALBOT, Elizabeth 69;
    Thomas 69, 70
TANNER, Joseph 33
TAPPAN, Benjamin 6; Benjamin
    L. 6; Benjamin S. 4, 5, 11,
    13, 34, 40, 43, 45, 60,
    68, 79, 99; Edmund T. 79
TARKINGTON, Benjamin 38
TATE, James 89; Margaret 89
TATUM, Alesalom 63, 64
TAYLOR, Elizabeth 74, 75;
    Emily C. 115; Frances 116;
    James 116; James H. 115;
    John 116; Tabitha 116;
    William D. 42, 74
TENNISEN, Joseph 159
TENNISON, Joseph 160;
    Shelbourn 160; Shelbourne
    159
TERRILL, Bird 157; James 5,
    16; James B. 158; John
    157; Nancy 157; Sallie 157,
    158; Sufrona 157; Timothy
    157,158
TIGNOR, Isaac 59
TINDALL, Henry 110; Mary 110
TINNEN, Mary 58
TISDALE, James 36; James R.
    60, 68, 75, 79, 80; John
    7, 21, 33
THOMAS, Atha 166; James 35;
    Nathaniel H. 61, 69, 79,
    82, 87, 91; Phineas 69;
    Samuel T. 159
THOMPSON, David 71; Elijah 113;
    James E. 53; Jason 11, 14,
    22; John 24, 63; Joseph L.
    53; Martha A. R. 100; Rachel
    53; R. C. 104; Robert C. 27,
    104; Susan 24; Thomas A. 6,
    24; William 53

THORNHILL, Thomas T. 34
THWEATT, Elizabeth 25; Isham
    R. 32, 61, 62, 76; Peter
    25; William 25
TOLAND, Henry 33
TOLLOSSE, Rodham 66
TOMPKINS, James H. 142
TONEY, Elvy 51, 52; John
    51, 52; Littleberry 51;
    Mary 51; Polly 51
TONY, Elvy 84; John 84;
    Littleberry 84; Mary 84
TOON, Beverly B. 140, 152,
    156
TROTTER, Benjamin 44, 59,
    60, 65, 67; Isham R.
    105; Sally 105
TRUETT, Alpheus 130
TUCKER, Rodden 13
TULLOSS, John W. 168;
    Nancy P. 109; Parthenia
    N. 128; Robert C. 109,
    110, 128
TURMAN, Charles 28; Luke
    28
TURNER, James 65; John 71;
    John Jackson 100; Lewis
    21; Stephen 83
TWOOMEY, Isaac 117
TYRRILL, Hezekiah 63, 64, 90,
    100; James 63, 64, 90,
    100; Joel 90, 100;
    Joseph 63, 64; Mary 63, 64,
    90, 100; Martha 63, 64,
    90, 100; Nancy 63, 64, 90,
    100; Timothy 63, 64, 90,
    100; William 64, 90, 100
VANLEER, Anthony W. 16, 17;
    Benard 16, 17; W. 11
VAUGHN, Arch 117; Catherine
    153; Celia 117; Daniel 62;
    Elizabeth 164; Franklin
    117; Isaac L. 143; James
    19, 117; John 117; Martha
    A. E. 136; Richard 104;
    Robert C. 117; Tennessee
    117; William 17
WADDY, E. R. 163
WADE, Clement W. 140; Henry
    P. 140; John F. 140; Lucy
    D. 140; Martha A. 140;
    Sarah Ann 102; Thomas B.
    140